THE CITIZEN'S LIBRARY

OF

ECONOMICS, POLITICS, AND SOCIOLOGY

EDITED BY

RICHARD T. ELY, Ph.D., LL.D.

PROFESSOR OF POLITICAL ECONOMY, UNIVERSITY OF WISCONSIN

COMMISSION GOVERNMENT IN AMERICAN CITIES

THE CITIZEN'S LIBRARY OF
ECONOMICS, POLITICS, AND SOCIOLOGY

Edited by Richard T. Ely, Ph.D., LL.D.

Half Leather   12mo   *$1.25 net each*

AMERICAN CITY, THE. A Problem in Democracy. By D. F. Wilcox.

AMERICAN MUNICIPAL PROGRESS. Chapters in Municipal Sociology. By C. Zueblin.

CHILD PROBLEMS. By George B. Mangold.

COMMISSION GOVERNMENT IN AMERICAN CITIES. By Ernest S. Bradford.

COLONIAL ADMINISTRATION. By Paul S. Reinsch.

COLONIAL GOVERNMENT. By P. S. Reinsch.

CUSTOM AND COMPETITION. By R. T. Ely. *Preparing.*

DEMOCRACY AND SOCIAL ETHICS. By Jane Addams.

ECONOMIC CRISES. By E. D. Jones.

ECONOMICS OF DISTRIBUTION. By J. A. Hobson.

EDUCATIONAL AND INDUSTRIAL EVOLUTION. By Frank Tracy Carlton.

ELEMENTS OF SOCIOLOGY. By F. W. Blackmar.

ESSAYS IN THE MONETARY HISTORY OF THE UNITED STATES. By C. J. Bullock.

FOUNDATIONS OF SOCIOLOGY. By E. A. Ross.

GOVERNMENT IN SWITZERLAND. By J. M. Vincent.

GREAT CITIES IN AMERICA. Their Problems and their Government. By D. F. Wilcox.

HISTORY OF POLITICAL PARTIES IN THE UNITED STATES. By J. Macy.

INTERNATIONAL COMMERCIAL POLICIES. By G. M. Fisk.

INTRODUCTION TO BUSINESS ORGANIZATION. By S. E. Sparling.

INTRODUCTION TO THE STUDY OF AGRICULTURAL ECONOMICS. By H. C. Taylor.

IRRIGATION INSTITUTIONS. A Discussion of the Growth of Irrigated Agriculture in the Arid West. By E. Mead.

MONEY. A Study of the Theory of the Medium of Exchange. By David Kinley.

MONOPOLIES AND TRUSTS. By R. T. Ely.

MUNICIPAL ENGINEERING AND SANITATION. By M. N. Baker.

NEWER IDEALS OF PEACE. By Jane Addams.

PRINCIPLES OF ANTHROPOLOGY AND SOCIOLOGY, THE. In their relations to Criminal Procedure. By M. Parmelee.

RAILWAY LEGISLATION IN THE UNITED STATES. By B. H. Meyer.

SOCIAL CONTROL. A Survey of the Foundation of Order. By E. A. Ross.

SOME ETHICAL GAINS THROUGH LEGISLATION. By Mrs. Florence Kelley.

SPIRIT OF AMERICAN GOVERNMENT. By J. A. Smith.

STUDIES IN THE EVOLUTION OF INDUSTRIAL SOCIETY. By R. T. Ely.

SURVEY OF SOCIOLOGY. By E. Vincent. *Preparing.*

WAGE-EARNING WOMEN. By Annie Marion MacLean.

WORLD POLITICS. By P. S. Reinsch.

THE MACMILLAN COMPANY
64-66 Fifth Avenue,   New York

COMMISSION GOVERNMENT IN OPERATION — *Des Moines, Iowa.*

COMMISSION GOVERNMENT

IN

AMERICAN CITIES

BY

ERNEST S. BRADFORD, Ph.D.

New York
THE MACMILLAN COMPANY
1912

All rights reserved

COPYRIGHT, 1911,
By THE MACMILLAN COMPANY.

Set up and electrotyped. Published November, 1911. Reprinted August, 1912.

Norwood Press
J. S. Cushing Co. — Berwick & Smith Co.
Norwood, Mass., U.S.A.

PREFACE

OF the recent developments in the field of municipal politics, none has attracted more attention than the introduction and rapid spread of the Commission Form of city government, so called from the commission or board which constitutes the governing body. Starting at Galveston after the disastrous Flood of 1900, it was installed by Houston in 1905, and two years later spread rapidly in all directions, being adopted by Dallas and other Texas cities, Des Moines and Cedar Rapids, Lewiston (Ida.), and by the states of Kansas, South Dakota, and North Dakota, during 1907. Accepted by a constantly increasing list of municipalities, in August, 1911, it numbered among its adherents, more than a hundred and fifty American cities, of varying population and representing all sections. Though the Commission System changed somewhat in its transit from the Gulf to the North Central states, to New England and the Pacific coast, modifications or additions being found in each locality, certain basic features prove upon examination to have remained, and, common to all the forms, constitute the elements which distinguish the commission type.

The Commission Plan gives to a small board of city directors elected by the municipal stockholders — that is, the voters — all the corporate powers of the municipality. This commission is the governing body of the

PREFACE

city. The board selects subordinate officials and employees, fixes their salaries and duties, passes ordinances, levies taxes, and appropriates money. Each member is at the same time the head of a department, responsible for it to the board as a whole and known to all the people. The exercise of the large powers so granted are safeguarded by certain "checks" which, in addition to the definite division of duties among the members, consist of complete publicity of proceedings, the referendum and the recall in a majority of commission charters, and frequently other provisions.

The council-mayor plan has thus been modified. The size of the body has been reduced; its members are elected at large instead of by wards; bulky council committees with loose administrative oversight of departments give way to responsible single heads. The mayor is merged into the council, usually losing his veto, but gaining a vote as one of the five, and being frequently the head of a department which is charged with the duty of general municipal oversight. The name of "Mayor" is usually retained, together with certain emergency powers.

Under this plan, the organization of a city is similar to that of a business corporation. The board of directors of the corporation, it is true, frequently contains men who are not executive heads of divisions, and who act purely in an advisory (legislative) capacity; while each member of the city commission is also chief of an administrative department; yet this difference is scarcely fundamental. The corporation in which every member of a small board of directors is also president or secretary or other important executive officer corre-

PREFACE

sponds almost exactly to the commission form of municipal government. In a great number of companies the administrative heads are the leading directors. It is true that in the municipality, the voters cast one ballot each, no matter what their property holdings, it being assumed that the individual interest in the municipality is equal; while the *stock* of the corporation votes, and one person may cast ten votes to his neighbor's one. Yet this does not change the principles underlying the powers of the board or the methods of administration. In combining the policy-determining and the appointing power with executive oversight in the hands of one small body, elected by the members of the larger organization, the municipal commission and the corporate directors are alike.

The term "commission government" or "commission" (in that sense) appears in the statutes granting cities the right to use this new plan in South Dakota, North Dakota, Texas,[1] Mississippi, Minnesota, and New Mexico; and in the charters of Dallas, Marshall, Waco, Clarksdale (Miss.), and other cities. Even where the law retains the old name "council," or "mayor and council," the councilmen are frequently referred to locally, as in Houston, as commissioners; and the substance of their powers and the general form of organization are of the commission type. Commission government in cities should not be confused, however, with "government by commission," in the sense in which that phrase has been applied to the multiplicity of boards in state and national govern-

[1] The general law of Texas applies to cities of less than 10,000 population.

PREFACE

ments. There is a vast difference between a single small board, exercising all the powers of a municipality, and a multitude of boards, each possessing jurisdiction over some small division of federal or state governmental activity.

When one reflects that the commission form of government has been in use in America for less than a decade, the number of cities which have adopted it appears remarkable. Is this a fad in municipal politics, which will gradually disappear; or is it based on sound principles which insure its success and a permanent hold on the governmental good sense of our people? Are the cities which have tried it typical American municipalities? What effect has it upon the personnel of officials? Does the plan lessen or stimulate that active public interest so essential under a democratic form of government? Is it likely to succeed in the larger centers? These questions are being asked by many citizens, and the answers depend upon a careful study of many related facts. To inquire as to the rise of the plan, the reasons for its adoption, and the degree of success attained where it has been tried; and finally to analyze the idea into its elements, and to try to account for certain of the results which have followed its introduction, is the purpose of this brief volume.

To secure the necessary data, all the commission charters and many others which contain certain commission features were examined; correspondence was had with officials and citizens of the commission cities; annual reports and proceedings were inspected, and personal visits were made to Galveston, Houston, Des Moines, Cedar Rapids, Huntington, and other cities; business

PREFACE

men were interviewed, meetings of the commission attended, officials questioned, and local conditions and peculiarities noted. In order to insure as impartial an impression as possible, in each place, information was first sought from representative citizens of all classes, as to conditions under the former and the commission system; afterward, the city hall was visited and administrative authorities consulted. It proved necessary to discard a considerable amount of evidence on account of lack of definiteness or evident bias on the part of the informant.

The results as here recorded may be verified by visiting the cities mentioned. It is hoped that the data presented, while not as complete as it will be possible to obtain after a longer period of trial, may throw some light on the workings of the plan so far as adopted. No claim is made that the subject has been exhausted; only the broader aspects have been sketched; in so new a field, much remains to be studied in detail. Every effort has been made to insure accuracy of statement, although in the multitude of items noted or tabulated, some errors may have escaped notice. While the right is reserved to modify the conclusions reached, according to later and more complete information, it is scarcely probable that the experience of our cities with the new form of government will be greatly different in the next few years from that already recorded. Nevertheless, the student or the citizen should not hesitate to note and condemn imperfect features whenever evident in individual charters, and to point out needed additions or modifications.

In connection with this study, undertaken primarily for the Department of Political Science of the University

PREFACE

of Pennsylvania and important parts of which were prepared for the annual meetings of the National Municipal League, I wish to acknowledge the valuable criticisms of Professor Leo S. Rowe of the University of Pennsylvania; to thank Mr. Clinton Rogers Woodruff, Secretary of the National Municipal League, for permission to reprint here portions of the studies of the subject presented at the Cincinnati and Buffalo conferences for Good City Government, and to express my hearty approval of the work of that body. I am indebted to Professor Richard T. Ely, of the University of Wisconsin, for many suggestions. To Dr. Charles W. Eliot I am under obligation for helpful ideas contained in his writings on Commission Government; to Mr. Horace E. Deming, author of "The Government of American Cities," for certain chapters in that volume; and to Professor Henry Jones Ford, for the initial impulse received toward the examination of this topic. Dr. Frank G. Bates, recently of the University of Kansas, furnished data regarding the commission forms in that state. Professor Paul S. Reinsch, Dr. Chester Lloyd Jones, and Dr. Howard L. McBain, of the Department of Political Science of the University of Wisconsin, and Dr. W. P. Sterns and Mr. Charles E. Edgerton, of Washington, D. C., read the manuscript. I take this occasion also to express appreciation for assistance from the staff of the well-equipped Legislative Reference Library of Wisconsin; Mr. Ford H. MacGregor, of the Municipal Reference Department of the University of Wisconsin; Dr. Clarence B. Lester, of the Legislative Reference Library of New York; and Mr. Robert A. Campbell, Municipal Reference Librarian of California.

PREFACE

Mr. E. R. Cheesborough, of Galveston, a close student of the commission form since its inception; Mr. J. Z. Gaston, Commissioner of Finance and Revenue, and Mayor H. B. Rice, of Houston; Mr. James G. Berryhill, attorney, "father" of the Des Moines plan; John MacVicar, Commissioner of Streets and Public Improvements of Des Moines, and Secretary of the League of American Municipalities; Charles D. Huston, former Commissioner of Streets, and Mayor Matt J. Miles, of Cedar Rapids; Mr. George I. Neal, of Huntington; and many others,— coöperated in furnishing data without which any study of the commission system would have been most fragmentary.

The various commission forms of government, says Dr. Eliot, "are the most promising experiments which the last ten years have seen in the direction in which good citizens want to advance." The reasons for the promise contained in these experiments may be found in a study of the results of operation in the commission cities, and analysis of the principles underlying this type of municipal government.

WASHINGTON, D.C., August, 1911.

CONTENTS

PREFACE v

PART I

SPREAD OF THE COMMISSION FORM

CHAPTER
I. GALVESTON 3
II. HOUSTON 23
III. DES MOINES 33
IV. CEDAR RAPIDS 54
V. CITIES OF KANSAS 63
VI. STATES OF UPPER MISSISSIPPI VALLEY 70
VII. TEXAS AND OKLAHOMA 76
VIII. MASSACHUSETTS 80
IX. WEST VIRGINIA, TENNESSEE, AND THE SOUTH . . . 88
X. COLORADO AND THE PACIFIC STATES; PREFERENTIAL VOTING 100
XI. SUMMARY OF COMMISSION CITIES 112
XII. THE CITY BUSINESS MANAGER — STAUNTON, VA. . . 119

PART II

A COMPARISON OF FORMS OF COMMISSION GOVERNMENT

XIII. COMMISSION GOVERNMENT: ESSENTIAL FEATURES . . 127
XIV. THE SMALL BOARD 139
    Other Elective Officers 146
    Complete or Partial Renewal of Commission . . 149
    Length of Term 159

CONTENTS

CHAPTER		PAGE
XV.	ELECTION AT LARGE: A REDEFINITION OF REPRESENTATION	162
	Time Requirements	166
	Salaries	170
	Qualifications	179
XVI.	CONCENTRATION OF MUNICIPAL AUTHORITY	181
	General Powers	184
	Appointing Power	186
	Administrative Control	188
	Financial Powers	190
	The City a Business Corporation	191
XVII.	EACH COMMISSIONER HEAD OF A DEPARTMENT	197
	Assignment of Departments	200
	Duties of Departments	204
	The Mayor	204
XVIII.	"CHECKS": PUBLICITY	214
XIX.	REFERENDUM AND INITIATIVE	220
XX.	THE RECALL	234
XXI.	NONPARTISAN PRIMARIES AND ELECTIONS; PREFERENTIAL VOTING	247
XXII.	MUNICIPAL CIVIL SERVICE; OTHER PROVISIONS	262
XXIII.	SUMMARY OF "CHECKS"; CLASSIFICATION OF COMMISSION CITIES	271
XXIV.	UNUSUAL AND PARTIAL FORMS OF COMMISSION GOVERNMENT	282
XXV.	LIMITATIONS OF THE COMMISSION FORM	291
XXVI.	OBJECTIONS TO COMMISSION GOVERNMENT	299
XXVII.	CONCLUSION	304
PREFERENTIAL BALLOT PROVISIONS OF GRAND JUNCTION		307
TEXT OF IOWA LAW ("DES MOINES PLAN")		312
LIST OF REFERENCES		339
INDEX		355

CHAPTER I

GALVESTON

THE most far-sighted student of municipal affairs could scarcely have predicted that the devastation of a Southern seaport by a great storm would lead to a change in the form of government of a hundred American cities, within less than a decade. The installation of a board of five as the governing body of a city of Texas, at a crisis in its civic life, resulted in such administrative efficiency as to lead other municipalities to adopt for their ordinary needs a form of government devised originally to meet an emergency; and the success of the new plan in these cities has led to its wide acceptance by others.

On September 8, 1900, a hurricane, driving up from the southeast with unusual violence, swept the waters of the Gulf of Mexico over Galveston. The bridges which connected the island-city with the mainland went down in the flood. Trees were uprooted; dwellings were crushed; schoolhouses, churches, and fire stations were wrecked; the waterworks and lighting plants destroyed. The very streets were washed away, the wood-block paving floating off in great strips. In place of level streets and regular blocks of stores and dwellings was a chaos of fallen brick, ruined houses, stubs of telegraph poles, and sand. The dead numbered about six thousand. One does not realize what a degree of order civilization enforces in cities until a stroke of nature sweeps it all away and men start anew.[1]

Those who survived faced a desperate situation. If the city was to exist again, order must be restored, the dead buried, stores and homes rebuilt, and the general machinery for supplying the needs of the citizens set running again. Scores of people were leaving Galveston. City scrip sold at fifty cents on the dollar; and in addition to a floating debt of $200,000, previously outstanding, the municipality defaulted in the payment of interest, on its bonds, which fell to sixty. The important part that government plays in ordering the larger aspects of city life was revealed at a flash; and to the mayor and ward aldermen[2] citizens looked for the measures needed to renew confidence and restore credit.

The city government failed them utterly in the crisis. Nothing was done but to pass resolutions. Alderman McMaster proposed that the mayor and aldermen resign, and an emergency board be appointed by the governor of the state; but his motion was laid on the table. The governor was appealed to for financial aid, but he declined to allow state money to be advanced to a city which under normal conditions permitted its expenditures to exceed its income, and made up the deficit by issuing bonds.

---

[1] See George Kibbe Turner in *McClure's*, October, 1906.

[2] Galveston was governed previous to 1890 by a mayor and 12 ward aldermen; from 1890 to 1895 by a mayor and 16 aldermen, four of whom were elected at large; from 1895 to 1900 again by a mayor and 12 aldermen, all elected at large.

GALVESTON

Then the Deepwater Committee, an organization of substantial business men previously formed for the improvement of the harbor, took up the matter; and a subcommittee [1] was appointed, which secured the charters of several cities, including the law governing the city of Washington, D.C., the act creating the Taxing Commission of Memphis after the great yellow fever epidemic of 1878, and a copy of the so-called model charter of Baltimore, Md. With these before it and drawing largely also from the business experience of its members, the subcommittee framed a new charter, which the Deepwater Committee presented to the legislature for adoption, issuing at the same time an address to the people, a part of which was as follows: [2] —

"We believe that municipal government, as it has been administered in this community for the past twenty years, is a failure. It did not require the storm to bring a realization of this fact, but it brought it home with greater force upon us. We are seeking relief from the municipal destruction and despair staring us in the face. It is a question with us of civic life or death. This committee has labored diligently and earnestly to prepare and present to the people of this city, and to the legislature, remedial legislation adequate for the grave emergency confronting us. Months have been given to its preparation. It is hoped that the central idea of this new charter — that of a commission — em-

[1] Composed of Messrs. R. Waverley Smith, chairman, previously city attorney for four years, upon whom fell a large share of the burden of drafting the new charter; former Congressman Walter Gresham; and F. D. Minor, attorney.

[2] See article by E. R. Cheesborough, of Galveston, in the *Galveston Tribune*, December 31, 1909.

bodies the practical solution of that hitherto unsolved problem : how to govern, cheaply and well, a municipal corporation. We are asking for a charter, placing the entire control of the local government in the hands of five commissioners, designed to benefit the people rather than to provide sinecures for politicians."

The legislature granted the charter desired on April 19, 1901, after a long and bitter struggle, and it went into operation September 18, 1901, a year after the storm.

The Galveston Plan

The new charter, which is in effect to-day except in certain particulars to be noted,[1] was unique in its provisions. The controlling idea was to create a governing body which should resemble as nearly as possible the board of directors of a business corporation, concentrating both power and responsibility in a small commission or board, which takes the place of mayor and council. To the Board of Commissioners was given power, (*a*) " to appoint all officers and subordinates in all departments of said city " ;[2] (*b*) "to make and *enforce* such rules and regulations as they may see fit and proper for . . . the organization, management, and operation of all the city departments of said city and whatever agencies may be created for the administration of its affairs " ;[3] (*c*) " to make all laws and ordinances not inconsistent with the constitution and laws of this state, touching every object, matter, and subject within the local government in-

[1] The charter was amended March 30, 1903, making all the commissioners elective, instead of two elective and three appointed by the governor.
[2] Charter, Sec. 8.   [3] Charter, Sec. 12.

GALVESTON

stituted by this act."[1] Under these provisions the Board passes (by majority vote) ordinances and city regulations; appoints and removes all city officials and employees; determines the salaries and fixes the qualifications of officials and employees; and grants all franchises.

One of the commissioners is called the mayor-president, who presides at all meetings; he has no veto, however; he votes as one of the five, and a majority settles every question. The duty of the mayor-president is to oversee the city business as a whole, and the law provides that he shall give six hours a day to his municipal duties. Of the other four, one commissioner has charge of the police and fire departments; one is commissioner of streets and public property; one is waterworks and sewerage commissioner; and the fourth is commissioner of finance and revenue, the Board by majority vote determining what department each member shall have charge of. Each commissioner supervises the work of his department, not directing it in detail, — for this he has superintendents, — but looking after it in its larger aspects. In this respect the five commissioners are similar to a general manager and four assistant managers, each the head of a particular division. As a group, this body constitutes the board of municipal directors, determines the policy of the city (so far as the city may be said to have a policy) and of the departments; each commissioner, as an individual member of the Board, sees that such policy is carried out in his particular department; and also the Board as a whole has general oversight of administrative matters. The Board of Commissioners thus acts in two capacities:

[1] Charter, Sec. 17.

first, as a council, or ordinance-making body; and second, as the administrative board of the city, each commissioner being the head of a definite department. Not only power, but responsibility as well, is concentrated in this small board; there is no one else to blame if matters do not go right. In the usual city government the council may and often does try to shift responsibility to the mayor or the heads of departments, while these in turn attempt to throw it upon each other or back upon the council. It is always difficult to prove who is at fault, authority being so much divided under the aldermanic form. With the commission plan, mayor, council, and department heads are one; a single group of five is accountable for all matters municipal. The commissioners are elected at large, that is, by the voters of the entire city, not by wards; every elector votes for all five commissioners. Citizens know who is in charge of each department and to whom to go with complaints. In place of the old theory of city government, "Distribute authority among many, so that no *one* shall have power to do much harm," has been substituted the principle, "Place the management of the city's business in the hands of a few, and watch those few." It is the same general idea as that employed by commercial corporations; the stockholders elect a board of directors, which, under the charter, exercises all the power needed to run the business successfully.

The Board of Commissioners appoints in Galveston the following city officials, provided for in the charter: a city secretary, who keeps the minutes of the meetings of the Board, and conducts necessary correspondence; a city treasurer, city attorney, recorder or judge of the corporation court, assessor and collector of taxes, chief of police, chief of the fire department; an engineer, who is also superintendent of streets; an auditor, a secretary of the waterworks and sewerage department, harbor master, sexton, superintendent of waterworks and sewerage, an engineer of the waterworks, an assistant engineer of the waterworks; and if deemed necessary by the Board, an inspector of waterworks and sewerage plumbing, an assistant chief of police, an assistant chief of the fire department, and an assistant city engineer.

The respective duties of these officials are prescribed in the charter. In addition, the Board is given power [1] "from time to time to require further and other duties of all officers whose duties are herein prescribed, and to define and prescribe the powers and duties of all officers elected to any office under this act whose duties are not herein specifically mentioned, and to fix their compensation when not herein fixed." Besides the right to require bonds of officers, and to fill vacancies, the Board of Commissioners has also "authority from time to time to create and fill and discontinue offices and employments other than herein prescribed according to their judgment of the needs and requirements of the city, and in their discretion by a majority vote of all the members of the Board to remove, for or without cause, the incumbent of any such office or employment, and may, by order or otherwise, prescribe, limit, or change the compensation of such officers or employees," [2] but no salary of such created office shall exceed $900 per annum.[3]

These provisions give elasticity to the administration of municipal affairs, lodging in the Board that discretion

[1] Charter, Sec. 21.   [2] Charter, Sec. 29.   [3] Charter, Sec. 24.

which is so needful to the successful conduct of any business. Many of the commission charters similarly recognize the need of allowing the Board some latitude of action, the Kansas law for cities of the first class permitting the Board to appoint "such other officers and servants as they may deem necessary for the best interests of the city."

As a check upon the large powers granted to its commission, Galveston depends upon publicity, and also upon care in selecting its Commissioners. All legislative sessions of the Board, whether regular or called, are open to the public. Newspaper men are present and report all the business transacted; citizens may attend; but the idlers and "city hall loafers" so frequently seen at council meetings are noticeable for their absence. In the selection of commissioners a vigorous city club takes an active part, noting the work of the various officials, and backing for reëlection those who have proved to be capable. Its energetic support has played no small part in the continued reëlection of a majority of the Commissioners, although opposed by the old-time politicians. With the coöperation of the best elements in the community, it has looked after the nominations, the campaign literature, and the election of the men who have served the city well, thus rendering it unnecessary for the Commissioners to fight for their own reëlection.

Results

Any study of the results of commission government in Galveston should take account of the double task which confronted the new administration. The city had first to be rebuilt; after the entire grade had been raised enough to protect the city from the sweep of future floods, streets must be paved, the water and lighting plants reconstructed, and the credit of the city restored. Then, after the period of stress had passed and the civic spirit roused by the crisis had returned to its usual level, the daily problems of city governing must be met and the departments administered month after month economically and efficiently. A system of government may be successful in meeting unusual conditions and yet prove unable to cope effectively with the ordinary duties of municipal administration; on the other hand, it may succeed in both crisis and calm, provided it be based upon correct principles. Not only should the degree of success attained in rebuilding Galveston be considered, but also the extent to which the commission form has proved capable of directing regular municipal business.

The Commission secured and paid for the services of a board of three eminent engineers, which devised the plans for the great Sea Wall, and for raising the grade of the city.[1] The county of Galveston, of which the city of Galveston comprises 80 per cent financially, constructed the sea wall, and the United States government

[1] The plan adopted in raising the grade of the city was not only remarkable in itself, but was one that called for the highest public spirit on the part of the people. A canal $2\frac{1}{2}$ miles long, 300 feet wide, and 20 feet deep, was excavated from Galveston Bay through the residence section of the city. The people, for the mere payment of taxes, leased their lots to the city, and houses were moved to vacant lots. Five self-loading, self-propelling, and self-discharging hopper dredges were employed. Sand was sucked up from the bottom of the bay, and brought in through the canal and discharged through pipe lines, the water draining back into the canal. The work completed, the canal was refilled and houses replaced.

extended the same to protect Fort Crockett. The raising of the city grade was financed and carried out by the city, with aid extended by the state of Texas. The total cost of the Sea Wall and grade raising was over $4,750,000, not including the cost of raising over 2000 buildings, and other improvements,[1] nor the grand causeway connecting Galveston with the mainland, now being completed by the county, assisted by the steam railroads and a new interurban electric railway, at a cost of $1,500,000.

Between September 18, 1901, and December 31, 1910, the Board of Commissioners of the city financed and carried out the following public improvements: —

Raising the grade of the city	$2,000,000.00
Additional protective improvements	179,388.65
Additional grade raising	176,327.76
Waterworks improvements	312,242.11
Brick paving in streets	237,902.36
Drainage	319,651.63
Sewer extension	290,231.04
Rock and shelled streets	279,647.77
Addition to electric light plant	37,459.76
Total improvements	$3,832,851.08
Paid for in bonds	2,759,170.88
Paid for out of current funds	$1,073,680.20 [2]

[1] The county of Galveston assumed $1,500,000 in the building of the Sea Wall. The United States government extended the wall around its property at Fort Crockett in the southwestern part of the city at a cost of $700,000 more; and the state of Texas was persuaded to remit the state taxes on Galveston property for 17 years, and allowed the sum of these taxes to be used toward the $2,000,000 (and over) which was required for raising the city's grade to the top of the Sea Wall. — George Kibbe Turner in *McClure's*, October, 1906.

[2] Data furnished by city auditor, February, 1911. See also "Galveston's Commission Form of City Government," by E. R. Cheesborough, reprinted for the Galveston Deepwater Committee, 1910.

GALVESTON

In addition to the above, the city paid out of its general fund the cost of repairing storm damage to the city hall and fire engine houses, three new engine houses, three new engines, and new equipment for the fire department.

The Commissioners also adjusted the city's bonded debt, secured a reduction in interest rate on the bonded debt of the city for a period of five years, and then resumed payment of full interest.

The city also has maintained a public hospital at a cost of $32,000 per annum above the income.

The Sea Wall is completed; the grade raising is done; the bonds of the city are back at par; Galveston is on its feet again, and the great storm is only history. As an emergency form of government there can be no question that the Commission has proved to be wonderfully prompt, energetic, and economical.

Meeting Usual Problems

But after the city had been restored, the Commission faced a serious condition. Under the old mayor-council administration, the city's income each year had run behind its expenses, as already noted, leaving an annual deficit. This deficit was made up by the sale of bonds, until $2,850,000 of these bonds had been issued, in the period between 1876 and 1897, for which there was but little to show.[1] These bonds had seriously impaired the credit of the city. Besides, a floating debt of about $200,000 was outstanding in the form of scrip or due bills given in settlement for services, labor, and supplies. These were elements in a bad municipal situation which

[1] See statement of Board of Commissioners, 1907.

existed prior to 1900, and which must have been reckoned with, even though the storm had not forced earlier action.

The floating debt has been paid without the issue of bonds, and $1,124,326.62 of the bonded debt (including $555,000 of grade-raising bonds)[1] has been retired. The assessment and the collection of taxes have been consolidated, one officer now doing both — not a difficult task, since the labor in these divisions comes at different times of year. Back taxes, which had been allowed to remain long unpaid, were vigorously collected; the fact that during the four and a half years following the installation of the new government, $90,000 more was secured than in the same period immediately preceding, is evidence of the energy of the Commissioners in this respect.

In current taxes the Commission has made an excellent record. The city moneys, on deposit with various banks, and interest on taxes, were made to yield a revenue of $136,451.30, up to December 31, 1910. Under the old form of city government no interest was collected on bank balances and but little on back taxes. The waterworks income was increased by $115,000, with practically no addition to the expenses of operation. A new vehicle tax used exclusively for street paving yielded $67,102 (between January 1, 1903, and December 31, 1910). The street railway companies paid $40,000 as their share of new paving, spread over a period of six years.

Expenses, too, were cut wherever practicable. The police department cost in five years $60,000 less, through

[1] Data furnished by city auditor, February, 1911.

decreases in salaries and in number of men, and on account of the city receiving all fees, and various other economies. The fire department is better equipped and more efficient. An entirely new electric lighting plant operating on a more economical basis has been installed.

Diligence in collecting city income has been accompanied also by prompt payment in cash of employees' wages and current bills.

In finances, then, through the exercise of care and economy, income has been increased, expenses have been diminished; old obligations have been retired; current revenues have been able to care for street paving; and many permanent improvements have been made without the issue of bonds.

The results in other departments are favorable. Health and quarantine regulations — of vital importance to a seaport city — have been enforced with a strictness formerly unknown. Sidewalks have been cleared of fruit stands and other obstructions which had encumbered them for years. Open gambling of all forms has been completely abolished and saloons barred from the residence section. Improvements in the fire department have already been mentioned. It is the testimony of nearly every one interested that the streets are kept cleaner than before. The lighting is good; the pumping stations supply pure water at low cost. The more details of city administration that one examines, the more small improvements and economies are disclosed. Every citizen encountered tells of some specific feature wherein the new government is superior to the old; and investigation confirms the statements.

COMMISSION GOVERNMENT

A Meeting of the Commission

A meeting of the Board of Commissioners offers a striking contrast to that of the usual council. The meetings are held usually once each week, at 6 P.M., but special meetings may be called oftener. Six men sit around a table — five commissioners and the city secretary. Every commissioner is there. At one end presides the Mayor-President. The city attorney, city engineer, chief of police, and city physician usually attend also, and frequently other officials. Citizens may or may not be there, though all sessions are public. The meetings are usually short, from half an hour to an hour. The mayor-president calls to order; he is addressed as "Mr. President." The minutes are read and the regular order of business followed, but rapidly; and as there has been more or less informal discussion previously, each man knows about what is coming up for consideration. Everything is concise and direct. The commissioner of streets and public property submits a recommendation to pave certain streets; it is referred to the city engineer for an estimate as to cost. The Commission approves plans for a new fire station, and accepts the bond of a recently appointed city officer. A committee of citizens presents a petition to bar saloons from a residence district. The members of the committee leave as soon as the petition is received, seeming to have great confidence that their request will receive attention. The Commissioners discuss the petition in a businesslike way, some favoring, some opposing; but there is little "playing to the galleries." Adjournment is prompt when the business is done.

GALVESTON

All the members of the Commission at Galveston are business men. The commissioner of waterworks and sewerage is head of a wholesale grocery firm; the police and fire commissioner is an insurance agent and stockbroker; he was formerly alderman. The first mayor-president, Judge William T. Austin, a well-known lawyer and a public-spirited citizen, held that office until November, 1905, the date of his death; he was followed by Mr. H. A. Landes, a wholesale merchant of long experience, a bank director and a member of the school board. In 1909 Judge Lewis Fisher, formerly county and later district judge, was elected mayor-president. The commissioner of finance and revenue is head of a large cotton commission firm, president of a wholesale shoe and hat company and of a bank, and president of the Galveston Cotton Exchange. The fifth commissioner is an active real estate agent. These are the men chosen to administer the affairs of this city of 40,000 — representative business men, of good but not unusual caliber. "While your mayor-president and commissioners are excellent men, are capable and attend strictly to business, there is really but one exceptionally strong man on the Board," said an observant journalist who made a careful study of the Galveston commission. "I think that the plan itself is largely responsible for the splendid showing made by your city government."[1] A study of the personnel of the Commission in other cities tends to confirm the opinion that the form is a large and deciding element in the success achieved, although the

[1] George Kibbe Turner, quoted by E. R. Cheesborough, in the *Galveston Tribune*, December 31, 1909.

men chosen are usually of a higher type than those elected under the former system.

It has been argued that the success of the Galveston plan is due not only to the exceptional men secured as officials, but to the fact that Galveston presents fewer problems of government than most other cities. The contrary is the case, as any one familiar with Galveston realizes. A port with a large floating population, a summer resort where on Sundays the town is filled with excursionists from inland, is harder to govern than the average manufacturing city or commercial center. Moreover, George Kibbe Turner found that of the many laborers residing in Galveston " one fourth are negroes, and a large proportion of the remainder are foreign born. There are many saloons, and saloons usually participate in politics. There are also a large number of merchants and bankers in Galveston, but the middle class, the backbone of every community, is the smallest, in proportion to the population, of any city that I have yet visited. If under these conditions Galveston can produce and maintain a successful system of city government, then any other city in America, by adopting the Galveston plan, can do likewise," [1] — an assertion which other cities are proceeding to test.

Of the first commission, three members were appointed by the governor of Texas and two elected by the city. A decision by the Court of Criminal Appeals of the state, however, compelled a change in 1903 to a board entirely elective. A drayman, arrested for violat-

[1] Quoted by E. R. Cheesborough, in the *Galveston Tribune*, December 31, 1909.

ing a sanitary ordinance, and fined by the local authorities, appealed to the district criminal court on the ground that the city government was unconstitutional, since the citizens were deprived of the right of suffrage guaranteed by the constitution of Texas, a majority of the commissioners being not elected, but appointed. The district court held with the city, but the court of criminal appeals of the state, which has final state jurisdiction in criminal matters, when the case was carried up to it, reversed the decision of the lower court, holding [1] by a vote of two to one that the feature of the charter by which citizens were deprived of a voice in the selection of the officers who were to govern them, was unconstitutional. Later, the Supreme Court, which has final jurisdiction in the state over civil matters, sustained the charter,[2] holding the appointive feature constitutional, and the commission government valid in *civil* affairs. But since criminal matters, in which the Court of Criminal Appeals has final jurisdiction in the state, included the enforcement of police regulations, it was deemed necessary to amend the charter in this respect, conforming to the decision of the body that must pass eventually on some of the acts, at least, of the Commission. An amended charter, eliminating the appointive feature and making all the commissioners elective, was presented to the legislature, then in session, passed promptly, and signed by the governor. An election of five commissioners was ordered, and the same five commissioners who were then in office were reëlected by large majorities.

[1] *Ex parte* Lewis, 45 Tex. Crim. Rep. 1.
[2] Brown *vs.* City of Galveston, 97 Tex. Rep. 1.

Reëlection of Commissioners

The fact that all the commissioners, except the mayor-president, have remained the same since the beginning should be attributed partly to the satisfaction of the people, and partly to the vigorous support of the better citizens; it also indicates possibly an awakening on the part of the voters to the value of experience in public as well as in private business. Continuity in office adds greatly to the quality of the service rendered, provided there is constant and active supervision, either by the public, or by a superior officer. Commercial and manufacturing corporations find that their managers become more expert as they gain familiarity with the details of the business. Why should not the same be true of city administrators? Six terms of two years each, as at Galveston, mean much to the commissioners in their added knowledge and greater ease of handling municipal affairs.[1]

The only referendum provided for in Galveston is on bond issues; bonds cannot be issued by the Board unless first authorized by a majority of the qualified voters of the city who are taxpayers, voting at an election as required by state law.[2] There is no referendum on franchises or other ordinances; nor is there provision for the initiative or the recall. Any member of the Board may be removed for the same reason and in the same manner as county officers. City officers other than commissioners may be removed by the Board for incompetency, corruption, or malfeasance in office, after

[1] The same commissioners were reëlected in May, 1911.
[2] Laws of 1899, chap. 149.

written notice and a hearing. In such cases the Board of Commissioners acts as a court, having exclusive jurisdiction.

The salaries paid to the Commissioners, while not large, are more than those formerly paid to councilmen. The mayor-president receives $2000 a year; each of the other commissioners, $1200. The mayor-president gives at least six hours a day; the others what time is needed. In Houston, with about twice the population of Galveston, the commissioners are compelled to give their entire time, and they receive double the salaries paid in Galveston.[1] Most of the cities operating under the commission plan pay their commissioners and require them to give a bond for the faithful performance of their duties.[2]

The administration of the schools of Galveston is not under the Commissioners, but under a "board of trustees," — unsalaried and elected by the people at a special election. The taxes are levied and collected by the city and paid over to the school treasurer, but otherwise the Board of Commissioners has nothing to do with the schools.

Exact comparisons with the situation prior to 1900 are difficult to draw, since conditions have changed somewhat since the flood. In some departments less money has been spent than formerly; in others, more; the tax rate has not greatly changed. But in the large and fundamental aspects of administration — improved income, economy in expenditures, cleaner streets, a more active health department, and in the increased respect

[1] For discussion of "part time or entire time," see pp. 167–171.
[2] For salaries, see table on pp. 172–180.

of citizens for their municipal government — the evidence is conclusive. Making due allowance for differences in conditions, and discounting the overenthusiastic statements of certain advocates of the new system, it is clear that Galveston under the commission plan is governed much better than previously; and the change seems to be due more largely to the improved form of government than to the unusual public spirit roused by the great disaster. A small board, elected at large, with ample powers, each member being placed in charge of a department for which he is responsible, with publicity and a strong citizens' organization as the main safeguards against misuse of power, — this is the substance of Galveston's contribution to the science of municipal government.

Ten years have elapsed since the storm. Two structures, erected as a result of that catastrophe, hold a continuing interest for men — the Sea Wall, and City Government by Commission.

CHAPTER II

HOUSTON, TEXAS

HOUSTON had no great storm; no such crisis as that at Galveston confronted her; and her adoption of the commission form was due not so much to the need of the hour as to the example set by her neighbor city and a desire for better government. For this reason Houston's experiment, and her success under normal civic conditions throughout, is of much interest to the average American municipality.

For three years Houston observed how well the plan was working in Galveston, forty miles away on the Gulf; she noted Galveston's steady rise to her old-time strength and population, and finally decided to adopt the same form of government for her population of 80,000. There was a struggle before the citizens succeeded in persuading the state legislature to grant the new charter; but in spite of vigorous opposition, it was at last accomplished. The new plan was submitted to popular vote in December, 1904, and though the vote was small, the proposition carried by a good majority; and on March 18, 1905, the new charter was granted. The first election under it took place three months later, and the officials so elected assumed office on July 5, 1905.

Many of the old forms were retained in Houston, though the substance was new. There are five commissioners, elected not by wards, but by the entire body of voters, and possessing large powers, as in Galveston, but they are called the "City Council," — a mayor and four aldermen. There were committees nominally, on finance and revenue; police and fire; water, light, and health; and streets, bridges, and public grounds, having each a chairman and three other members; but in actual practice the chairman was made the administrative chief of his department; the other members of his committee leave the management of the business almost entirely to him. In Houston the entire time of the commissioners is required, and their salaries are $2400 each, with $4000 to the mayor.

There are certain other features different from those of the Galveston charter, one of which is the greater power of the mayor. In Galveston, the mayor-president is only one of five, — the chief, it is true, but with only a single vote and no veto. The mayor of Houston has a veto on every ordinance, and also a "right to vote as a member of the City Council." He may thus have a vote on his own veto. Moreover, he possesses the power to appoint all heads of departments, subject to confirmation by the four aldermen, and may "appoint and remove all officers or employees ... for cause, whenever, in his judgment, the public interests demand,"[1] "and no officer whose office is created by ordinance shall hold the same for any fixed term, but shall always be subject to removal by the mayor, or may be removed by the City Council."[1] The City Council includes the mayor. The City Council "may increase or diminish the compensation of all officers," except

[1] Charter, Art. V, Sec. 2.

themselves, "and abolish entirely any office at any time, except as to the officers above mentioned."[1] The City Council may "establish any office" necessary, "fix its salary and define its duties"; but "any incumbent of any office, except the Controller, may be removed at any time, by the mayor, *with or without* the concurrence of the Council."[2] The mayor, therefore, may remove, upon his own motion, — a second element of his large power. He may be suspended or removed from office, however, by a majority of all the aldermen elected (three out of five).

The commission, as in Galveston, may be convened at any time. The City Council, says the charter, "shall be continuously in executive session, or open and ready to be convened therefor at any time."[3] Its sessions are often very short. The regular meetings, at 4 P.M. every Monday, are little more than a ratification of matters agreed to previously, in informal conference. The council chamber, with the mayor's high desk in front and the chairs of the aldermen arranged in the usual semicircle, is not much used at Houston; the real work is done around a table in the office of the mayor or other member of the Council.

A city controller is elected by the Council every two years, according to the charter; he cannot be removed except by impeachment proceedings, requiring a majority vote of all members of the Council. He acts as an additional guardian of the fiscal affairs of the city, keeping the accounts and making such financial reports as are required.

[1] Charter, Art. V, Sec. 1.   [2] Charter, Art. VII, Sec. 8.
[3] Charter, Art. VII, Sec. 11.

COMMISSION GOVERNMENT

Specific provisions as at Galveston are intended to insure publicity. The Council must not only sit with open doors, but the journal of its proceedings shall also be public; and on every ordinance the yeas and nays shall be recorded. Other minor provisions include the usual prohibition of passing an ordinance on the same date on which it is introduced.[1]

A distinct addition to the provision of the Galveston charter is the referendum on franchises as well as on bond issues. In Houston not only must all issues of bonds amounting to over $100,000 be submitted to the taxpaying voters, the approval of a majority of whom is necessary to empower the City Council to issue the bonds,[2] but a petition signed by five hundred legally qualified voters compels the City Council to order an election at which the voters, by majority vote, may approve or reject any franchise.[3] All grants for a longer period than thirty years *must* be submitted to popular vote, without the necessity of a petition; no grant, however, shall be made for more than fifty years, the same limit being set also in the Galveston charter. Other provisions as to compensation, regulation of rates, and examination of accounts guard the issue of franchises still more fully.[4] Galveston leaves almost complete control of franchises to the Board of Commissioners, with only a few specified requirements.[5]

It may be noted, in passing, that two aldermen appointed by the mayor, together with the assessor and collector of taxes, constitute the board of appraisement

---

[1] Charter, Art. VII, Sec. 6.   [2] Charter, Art. IV, Sec. 1.
[3] Charter, Art. II, Sec. 18.   [4] Charter, Art. II, Sec. 17.
[5] See charter of Galveston, Sec. 45.

(equalization of taxes), and appeal from their decision is to the City Council, which is the final authority.

Members of the City Council, like the Galveston commissioners, may not be pecuniarily interested in any contract let by the city; and all contracts involving $1000 or more must be advertised and let to the "lowest secure bidder." Also, any taxpayer may maintain an action to restrain the execution of an illegal contract by the city.

The city possesses the power to acquire public utilities. There is no initiative on ordinances, nor "recall" of officers.

In Houston, then, a board of five directors, including a powerful general manager called a mayor, directs municipal affairs, with authority to pass ordinances, appoint and remove all other officers and employees, determine salaries and qualifications, and grant franchises, subject, upon proper petition, to popular approval. Power is concentrated in this single body, and public attention is focused upon it. To locate responsibility each alderman is head of a certain "committee" or department; to assure control by the voters, the charter provides for publicity of proceedings, the recording of each councilman's vote on every ordinance, the publication of ordinances granting franchises, a referendum on franchises and on bond issues of over $100,000, and certain other restrictions.

Financial Results

The commission form provided for Houston, similar in most of its essentials to that of Galveston, produced similar results. In the first eight months under the new régime, a floating debt of $400,000 was retired, without a bond issue. Back taxes were collected vigorously. The offices of controller and of secretary were consolidated, saving $2100 a year, the salary of the former secretary. The cashier of a well-known bank was appointed treasurer at a nominal salary — $600 a year, as against a former annual expense of $2720. Interest on city deposits in the past five years has amounted to more than $40,000.[1] Not a cent was previously received from this source. Improvements have been made without the issue of bonds. Park property was purchased to the amount of $56,000 in 1907 and $18,000 in 1910; $42,000 was spent during 1907 alone, for paving. The amount of $340,323.63 has been put into eleven new schoolhouses since 1905; $98,000 has been appropriated for deepening the channel to the Gulf. New bridges have been built and new sewers constructed. The price of gas, when the commission assumed charge of the city, was $1.50 per thousand cubic feet; now it is $1.15 per thousand cubic feet. In July, 1905, arc lights for the city streets were costing $80 per year. Now they are $70. These reductions have been made without friction or litigation; the commission seems to have shown no disposition to prevent the public service companies from earning a fair return on their investment, at the same time insisting that the citizens shall be benefited by lower rates. About $1000 a year has been saved to the city by the early settlement of its electric light account each month, a discount of two and a half per cent being allowed by the local lighting com-

[1] Figures furnished by the commissioner of finance and revenue, up to January 1, 1911.

pany for the prompt payment of monthly bills. Employees have received their wages in cash, at the same time being required to give a full measure of work in return. The tax rate, instead of increasing, was reduced from $2 to $1.90, then to $1.80, and is now $1.70, per $100.

That the people have confidence in their new commission is evident from the fact that a proposition to purchase and operate the municipal waterworks plant, overwhelmingly voted down in August, 1903, was carried by a majority of three to one in May, 1906, after ten months of the new government. The purchase price was $901,700.

The installation of water meters has been begun by the city, and the wasting of water is being gradually checked.

In the field of police control, and law enforcement, as important to the welfare of a city as financial efficiency, results have been good, though not so striking as in some other cities. Gambling is believed to have been largely suppressed; gambling houses entirely abolished; pool rooms are shut; saloons are closed at one o'clock every night, and on Sundays. In the department of health, more attention has been paid to the collection of garbage and other waste, a small but efficient crematory being operated at low cost. In the single item of city prescriptions, a typical saving has been effected. The city has been accustomed to furnish drugs free to those sick who are unable to pay for them. The former method was to send the prescriptions to be filled at a drug store, at an average cost of thirty-five cents for each prescription. With the advent of the commissioners, the city established a free dispensary, buying its own drugs at wholesale, and the cost of prescriptions fell to an average of eight cents apiece.

Personnel of the Commission

Of the commissioners at Houston, two have held their positions since the beginning. The present mayor and head of the commission was mayor previously, but was unable to accomplish much under the old system. He is a politician of considerable ability, vigorous and aggressive, and a man of some property.

The present commissioner of finance was a merchant, and formerly an alderman. He is popularly known as the father of the commission system in Houston; he fought for the plan when it had few friends, and after its installation was placed in charge of the revenues. "Our commissioner of finance," said a merchant, "saves us much money each year. He and the other commissioners refused to pay the brick trust extortionate prices for paving brick, and finally brought a shipload from New York at a much lower cost."

The other three commissioners, after two terms each, were replaced in 1909 by others. The first commissioner of water, light, and health, James A. Thompson, had been an alderman under the last previous administration; before that he was a printer. He was classed by citizens, together with the mayor, as a combination of politician and business man. The first head of the department of streets, bridges, and public grounds was a blacksmith, later a justice of the peace, and finally city commissioner. A majority of the members of the first

HOUSTON, TEXAS

commission and of the present commission,[1] were active in local politics, in some capacity previously.

Differences in policy developed early in the Council, the most marked being over the question whether to save money and leave streets unswept and unpaved, or to raise funds and make improvements. Such differences are bound to arise in any board; but in Houston the mayor has dominated.

Interviews with citizens of all types bring out an astonishing unanimity of opinion as to the marked improvement manifest in nearly every department. Merchants, lawyers, insurance men, cotton brokers, bank cashiers, railroad officials, emphasize the businesslike character and efficiency of the commissioners' administration, one declaring that Houston is now saved thousands of dollars each year in street paving alone, and that the city could well afford to pay their "directors" double the salaries which they are now receiving, purely as a business proposition. The proprietor of one of the largest stores stated frankly that he is now reporting his property for taxation at a higher valuation than under the old government because he has confidence that the money will be well spent. A banker called attention to the fact that previously with high taxes the city was nevertheless heavily in debt; now, with lower taxes, a large share of the debt has been paid, and at the same time the streets are better cared for, the sewerage system is being extended, and other improvements carried on.

The principal opposition to the new government, so far as ascertained, came at the beginning from politicians who were displaced by the change.

[1] March, 1911. The same members were reëlected for 1911 and 1912.

COMMISSION GOVERNMENT

Several large taxpayers expressed belief that it is better to have the commissioners elected at large than by wards, and to give their entire time to the city government. "We depend on getting good men, paying them well, and having them give their whole time to the city's affairs," said one. "It is true that some of our best business men cannot afford to be city aldermen (commissioners) for the salary paid, but nevertheless, very good men can be had. One manager for each department is an especially valuable arrangement for looking closely after the city's work."

CHAPTER III

DES MOINES, IOWA

In the fall of 1905, business took James G. Berryhill, an attorney of Des Moines, to Galveston. The commission plan had then been in operation in the latter city for four years, and was beginning to attract attention. Friends of the attorney urged him to study the system, while there, and ascertain whether it offered a really better method of city government. Upon his return to Des Moines, a meeting of citizens listened with interest to his account of the changed conditions in the Texas city. Other meetings were held, and a period of active discussion followed. A commission was appointed to prepare a bill for presentation to the Iowa legislature. The plan submitted included not only the small council, elected by the entire city, and exercising both ordinance power and administrative oversight, but also certain additional features, among others the compulsory submission of franchises to popular vote, the Los Angeles "recall," and nonpartisan nominations and elections.

This bill, presented to the legislature during the winter of 1905–1906, failed of passage; public sentiment had not sufficiently developed. Discussion continued, the movement for a change of charter gathering momentum. A group of citizens urged the so-called "Indianapolis Plan," recently adopted in that city, under which much power was vested in the mayor, while legislative authority centered in a large council elected by small subdivisions of the city. A committee from Des Moines visited Indianapolis; and upon its return, the comparative merits of the Galveston plan and the Indianapolis method were presented at a public debate held early in 1907, under the auspices of the Commercial Club. The Galveston form was endorsed by a decisive majority of the committee of three hundred citizens who had been named as jurors. A bill was again drawn and presented to the legislature, and became a law on March 29, 1907. This act, a general law permitting any city of over 25,000 population to adopt the commission form, if approved by a majority of its electors, has since been extended to all cities of over 7000 population.

The former government of Des Moines consisted of a mayor and nine councilmen, seven elected by wards and two at large. The mayor did not have large powers. Besides having a veto, he appointed the board of public works and the chief of police, subject to confirmation by the Council. There had been, however, continued conflict between the mayor and the Council. The members of the board of public works remained in office after their term had expired, and the mayor was unable to replace them on account of opposition in the Council. A police and fire commission controlled the personnel of those departments under what were supposed to be civil service regulations; but politics ruled. In the council a group of aldermen combined to expend most of the appropriations for public improvements in certain wards, while the other wards were denied recognition.[1] The Council was slow and weak in administra-

[1] See Address before the Iowa Bar Association, July 9, 1908, by James G. Berryhill.

DES MOINES, IOWA

tion because of a lack of concentration of power; it was neglectful of the interests of the city because it was not accountable to the electorate as a whole. These two flaws in the municipal machinery, common to many cities, had become so evident that special attention was given to their elimination in the new measure. The commission law abolished election by wards; reduced the Council to five, including the mayor; provided that all officials, except these five, should be chosen by the Council — features copied from the Galveston plan; it took the Houston referendum and greatly broadened it; added a "recall" for unsatisfactory councilmen; the initiative; a nonpartisan ballot for primaries and elections, and certain other interesting provisions, all designed to simplify the form of government, to concentrate authority, and to provide definite and easy popular control, free of partisanship.

The Iowa law, or, as it is sometimes called, the "Des Moines Plan," has been the model for so many recent charters that it is of interest to quote its most important provisions.[1]

Each city adopting the commission plan "shall be governed by a council, consisting of the mayor and four councilmen,[2] chosen as provided in this act, each of whom shall have the right to vote on all questions coming before the council. Three members of the council shall constitute a quorum, and the affirmative vote of three members shall be necessary to adopt any motion, resolution, or ordinance, or pass any measure, unless a greater

[1] The text of the law is given in full, pp. 308–333.
[2] In cities of less than 25,000 population, a mayor and two councilmen. See law as amended in 1909.

number is provided for in this act. . . . The mayor shall preside at all meetings of the council; he shall have no power to veto any measure, but every resolution or ordinance, passed by the council, must be signed by the mayor, or by two councilmen, and be recorded before the same shall be in force."

Furthermore, "the council shall have and possess, and the council and its members shall exercise all executive, legislative, and judicial powers and duties now had, possessed, and exercised by the mayor, city council, solicitor, assessor, treasurer, auditor, city engineer, and other executive and administrative officers in cities of the first and second class, and in cities under special charter, and shall also possess and exercise all executive, legislative and judicial powers and duties now had and exercised by the board of public works, park commissioners, the board of police and fire commissioners, board of waterworks, trustees, and board of library trustees" in all cities where such exist. "The executive and administrative powers, authority and duties in such cities shall be distributed into and among five departments, as follows: —

"1. Department of Public Affairs.
"2. Department of Accounts and Finance.
"3. Department of Public Safety.
"4. Department of Streets and Public Improvements.
"5. Department of Parks and Public Property."[1]

Acting as a body, the Council assigns each of its members to be head of a department, except the mayor, who always has charge of Public Affairs; it performs

[1] Law as amended in 1909, Sec. 1056–a 25.

the usual legislative function of passing ordinances and making regulations for the city; it appoints, by majority vote, at its first meeting, or as soon as practicable thereafter, "a city clerk, solicitor, assessor, treasurer, auditor, civil engineer, city physician, marshal, chief of fire department, market master, street commissioner, three library trustees, and such other officers and assistants, as shall be provided for by ordinance and necessary to the proper and efficient conduct of the affairs of the city; and . . . a police judge in those cities not having a superior court." The Council may remove officers and assistants so appointed, determine the duties to be performed by each department and the duties of officers and employees, may require an officer or employee to perform duties in two or more departments, and from time to time "create, fill, and discontinue offices and employments, other than herein prescribed, according to their judgment of the needs of the city; and may, by majority vote of all the members, remove any such officer or employee, except as otherwise provided for in this act; and may, by resolution, or otherwise, prescribe, limit or change the compensation of such officers or employees."

As individual members of the Council, each councilman is assigned to a specific field of activity, in which he exercises administrative control, and for the successful conduct of which he is held responsible by his fellow members, and, to a considerable degree, by the public. The numerous Council committees of several members each, under the usual aldermanic plan, are replaced in Des Moines and the other commission cities by five committees of one person each, that person being the definite head of the department which is allotted to him. There is no gap between Council and departments; committee chairman and department chief are one.

The mayor, in charge of the department of Public Affairs, has general oversight of the city's business. Under his control, also, are the corporation counsel, the police court, the city library, and the civil service commission.

The councilman in charge of Accounts and Finance has supervision of the accounts of the city, inspects all city records and audits the accounts of every officer or employee who receives or disburses money. He purchases supplies, and has charge of all public printing. His duty is to report to the Council on all bills, payrolls, and claims before they are allowed. He sees that public-service corporations make proper reports to the city, and collects license fees, franchise taxes, rentals, and similar moneys. Under him are the assessor, auditor, treasurer, license collector, city clerk, and market master, and their employees.

The Department of Public Safety includes the police and fire departments, the city physician and board of health, the inspector of plumbing, the city electrician, the electrical inspector and all associated employees. The head of this department has direct supervision of the regulation of saloons, the suppression of gambling, the maintenance of order, and the protection of property.

The Department of Streets and Public Improvements deals with the paving and cleaning of streets, the construction of sidewalks, sewers, bridges and other improvements, lighting, and all city contracts. It includes the city engineer, the street commissioner, supervision

DES MOINES, IOWA

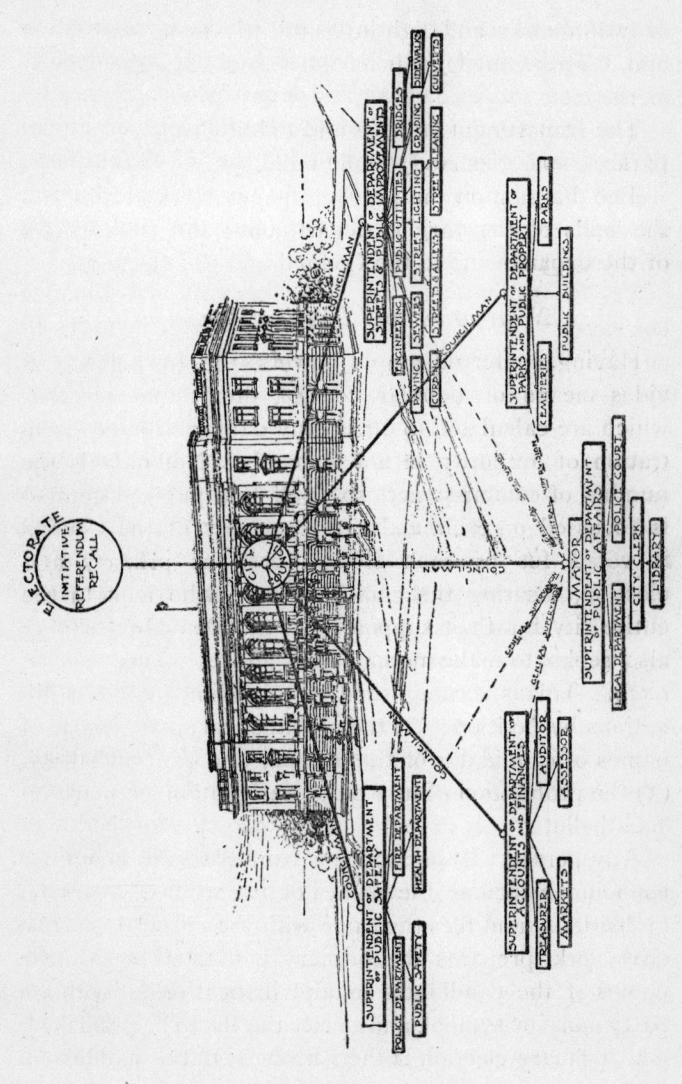

of waterworks and lighting, and the many inspectors and laborers engaged in constructing the public works of the city.

The Department of Parks and Public Property controls parks, cemeteries, and public buildings.

The diagram on the previous page shows graphically the fields of the various departments, and the relation, of the departments to the Council and the electorate.

Nomination and Election Provisions

Having conferred ample powers, the Iowa law provides means of popular control, direct and positive, which are calculated to offset any danger from concentration of authority in a few hands. Not only is the number of commissioners so small that public attention is focussed on each, and every member of the Council is voted for by each elector, both at primary and election, insuring the choice of men who look to the entire city for their support; but the Des Moines plan also seeks to make nominations and elections *nonpartisan*. This is accomplished by providing for (1) nominations by petition; (2) the alphabetical arrangement of names of candidates on the primary and election ballots; (3) the prohibition of any party designation or mark on such ballots.

Any person wishing to be a candidate for mayor or councilman secures the names of twenty-five voters on his petition, and files the same with the city clerk. The city clerk prepares the primary ballot, arranging the names of the candidates in alphabetical order, with no party name or symbol, and causes the list to be published. The primary election is then held. Of the candidates for mayor the two receiving the largest number of votes at the primary become the nominees for election; and similarly, the eight candidates for councilmen who poll at the primary the largest number of votes are given a place on the election ballot, again with their names arranged alphabetically and party names prohibited. Each elector votes for a mayor and all four councilmen, a majority electing the mayor, and the candidates for councilmen who receive the four highest number of votes being elected. The voter, thus compelled to mark each name separately, since there is no party circle or square, a cross in which will carry a vote to a long list of candidates, must make a choice of men. This is an effective means of separating national from local issues. What interest has the city dweller, as such, in the *national* politics of the councilmen who light and pave the streets he uses, furnish him police protection, supply him with pure water, and for all these purposes spend his taxes? What parties there are in city elections should be determined by local considerations. It is impossible to eliminate city politics, even under the commission plan; but a councilman chosen for his ability or his popularity or for a well-known municipal policy which he favors is likely to serve the community better than if elected merely because he is a Republican or a Democrat.

Publicity requirements in the Iowa law are not markedly different from those of the two cities previously considered. All meetings of the Council are public; the yeas and nays are to be recorded on every resolution and ordinance; and monthly financial statements are published, together with the Council proceedings; an annual examination of the finances of the city must be made, and the results published.

Publicity provisions are supplemented by a broad referendum, the initiative, and the recall.

Referendum and Initiative

The referendum, under the Des Moines plan, is more comprehensive than that provided by the Houston charter, since it applies not only to bond issues and franchises, but to all ordinances; and the submission of all franchises to popular vote is mandatory, no petition of voters being necessary. A petition signed by 25 per cent of the entire vote cast for all candidates for mayor at the last muncipal election,[1] protesting against the passage of an ordinance, may be presented to the Council during the ten days between the final passage of all ordinances and the date of their taking effect; and upon verification of the petition by the city clerk, the Council must submit the ordinance in question to the voters "either at the general election or at a special election to be called for that purpose"; and the ordinance does not go into effect unless approved by a majority of the votes so cast. Franchises, as just noted, must in all cases be approved by a majority of the electors voting thereon.

A petition of 25 per cent of the voters, containing a request for a proposed ordinance, compels the Council either to pass the ordinance without alteration within twenty days, or submit the same without alteration at a special election (unless a general municipal election falls due within ninety days); and if approved by a majority

[1] See law (as amended in 1909), Sec. 1056–a 38, for exact wording.

of the votes so cast, becomes a binding ordinance of the city. If 10 per cent, but less than 25 per cent, of the voters petition for such an ordinance, the Council must submit the same at the next general election. This is known as the initiative, from the power of the voters to initiate or originate legislation. It is the positive side of the referendum.

Recall

An unsatisfactory mayor or councilman may be recalled and another substituted in his place, upon filing with the city clerk a petition signed by 25 per cent of the last vote for mayor, demanding the election of a successor of the person sought to be removed, and stating the grounds for such request. After the clerk certifies that the names signed are genuine signatures and of the number required, the Council is compelled to call an election, at which the voters may choose a successor to the official in question, or indorse the incumbent, by a majority vote. To nominate such a successor requires a 10 per cent petition.

The referendum and initiative insure popular control over measures; the recall, control of officials. If honest and efficient commissioners pass a bad ordinance, the referendum can be utilized. But if a member of the commission proves manifestly recreant to his trust and an unsafe public servant, his removal may be effected by means of the recall.

Civil Service Commission

The Des Moines plan provides also for a civil service commission of three members, appointed by the Council for six years,[1] and removable for cause by a four fifths vote of the Council. It also includes special provisions as to franchises, besides the referendum; it prohibits officials from being interested in city contracts or accepting substantial favors from public service corporations,[2] and punishes political assistance in return for a money consideration by fine or imprisonment.

The main idea of the Des Moines plan, says John J. Hamilton of Des Moines,[3] — " was frankly appropriated from the charter of Galveston. The recall of unsatisfactory officials was borrowed from Los Angeles. The charter of Dallas, Texas, perhaps most directly suggested the referendum and the initiative, although an enlargement of a right long possessed, by all cities, under an Iowa statute." Both were adopted as the result of general and local discussion, as was the elimination of partisanship from city elections. "The unqualified establishment of the merit system was an evolution from a less thorough but excellent plan already in operation. The double election, as a feature of municipal practice, originated in Des Moines, but had many precedents to suggest and justify it. The provisions for purity of elections and administration, for publicity and for the safeguarding of franchises, gave effect to local demands due, in part at least, to discussion which had long been going on in every part of the country. The abolition of the ward system was incidental to the adoption of the commission plan, being inherent in it."

[1] See commission law, Sec. 14, for details.
[2] Sec. 13 (amended law, Sec. 1056-a 31).
[3] John J. Hamilton, "The Dethronement of the City Boss," pp. 9, 10.

DES MOINES, IOWA

The Plan in Operation

The outcome of the first nominating primary and election was to place in power as members of the council (commissioners) a former police judge, two union labor men, a former mayor, and a former city assessor, a board not particularly favorable to the new plan. These men began their duties in April, 1908. The administration which went out left more than $175,000 of outstanding judgments and other claims. This amount the new government took up by issuing bonds, and with a clear field went forward to meet current expenses.

Among the first reforms instituted was the installation of modern bookkeeping methods. It was found that under the former system a justice had failed to turn over several thousands of dollars of fees due the city; and when inspection revealed the discrepancy, there was no way of telling whether all the funds were then turned over, since the justice, in many cases, had given no receipt to those who paid the fees. Money had also been allowed to remain a long time in the hands of the county officers before being paid to the city. Under the new system it has been secured promptly and regularly. Bills are paid as soon as audited.

The estimates which have been made as to the saving in cash to the city during the first year of the commission vary considerably, and in view of the ease with which figures can be made to prove a case, all comparative statements on this point should be examined with care. On the broad question as to whether the city has secured greater returns for the money expended, there is unanimity of opinion, not only at the city hall, where

COMMISSION GOVERNMENT

the city auditor and two commissioners have held office under both the old and new governments, but also in the banks and offices of the city, where are found well-informed business men who are familiar with municipal finances. All agree that much has been saved to the city by the careful business methods of the commissioners. Just how much has been saved, it is more difficult to say. The following statement by the city auditor, John W. Hawk, shows the condition of the working funds of the city during the years ending March 31, 1907, March 31, 1908, and the year ending March 31, 1909, which was the first year of the new administration: —

COMPARATIVE STATEMENT OF WORKING FUNDS.
1906, 1907 AND 1908.

For year 1906:
  Cash on hand April 1,
    1907 $70396.63
  Claims outstanding $55085.83
  Excess cash over claims $15310.80

For year 1907:
  Cash on hand April 1,
    1908 $72790.11
  Claims outstanding $191989.93
  Excess claims over cash $119199.82
  Loss 1907 $134510.62

  Claims outstanding April
    1, 1908 $191989.93
  Claims paid by Bond issue $175616.07
  Claims that were not paid
    by Bond issue $16373.86
  Cash on hand April 1,
    1908 $72790.11
  Excess cash over claims
    that were not paid by
    Bond issue $56416.25

DES MOINES, IOWA

For year 1908:
  Cash on hand April 1,
    1909 $164352.05
  Claims outstanding $59496.77
  Excess cash over claims $104855.28
  Gain 1908 $48439.03
Gain 1908 over 1907 $182949.65

On April 1, 1910, the excess of cash in the working funds over claims outstanding was $38,118.53; on April 1, 1911, $15,342.77, although the auditor states that this last amount should properly be $41,993.18, since $26,540.41 of the claims outstanding were for amounts covering a period of five years, for litigation in street railway and waterworks cases, but the actual amount of which was not known till April 1, 1911. These figures indicate at least the successful attempt of the city to live within its income. Just how much more they signify can be determined only after a more thorough study of the objects for which city funds were expended than has yet been made. Expenditures should be compared in detail for several years both before and after April 1, 1908.

In the cost of paving, grading, laying of sewers, and construction of bridges, it is not possible to make comparisons of value, since varying conditions of labor, materials, length of haul, character of soil, and the like, offer few instances of jobs sufficiently similar in size and kind. In street lighting, however, conditions are so far alike that it is possible to compare the cost in the year preceding April, 1908, with the year following. The cost of arc lamps for street lighting in 1907 was $95 per year; in 1908, the rate was first reduced to $75, and then to $65 for all-night arcs. A claim of the electric company for $4500 was cancelled. In addition, 603 lamps, formerly on moonlight schedule, now burn all night and every night, 4000 hours per year, a gain of 1818 hours per lamp per year. The auditor's annual report for the year ending March 31, 1909, showed the saving over the cost of lighting during the previous year amounted to $5,548.97, with an average of 71 more lamps in 1908 than in 1907.[1]

In the cleaning of catch basins, a simple operation which varies little from year to year, the average cost was $1.40 in 1907, with 2272 basins cleaned; 3860 were cleaned in 1908 (year ending March 31, 1909) at an average cost of $1.12 each. The chief clerk of the Department of Streets and Public Improvements states that in the old days it took three men, in one case, a day and a half to lower the level of a catch basin, a job of a few hours under present business methods.

In the character of the work done by officials and employees, there has been a marked change. Men formerly retained on account of their influence with council members are now subject to prompt dismissal for incompetency or drunkenness. The foreman in charge of a sewer repair gang was dismissed because the work of his gang was costing too much, a reason unheard of before. More work is done, and with a better spirit on the part of both heads of the departments and employees, than ever before in the history of the city.

The evidence of citizens as to the results secured is specific.

Said a wholesaler of coffees and spices: "The streets and alleys downtown are cleaner under the new plan;

[1] First Annual Report, City of Des Moines, 1908, p. 187.

sidewalks are being laid of uniform width and material, of cement, with an iron strip for edging. One or two pieces of bad paving have been rejected."

"Police regulations are better enforced," said a lawyer; "saloons are about the same as usual, but slot machines have been suppressed, and the red light district broken up, its denizens being mainly driven out of the city, not merely scattered."

"The fire department, usually efficient, is even more so under present conditions; and both policemen and firemen present a neater appearance," affirmed a third. These statements were repeatedly corroborated.

The cashier of the Iowa National Bank declared: "Since there has been a clear-cut division of municipal work, officials seem to take an interest in their duties."

"The new method," said the secretary and manager of the Brown-Hurley Hardware Company, "makes it possible to locate responsibility at the city hall for any act or failure of the city government. There is every reason to believe that the plan will be continued." He also emphasized the value of good streets in the business section.

One of the largest property owners in Des Moines, pointing out the superiority of the new system over the old, stated that formerly "it was frequently impossible to find an official at the city hall. The councilmen, being practically unpaid, gave little or no time to the city's affairs, meeting nights after their own business was finished. Now that men are paid to devote their whole time to the work of the city, they can be found at the city hall during the day, looking after their departments." A large retail clothing merchant remarked also on the prompt attention to business by paid commissioners.

The editors of the Des Moines *News*, the *Capital*, and the *Register and Leader* speak enthusiastically of the changes wrought by the new law. Professors in the Des Moines colleges now favor the plan which some of them at first opposed. The president of the Williams Buggy Company called attention to the fact that several of the councilmen held office under the old government, the same men who are accomplishing so much more for the city under the new system.

The Councilmen

Of the present commissioners, three were reëlected in April, 1910. Of these, John MacVicar, previously mayor twice, is head of the Department of Streets and Public Improvements. He has been secretary for several years of the League of American Municipalities, and has taken a wide interest in city affairs. Charles W. Schramm, formerly city assessor, now superintending the Department of Accounts and Finance, was also reëlected. In his department, the auditor was deputy auditor for six years, and auditor for two years, before the new government went into operation.

The first mayor was a former police judge, personally popular, though not particularly favorable to the new plan at the outset. He was succeeded in 1910 by Professor James R. Hanna, of Des Moines College.

John L. Hamery, the first commissioner in charge of Public Safety, was a union labor man, a journeyman printer by trade. He was a reform alderman in 1907, and made a good record in police matters during the two years of his commissionership, cleaning up the city

DES MOINES, IOWA

with energy and decision. He was defeated for reëlection in 1910 by a narrow margin.

The head of the Department of Parks and Public Property used to be a coal miner, and was deputy sheriff for one term. He is also a union labor man. He was reëlected.

The East Side of Des Moines — for the city is divided by the Des Moines River — contains the state capitol and a business section of its own, not so large, however, as that on the West Side. The first mayor and the commissioner of parks came from east of the river; the others lived on the West Side. The new commissioners are also fairly evenly distributed. There are both Republicans and Democrats on the board; union labor is represented; and there is no tendency discernible to choose the commissioners from any single section of the city, nor from any one profession or class.

Attend a meeting of the commission, that is, of the new Council, of Des Moines. Around a plain table, on which there are a telephone, a copy of the city ordinances, and various papers, sit five men and the city clerk discussing plans, receiving communications, passing occasionally an ordinance or resolution. A large map of the city hangs on the wall close at hand, showing wards and streets and water mains and city buildings. Reporters and a few citizens usually are present. Most meetings are open to the public.[1] There are no long

---

[1] " Whenever the council shows a disposition to hold many 'executive sessions,' " said a newspaper man, " the newspapers stir up the public, and everybody wants to know the reason for excluding citizens. Then the council has to divulge its plans."

speeches, no parliamentary wrangles, though decided differences of opinion have often developed. The business is commonly completed in an hour or less. Meetings are frequent, often every day at 10 A.M. The commissioners give all their time, and receive $3000 a year each, except the mayor, whose salary is $3500.

This, then, is the Des Moines plan of commission government. A city board of directors, elected at large by the municipal stockholders — the voters — are given adequate power to transact all business, subject, however, to recall for cause; and their ordinances may, upon petition, be referred to the stockholders for approval. Their proceedings must be published each month; their meetings are public; their municipal duties are their only business; and they are paid. The showing made by the first three years' operation is likely to result in its continuance, in the opinion of those interviewed.

The referendum and recall enable the voters of the city, knowing now who is responsible, to effectively control their agents. Control is undoubtedly more easily exercised with these two features than without them, unless, as in the case of Galveston, the city is governed by unusually able and unselfish men, and its citizens are moved by an uncommon public spirit.

Constitutionality of the "Des Moines Plan"

The validity of the Iowa law was attacked before the district court of Iowa in and for Polk County, the decision being rendered November 23, 1907, and later affirmed by the state supreme court. On the point that the United States Constitution provides that " the United States shall guarantee to every state in the Union a republican form of government," and that the Iowa commission plan does not provide for representative government, and therefore not for a republican government, the court held that the "provision of the Constitution of the United States, invoked in this case, is a guarantee by the federal government to the state; and it does not apply to a city. Cities are unknown to the national Constitution. They are organized under the state constitution and state laws." " The new plan provides for a government by representatives chosen by the people, and is clearly republican in form; but even though it were not, it would not be affected by the provisions of the Constitution of the United States here invoked, for the reason that municipal corporations are mere creatures of the legislature and subject to its control."[1]

Upon the other points raised, mainly technical, the court held that the act was not special or local legislation; that the provision of the state constitution that "the powers of the government of Iowa shall be divided into three separate departments, the legislative, the executive, and judicial," relate only to the government of the state, and that the affairs of the city are not a part of the state government. Other minor contentions were overruled, and the act was held to be entirely constitutional.[1]

[1] See text of decision, Eckerson *vs.* City of Des Moines, *N. W. Reporter*, March 24, 1908, p. 179.

CHAPTER IV

CEDAR RAPIDS

CEDAR RAPIDS began operating under the commission law of Iowa at the same time as Des Moines. The city is the center of a thriving farming community; it contains also two of the largest cereal mills in the United States, a large starch works, and smaller mills and factories. The population numbers about 30,000;[1] probably one fourth of its inhabitants are of Bohemian birth or extraction. Having an assessed valuation of $25,000,000, and an annual expenditure for municipal purposes of about $300,000 (exclusive of special assessments), with a mixed population, and both farming and manufacturing as the source of its wealth, it is typical of many American cities of less than 100,000.

The proposition to adopt the board plan was carried at a special election in December, 1907, by a majority of only thirty-three. To-day, judging by the expression of opinion by citizens of all classes, it commands the support of almost the entire city. At the primaries there were nine candidates for mayor and forty-eight for commissioner; but in spite of the rush for offices, the officials finally elected were fairly typical business men.[2] The council of five replaced a mayor and ten aldermen, one alderman from each of the eight wards and two elected

[1] 32,811, according to census of 1910.

[2] For interesting details of the campaign, see John J. Hamilton, "The Dethronement of the City Boss," Chap. XIV.

at large. As mayor and head of the department of Public Affairs, the owner and foreman of a foundry and machine shop was chosen. Upon his death in August, 1909, the Commissioner of Finance, a lawyer and real estate agent, was selected to fill the place. The editor and publisher of a local newspaper, a member of the retiring council, took charge of Public Safety, including the police and fire bureaus. The owner of a printing establishment, who had been councilman for four years and mayor for four years, was made head of the department of Streets and Public Improvements. The manager of a stone and lime company, who had previously been a councilman for several years, took the place left vacant when the Commissioner of Finance became mayor. Four members of the new administration, therefore, were connected with the city government under the former system, and many of their assistants had been employed in the city hall. These "average men and politicians" constituted the first commission of Cedar Rapids, giving nearly all of their time to the city's affairs, though the Iowa law does not contain a specific requirement to that effect.

The new administration had scarcely taken office before it had a smallpox epidemic to deal with. The Council, as the local board of health, which the Iowa law makes it, found cases of the disease developing in all parts of the city, the result of nonenforcement of quarantine regulations by the previous board; and the detention hospital was soon filled. The commission went into continuous executive session, shut up schools and colleges, fumigated houses, and maintained a rigid quarantine; until in two months the detention hospital was closed and the disease stamped out.

Then the commission turned its attention to improvements, at the same time practicing economies that enabled it to close the first year with a surplus. The quarters of the fire department were repaired, and two new brick stations built. Streets were paved with brick, or macadam cement walks were laid; sewers were constructed and water mains extended, — all these being needed additions and the most extensive which had ever been made in a single year. There had never been any money left for these purposes in the former days. For the first time in the history of the city, paving not up to specifications was rejected, amounting in value to $75,000. It is not entirely clear that the inferior material might not have served the purpose fairly well; but the Council feared the effect of the precedent, and ordered the street relaid with better brick. The commission extended streets and erected street signs; it made arrangements for the building of a new concrete bridge across the Cedar River, which divides the city into east and west sides.

An island in the river, equidistant from the two sides and yet near the business center of the city, most conveniently situated for a city hall, had for years laid unimproved and unsightly. A junk dealer occupied part of the six acres with his yards; the rest was bare ground or a dump heap. The natural beauty and practical advantages of the site had led to several attempts previously to secure it for the city, but the jealousy of ward aldermen prevented. Among the first acts of the commission was the bringing of a civic improvement expert to Cedar Rapids, to prepare a comprehensive plan of municipal beautifying and improvement. He recommended, among other things, the securing of the island for civic purposes. An option was obtained, and the island purchased for $106,500, the old city hall property being sold for $66,500; and the new government was soon installed in temporary quarters on the new site; this natural and sensible location for the city center will, in due time, be occupied by an new municipal building.

In what was formerly the eighth ward lived many small home owners, mechanics and workmen, who are among the best citizens of a community. They were without sewer or water facilities, since there was no connection with the rest of the city. At some points the streets had not yet been cut through. When the commissioners decided that this section should be afforded modern improvements, as well as other parts of the city, it was seen that the cost of excavation and filling might be materially decreased, to the advantage of the abutting property owners, by lowering the grade. No one had thought of altering the old grade, which dated back to 1886. It was cut down, however, streets opened, sidewalks and gutters put in, and sewer and water connection provided, all in the first year of the commission. "Councilmen are alert and regardful of the public interest," said a citizen, "because they can be held responsible to *all* the citizens."

In spite of the many improvements effected, the tax rate has been slightly reduced. In 1907, the last year of the old régime, the annual valuation was $22,832,785; the city levy (one fourth valuation) was 41.6 mills. In 1908, the first year under the commission, the valuation was $23,522,112, and the city levy 40.6 mills; in 1909, with $24,823,976 as the value assessed, the rate was 40.3 mills.[1]

[1] Data supplied by Department of Accounts and Finance.

COMMISSION GOVERNMENT

At the beginning of their term, the commissioners had a careful examination made of the books of the city to determine its financial condition, and an inventory taken. They then began a systematic cleaning up of outstanding warrants, and the prompt meeting of current demands. One improvement was to pay bills every week, discounting them 2 per cent. These discounts in the course of a year amount to nearly enough to pay the auditor's salary, which is $1200, as may be seen from the following table furnished by the city auditor for the twelve months beginning December, 1908:—

MONTHLY DISCOUNTS IN CEDAR RAPIDS[1]

	December, 1908	$166.61
	January, 1909	75.93
	February, "	110.06
	March, "	64.45
	April, "	76.95
12 months	May, "	80.85
	June, "	131.45
	July, "	141.23
	August, "	58.67
	September, "	32.11
	October, "	66.92
	November, "	121.61
		$1126.84

Formerly the city not only did not save this discount, but paid interest on outstanding bills. A well-known business man stated that during his four years' service in the Council, the city issued warrants, in the absence of funds to pay for supplies, labor, and other items,

[1] "Amounts saved by city of Cedar Rapids, by discounting current bills at 2 per cent and paying same every Monday."

these warrants drawing 6 per cent interest after being stamped "no funds" and countersigned by the city treasurer. These the city employee had to cash at stores or banks at eighty-five cents on the dollar, thus losing 15 per cent of his wages.

City funds on deposit with banks drew $2100 interest on daily balances and time deposits during 1908 — another small economy.

The fiscal affairs of the city, systematized and carefully managed, are given publicity by a monthly bulletin of the proceedings of the Council, which contains a clear financial statement; and a simple index of ordinances and resolutions enables any desired item in the bulletin to be easily found.

In the cost of sewer extensions and street paving, fairly low prices are said to have generally prevailed in Cedar Rapids; and any improvement on this score is regarded as due not to the commission plan, but to active competition or other causes.

Approximately $370,000 of public improvements were installed during 1909, exclusive of water extensions and storm sewers, but including paving, sewers, sidewalks, curbing, concrete bridge, etc.

It is interesting to note that the new Sixteenth Avenue bridge of concrete, across the Cedar River, cost only $69,600, including approaches, the cost of the moving of the old bridge aside thirty feet, of maintaining it till the new bridge was ready, and then taking it down and piling the steel on the bank. The Second Avenue bridge of concrete, across the same river, cost under the old government $104,000, exclusive of the cost of approaches, and of moving the old bridge aside for temporary use.

The additional forty feet of length of the latter bridge is not sufficient, in a total length of six hundred feet, to account for so great a difference in cost.

Lighting rates have not changed under the new plan, a five-year contract fixing the amount due the lighting company from the city until 1911.

The park board was very efficient before; there has been no marked change under the single commissioner of parks.

The meetings of the commission proved to be similar to those at Galveston and Houston and Des Moines. The city secretary calls the roll swiftly, and records all votes. At a typical session attended, the bonds of the waterworks trustees were approved; various routine matters considered briefly; an opinion was read by the city attorney relating to the extension of a telephone franchise and the proposed increase in rates; the city engineer reported on an ice gorge in the river which threatened the new bridge, nearing completion, and received instruction to break up the gorge by dynamite, if necessary; and the Council adjourned.

A board of three water trustees still manages the city waterworks. The members are appointed by the Council and are subject to its control; but the method of having a separate and partially independent water board had been proved by experience to be so satisfactory that it was continued under the new government. There is also a separate library board of three trustees and a separate school board.

The civil service commission has been at work for the past few months, and many employees have been appointed under their supervision, including assistant

CEDAR RAPIDS

assessors and policemen. The board has also jurisdiction over the appointment of firemen.

Inquiries as to whether all sections of the city are receiving reasonable equality of attention, in the way of improvements, fire protection, and other municipal facilities, were uniformly answered in the affirmative.

Four of the first board of five resided on the East Side of the river; yet the West Side is said to have been not at all neglected. Three of the commissioners were reputed to be Republicans, and two Democrats; but there has been no national politics discernible in city appointments. Said a well-informed citizen: "There are probably 9000 Bohemian-Americans in Cedar Rapids, including about 1500 voters. Under the old régime the Bohemian section had a representative on the Council who saw that it got its share of improvements. Now it has no representative, but gets just as fair treatment. The Bohemian-Americans, as a whole, opposed the adoption of the commission plan, and under the usual treatment accorded to a defeated element, would have received no consideration. The present commission, however, has built the Sixteenth Avenue bridge largely for them; has provided for the building of three miles of water main extensions every year, and for the construction of $40,000 worth of sanitary sewers, in their section. They are now among the stanchest supporters of the new government."

The second election, in 1910, resulted in the return of Mayor Miles; the other commissioners were changed.

COMMISSION GOVERNMENT

Other Cities

In April, 1910, Keokuk and Burlington began operating under a commission. Sioux City, also, which had once defeated the proposition, reversed its decision and installed the plan. Marshalltown voted favorably in July, 1910; and Fort Dodge a little later the same year.

CHAPTER V

CITIES OF KANSAS

KANSAS has two commission laws, one applying to cities of the first class (over 15,000 population), the other to cities of the second class (between 2000 and 15,000 population). Both were first passed in 1907; in 1909, the former was amended, while the law relating to cities of the second class was repealed and a new act passed.

The law for cities of the first class provides for five commissioners, all elected at the same time, for a term of two years, with salaries ranging from $1800 for the mayor, and $1000 for each commissioner, in cities of between 15,000 and 20,000 inhabitants, to $4000 for the mayor and $3000 for each commissioner in cities of 60,000 population or over.[1] In cities of the latter size, the mayor and commissioners must devote all of their time to the public service; in cities having from 30,000 to 60,000 population, the mayor must give at least six hours a day, as is the provision of the Galveston charter. The mayor is ex-officio commissioner of the police and fire departments. Besides the usual commission features, including large appointive power and administrative control, there is a referendum on franchises, upon petition of 10 per cent of the voters; and a double initiative, a petition of 25 per cent requiring the submission of the proposed ordinance to popular vote at a

[1] For table of salaries, see pp. 172-180.

special election, and a petition of 10 per cent, submission to the next *general* city election. The recall is provided, upon petition of 25 per cent of the voters. The provisions for the initiative, the recall, nonpartisan primary and election ballots, similar to those under the Iowa law, and a civil service commission, were added in 1909. There is no general referendum on ordinances.

Cities of the second class have three commissioners, one elected each year for a term of three years.[1] The salaries range from $300 a year to the mayor and $250 for each of the other two commissioners, in cities of from 2000 to 7000 population to $1200 for the mayor and $1000 for each commissioner, in cities of 10,000 to 15,000 population. The departments are consolidated, the mayor having charge of police, fire, and health, and the other two commissioners being at the head of the departments of streets and public utilities, and of finance and revenue, respectively. There are the same provisions for nonpartisan primaries and elections as in cities of the first class, except that they do not apply to cities of less than 10,000 population. A general referendum may be had on any ordinance on a petition of 25 per cent, while all franchises *must* be submitted for popular approval. Any ordinance may be proposed, on a petition signed by 40 per cent of the voters, for submission at a special election; "but if the petition is signed by not less than 10 nor more than 25 per centum of the electors, . . . then the board of commissioners shall, within 20 days, pass said ordinance without change, or submit the same at the next *general*

---

[1] An amendment adopted in 1911 provides for the nomination of each candidate to a particular place on the commission.

city election." There is no civil service commission in cities of the second class, nor recall. A special election on the question of adopting the commission form is required, upon a petition of 40 per cent; and after four years of trial, the same percentage may compel an election to vote on the question of a return to the old plan, a majority vote determining the result in both instances.

In cities of the first class, a petition of 10 per cent requires the calling of a special election to vote on the adoption of the plan, while, after four years' trial, it is possible to return to the former system, upon a petition of 25 per cent and a majority vote in favor of such return.

Under these two Kansas laws, twenty-three cities have installed, or voted to install, the commission form. Leavenworth led the list, commencing operation in April, 1908; Wichita, Independence, Hutchinson, and Anthony began a year later; Kansas City, Kan., voted on the adoption of the plan on July 14, 1909, and the commissioners took office in April, 1910; while Coffeyville, Parsons, Pittsburg, Emporia, Abilene, Newton, Wellington, Iola, Marion, Neodesha, Cherryvale, Girard, Caldwell, Eureka, and Council Grove took action during 1910 or early in 1911. Kansas City had rejected the plan in June, 1908. Winfield, El Dorado, Hiawatha, and Fort Scott voted in the negative.[1] "In some instances the plan was welcomed as a means of destroying a particularly unscrupulous ring," says Dr. Frank G. Bates; "in others, where political conditions were healthy, it won support by its novelty. One force working for its

[1] For list of other cities which have voted against the commission plan, see pp. 290, 291.

adoption was that idea always lurking in the popular mind that there is sometime to be discovered a piece of political mechanism which, when set in motion, will give perfect city government without further attention from the voter than the occasional casting of a ballot."[1]

In Leavenworth, the commissioners elected were a wholesale hardware merchant, a furniture manufacturer, a lumber dealer, a soap manufacturer, and the proprietor of a large transfer business, who were nominated and elected to fill the unexpired term of the former administration. When they took office, conditions were very bad; in the latter part of 1907 "the city's funds were completely exhausted. There was not enough money in the treasury to pay for lighting and cleaning the streets, and the city employees were forced to go without their salaries. In order that the city might at least be lighted at night, enough money was raised by private subscription to defray this expense and that of cleaning the streets."[2] These conditions, responsible for the adoption of the plan, were met by rigid economy under the commissioners. Every expense item was cut, where possible, the commissioners even working without a salary at first. When the unexpired term was completed, the same commissioners, with one change, were reëlected by majorities of more than 2000, as against the customary majority of 300; and the work was continued. A new set of books was installed, and the accounts of the city kept like those of a business firm; wages and bills

---

[1] "Commission Government in Kansas," Proceedings of the American Political Science Association, December, 1910, p. 114.

[2] Statement issued January, 1910, by the Secretary of the Greater Leavenworth Club.

were paid promptly. After the administration found itself again on a secure financial basis, it began a much needed paving of streets, and in the past two years has paved six miles, as against twelve miles in the preceding twenty years. The streets have been kept clean and well lighted. In spite of the fact that its revenues were decreased by about $80,000 annually, by the closing of the saloons (this amount representing fines imposed upon illegal "joints" under the former régime), the city has paid off, since April, 1908, $20,000 of city bonds on which it had been paying interest for the past thirty years, and $119,750 of its one half share of the county debt; during the same time it has incurred a new bonded indebtedness of only $27,000 for public improvements.

After making due allowance for the active coöperation of a powerful organization of business men known as the Greater Leavenworth Club, which was largely responsible for the adoption of the commission plan, and has since assisted the commissioners in their efforts to improve municipal conditions, a large part of the improvements in streets and policing and finance seems to be due to the greater ease of action and the added feeling of responsibility on the part of the city's commissioners. Citizens of Leavenworth assert that the commission form has inspired confidence and awakened civic pride, pointing to the marked increase in commercial activities — building improvements, real estate transfers, etc. Further study is needed to determine how far these results are due to the form of government; but that the commission form produced a large share of the improvement is the almost unanimous opinion of those of highest standing in the community. In wards where the working people own their own homes, the commissioners are said to have been most strongly indorsed for reëlection.

Results similar to those at Leavenworth are reported from Wichita, a city of 53,000; from Hutchinson and Independence, each of about 15,000; from Topeka, the state capital; and Kansas City, Kan., with 82,331 population.[1] The Commercial Club of Hutchinson, after investigating the results in Des Moines and Cedar Rapids and presenting a statement containing reasons both for and against the plan, reported that " while the commission is not and cannot be a panacea for all ills," and that much depends on a wise choice of commissioners, it provides " the means by which the best government can be secured." After the commission plan had been in effect there only a year, a published statement of the mayor and commissioners affirmed that " the affairs of the city are transacted more expeditiously, more economically, and more satisfactorily to the city officers and, we believe, also to the people," than ever before.

Kansas City reports remarkable progress in making needed street repairs. Said the commissioner of streets and public improvements: " A committee of citizens came to me yesterday morning and asked for a street improvement. The improvement was made to-day. I used to be a member of the streets and grades committee in the old council, and I know it would have taken the old committee at least a week to consider that petition." A similar incident occurred in Cedar Rapids,

[1] Census of 1910.

Iowa. The vote on adoption in Kansas City carried by a majority of 1489 out of a total vote of 7211, 900 women voting for, and 725 women against, the proposition.

There are, on the other hand, assertions that liquor-selling joints exist still in the larger cities; that the financial statements are misleading, since a clever transfer of moneys from one fund to another makes possible an excellent showing for which no warrant exists in fact. Party slates are said to be made and elected as before; though this is denied by many who admit that *local* politics exist. It is evident, however, that conditions are much better than formerly, and that present sentiment in the cities of Kansas is overwhelmingly in favor of the commission plan,[1] in spite of certain weaknesses which should be noted.

Just why nonpartisan nominations should not be permitted to cities of less than 10,000 inhabitants does not appear. The absence of a general referendum on ordinances, in cities of the first class, while the initiative is allowed, shows a curious lack of proportion in this section of the law, rendered less serious, however, by the referendum on franchises. There is no merit system provided in cities of the second class. The expiration of the terms of all the commissioners at the same time, in cities of the first class, has also been criticized on the ground of sacrificing permanence in administration; but this is a debatable question. Further evidence on this point is needed.

[1] See also conclusions of Dr. Frank G. Bates, in *Proceedings of the American Political Science Association*, December, 1910.

CHAPTER VI

STATES OF UPPER MISSISSIPPI VALLEY

North and South Dakota

SOUTH DAKOTA passed, on March 12, 1907, a state law permitting its cities to adopt the commission plan, upon a petition of 15 per cent of the voters, and the usual approval at an election. The proposition cannot be submitted oftener than once in each calendar year. North Dakota passed a similar law March 20, 1907; but the petition requesting submission to the voters need contain the names of only 10 per cent of the electors; and, if voted down, the proposition cannot be renewed for four years. Both states place the number of commissioners at five,[1] grant to the board its usual broad powers, constitute each member the head of a department, and give the mayor a vote, but no veto. South Dakota provides for a referendum on any ordinance upon petition of 5 per cent of the voters; on all franchises, a compulsory referendum; an initiative upon a petition of 5 per cent; a recall, on 15 per cent; and nonpartisan primaries and elections. North Dakota had none of these except a compulsory referendum on bond issues, until 1911, when they were added. Publicity provisions appear in both laws, as in those of most states granting the commission form to cities.

[1] A recent amendment in South Dakota permits three; see Laws of 1911, Chap. 97, § 1.

Bismarck, the state capital, Mandan, and Minot have adopted the plan, in North Dakota; in South Dakota, Sioux Falls, the largest city, Pierre, the state capital, Huron, Dell Rapids, Yankton, Rapid City, Vermillion, Chamberlain, and Aberdeen.

In Sioux Falls, the new government has proved superior to the old, although the election of commissioners opposed to the law, due to a three-cornered fight which divided the vote of the best citizens, is said to have resulted in considerably less improvement than expected. In the other cities, also, better conditions obtain than formerly. The absence from the North Dakota law of restrictions such as the recall, initiative, and referendum, is regarded by many as responsible for the unfavorable vote in Grand Forks (March, 1910; vote, 459–506). Fargo also decided against a commission (July 22, 1910), the vote being light. In the latter city, the "liberal" element, including those opposed to the enforcement of the liquor laws, is reported to have vigorously fought the proposed change, as it did in Mitchell, S.D. Mitchell, Watertown, and Spearfish, S.D., rejected the plan in 1910.

Idaho

In Idaho, the city of Lewiston secured a commission charter from the legislature, March 13, 1907. It provides for seven commissioners, — a mayor and six councilmen, — of whom the mayor and three councilmen are elected each odd-numbered year for a two-year term, and the other three councilmen each even-numbered year for a two-year term. The salaries are small — $300 a year to the mayor, and not over $200 a year to each other member. Each councilman is head of a department. The mayor has a vote on all appointments, as well as a veto. Among the checks provided are a referendum on the granting of franchises and the sale of public property, compulsory referendum on bond issues, an initiative, and a recall.[1]

Wisconsin

The commission law of Wisconsin, as passed in June, 1909, provided for a mayor and two councilmen, the mayor to have a six-year term, and one councilman to be elected every alternate two years for a four-year term. The law applies to cities of the second, third, and fourth classes. There was a referendum on all ordinances, but neither recall nor initiative. The absence of these additional safeguards is ascribed as the reason for the rejection of the plan by Janesville early in 1910, and the hesitancy of other cities to adopt it. Eau Claire, Wis., (18,310 population, 1910) adopted the commission form, elected officers in April, 1910, and has begun operation. Appleton (16,773 population, 1910) voted favorably, February 6, 1911, and is also operating under the plan.

An interesting provision of the Wisconsin law is that mayor and councilmen need not be residents of the city

[1] The city of Boise, Ida., sometimes named in the list of commission cities, has two features of the board plan, as the mayor states, namely (1) a small commission — a mayor and four councilmen, (2) elected on a general ticket. The council appears not to possess administrative power, nor are its members heads of departments; hence it has not been included in the list. The mayor has large powers, appointing all the city officials and employees, except two. There is also a referendum on bond issues, and a nonpartisan nominating ballot, but neither initiative nor recall.

by which they are chosen as officials, at the time of their election, though they must reside there after election and give their entire time to their official duties. This makes it possible for one city to secure an administrator who has done well in a similar office in another municipality, after the successful German plan.

The legislature of 1911 amended the law, incorporating provisions for the recall and initiative; lengthening the term of the two councilmen to six years, and making minor changes.

Minnesota

The Minnesota constitution allows each city to frame its own charter. In addition, an act approved April 10, 1909, specifically authorizes the board of freeholders to "incorporate as part of the proposed charter for any city the commission form of city government." Such charter may contain provisions that commissioners shall be elected at large; that each member shall perform such administrative duties as are designated in the charter; and provisions for referendum, initiative, recall, and nonpartisan primary and election ballots. Mankato, Minn., has adopted a new charter under this law, after once voting in the negative; Fairbault, also, voted "yes" on February 7, 1911.

Illinois

The legislature of Illinois, in 1909, sent a special committee of five members to investigate the workings of the commission plan in the cities which had it. The committee visited Houston, Galveston, and Dallas, which had operated longest under the small board, comparing the principal features in use in those cities. Although originally opposed to the plan, the committee summarized it finding in these words:[1] —

"In every city we visited, we found the almost unanimous sentiment of the citizens favoring the commission form of government. We sought the opinion of bankers, merchants, laboring men — in fact, all classes of citizens. The enthusiasm of the people for this form of government is hardly describable. Extremists have gone so far in their enthusiasm as to favor the abolition of the legislature of Texas and [to] substitute therefor a commission of five to govern the state."

"Without doubt there has been a marked improvement in the conduct of the affairs of these cities under this plan of municipal government. Able, fearless, progressive, and conscientious men are in charge of public affairs. . . . Under the stimulus of great municipal movements, conducted in the same manner as the affairs of great private enterprises, these cities are entering upon an era of great prosperity, with the full confidence of their citizens in the integrity of their public officials and in the efficiency of the commission form of government. This report is respectfully submitted to the judgment of the committee on municipalities."

The bill introduced was not enacted into law, however, until the called session of 1910, when, after a recommendation by the governor in his special message, the legislature passed a law (approved March 9, 1910), permitting commission government to cities and villages of not over 200,000 population which should

[1] Report made to Senate (of Illinois) by Mr. McKenzie from Special Subcommittee, Springfield, 1909, pp. 10, 11.

STATES OF UPPER MISSISSIPPI VALLEY

vote to adopt it. A mayor and four commissioners are to hold office for four years. Ward divisions are abolished. A graded scale of salaries runs from $50 a year for mayor and $40 for each commissioner, in villages of 2000 population or less, to $6000 a year for mayor and $5500 for each commissioner, in cities of between 100,000 and 200,000 population. The act provides also for initiative, referendum, and nonpartisan primaries; and a recall which requires a preliminary petition signed by 75 per cent [1] of the vote cast for mayor at the previous election.

The list of cities which have voted to operate under this law, is found on p. 138; and other cities have the matter under active consideration.

Michigan

In Michigan, Port Huron has framed a commission charter, under the "home-rule" permitted in that state, and began operation, January 2, 1911. The charter vests the corporate powers of the city in a mayor and four city commissioners. Each department is put in charge of one member of this city commission. Nonpartisan elections, initiative, and referendum are included.[2]

Pontiac, Harbor Beach, Wyandotte, and Owosso, Mich., have also framed commission charters, and ten other cities are agitating the question.

[1] Amended in 1911 to 55 per cent.

[2] For details of provisions of this and other charters, see Tables I to XII, Part II, under proper subjects.

CHAPTER VII

TEXAS AND OKLAHOMA

THE example of Galveston and Houston was followed in 1907 by Dallas, Fort Worth, El Paso, Denison, and Greenville; and in 1909 by Austin, the state capital, Waco, Palestine, Corpus Christi, and Marshall; while under a general act applying to cities of less than 10,000 passed April 1, 1909, the smaller cities of Aransas Pass, Harlingen, Kenedy, Barry, Lyford, Port Lavaca, Marble Falls, Elkhart, Terrell, and McAllen (Tex.) adopted commissions in 1910 or early in 1911.[1]

Dallas allows the mayor a veto as well as a vote, as do Denison, Greenville, and Corpus Christi, showing apparently in this respect the influence of Houston. The charter of Dallas is particularly well arranged, the powers of the city being grouped under general heads such as "Revenue," "Police Powers," "Fire," "Health," "Municipal Service," etc., instead of the items being scattered, ungrouped, over many pages, as in the charters of most cities.

The charters of Dallas and Fort Worth, amended in 1909, and those of Austin, Waco, and Marshall, include the referendum, initiative, and recall; Palestine and Corpus Christi have the recall, and a referendum on franchises; Austin and Palestine have the Des Moines nonpartisan primary and election.[2] Cities hav-

[1] See table, p. 134.   [2] But see table, p. 251.

ing neither a general referendum on ordinances, nor the initiative nor the recall are Galveston, Houston, and Greenville; those having the recall, but no general referendum nor initiative, are Palestine, Corpus Christi, and Denison. In the absence of a recall, the right to remove commissioners by impeachment is usually retained, a process which in Northern cities has fallen into disuse, in practice. Five of the earlier commission charters of Texas provide no referendum, or one limited to bond issues or franchises; the newer charters and amendments in Texas and other states show a tendency to include provisions for a broad referendum and for the initiative and recall.

Dallas

Better paved streets is the report from Dallas; water meters installed; creeks oiled to destroy mosquitoes; parks purchased, for their future benefit to the city. Best of all, these improvements are being considered according to a systematic "city plan." The great value to a city of a " plan " — a municipal outline along which the city may develop, a definite policy of improvement for the future — must be evident to every citizen. This policy may be broad or narrow, including provisions for the development of parks and driveways, a unified sewerage system, abolition of grade crossings, putting wires underground, the installation of public comfort stations, vigorous repression of gambling and liquor selling, the wise control of public utilities, and enough substantial street paving; or it may include only one or two of these features. Having a "plan" means that our

American cities, most of which, up to the present time, have "just growed," shall hereafter intelligently direct their development — at least aim toward certain ends. Such a plan is as important for a city to have, as for a railroad company or an industrial concern. It is not in order, however, to more than suggest here this need, and to note that one effect of the commission form is the beginning of such "city plans" in Cedar Rapids, Dallas, and other municipalities. It indicates an awakened civic spirit and the growth of confidence in government as a helpful directing agency. While not impossible under the aldermanic form, civic improvements are easier to secure under a government readily responsive to public opinion.

Fort Worth, also, has done well under a commission, which it installed early in 1907; there the commissioners and mayor give all their time to the city's affairs. At Austin, the city engineer, who occupied the same position under the old government, is enthusiastic, asserting that under the small board he can conduct his department much more effectively than before. Each city reports some new feature wherein its commission excels the former council.

Oklahoma

In Oklahoma few cities have had a commission more than a year. Ardmore, Enid, and Tulsa began operation in 1909; Purcell commenced on January 1, 1911; while McAlester, Muskogee, El Reno, Sapulpa, Bartlesville, Miami, Wagoner, and Duncan voted to adopt, in 1910. Guthrie defeated the plan twice, first

TEXAS AND OKLAHOMA

by a majority of 239, later (April 5, 1910) by a majority of 87; Oklahoma City voted "no" three times, the last defeat having been in May, 1910; but both cities voted favorably early in 1911. Sapulpa voted against a commission at first, but later (July, 1910) in favor of it, as did Muskogee. Each city has framed its own charter, subject to the constitution and state laws.[1] After the board of freeholders has prepared the new charter, the electors vote on it, and if ratified by the voters, it is submitted to the governor for his approval. The constitution provides that "the powers of the initiative and referendum are hereby reserved to the people of every municipal corporation," and fixes the percentage of signatures to a petition for either at 25 per cent.[2] It also makes compulsory the submission of franchises to popular vote.[3] All of the charters examined contain provisions for the recall.[4]

[1] Constitution of Oklahoma, Art. XVIII, Sec. 3 (*a*).
[2] *Ibid.*, Sec 4.
[3] *Ibid.*, Sec 5.
[4] See table, pp. 240 ff.

CHAPTER VIII

MASSACHUSETTS

AFTER its disastrous fire in 1908, a calamity analogous to the Galveston flood in its destructive results, the city of Chelsea secured from the Massachusetts legislature an act[1] vesting the management of its affairs in a Board of Control, consisting of five persons, appointed by the governor. The governor, with the consent of the council, has power to fix the salaries of the members of this board, to remove them and to fill vacancies. The powers of mayor and aldermen devolved upon this board, to which was given power to "establish departments and appoint the officers thereof, fix their compensation, and give to them such of the powers and duties of the Board as it shall specify"; purchase supplies, remove officers or employees, make public improvements, prescribe the height of buildings, etc. Two of the commissioners are elective after 1909, one being elected at the state election in 1909, the other in 1910, and to hold office till January, 1913, when the terms of all five expire. In 1911 a mayor and aldermen are to be elected as formerly, except that the Board of Control is to retain the power to annul acts of the mayor and aldermen, including appointments and contracts.[2] The voters are given power to continue the Board of Control with

[1] Passed March 29, 1908.
[2] See Acts of 1908, Chap. 559, Secs. 10, 11.

certain supervisory powers; if the vote is favorable at the city election in 1912, the governor is to appoint the Board, to consist thereafter of three members. If the Board of Control is continued under this act, the city government will be of an aldermanic type, the aldermen constituting in effect one chamber, and the Board of Control a second chamber with the power to review the acts of the aldermen.

The present government of Chelsea is clearly not of the usual commission type. It belongs in a class by itself, or possibly with Washington, D.C., where the President of the United States appoints the three commissioners, with the consent of the Senate; or with the first commission of Galveston, three of whose commissioners were appointed by the governor, and two elected by the voters of the city. For this reason it is not included in the list of cities having the commission form of government. The division of municipal business is effected merely by an agreement among the members of the Board that each will assume for the year a certain definite field of responsibility.

The success of Chelsea's Board of Control in supervising the reconstruction of the city pertains to those unusual and emergency conditions referred to in the case of Galveston; and the experience of Chelsea is as yet of value mainly for cities which need a vigorous hand at the helm during some period of crisis.

Haverhill and Gloucester

In the same year, Haverhill (June 3, 1908) and Gloucester (June 11, 1908) received new charters from the legislature. Each charter provides for a board of five, known as the municipal council, consisting of a mayor and four aldermen, elected at large, and paid. The board has ordinance and appointing power, and each member is also the head of a department. In Haverhill the departments are distributed by ordinance into accounts and finances, public safety and charities, streets and highways, and public property; the mayor has "general charge of all departments and the administration of public affairs." It is interesting to note, in passing, a provision of this ordinance that the mayor shall also "use such means as he shall devise for increasing the business and manufacturing interests of the city," and either by himself or in conjunction with organizations of business men, formulate "such plans as he may deem advisable, and report the same to the municipal council."[1] The mayor has a vote as one of the five commissioners, but no veto.

In Gloucester, the mayor and aldermen are still nominally chairmen of committees; actually, heads of departments, these departments being, in 1909, administration; fire; highways, bridges, etc.; and public property; the mayor has charge of fuel and street lights, poles, licenses, and police.[2] Both cities have the referendum and the initiative; Haverhill only has the recall, and nonpartisan primaries and elections. In Gloucester, the term of the commissioners is one year; in Haverhill, two years, the mayor and two

[1] See Ordinance defining duties of heads of departments (February 11, 1909), Art. 2, Section 7.

[2] Annual Reports of City of Gloucester, 1909, pp. 203, 204. The division into departments is somewhat different in 1911.

MASSACHUSETTS

aldermen being elected each even-numbered year, and the other two aldermen each odd-numbered year. The salaries in Haverhill are $2500 to the mayor and $1800 to the aldermen; the mayor of Gloucester receives $1200, and the aldermen $1000 each. The former city has a population of 44,115; the latter, 24,398. Under the former charter of Haverhill, no compensation was paid to any of the twenty men — mayor, board of aldermen (seven members), and common council (of twelve), who composed the city government.

The men elected in Haverhill as commissioners are business men. "The mayor is a large property owner and proprietor of as large a business as is to be found in Haverhill. The head of the department of public property is a retired contractor and president of the Haverhill Coöperative Bank. The head of the department of accounts and finances is an owner of considerable real estate and for many years connected with the largest bank in Haverhill. The head of the department of streets and highways is a civil engineer of wide reputation. The head of the department of public safety and charity is a man who was at the time of his election a machine operator in one of the largest factories. . . . Never before in the city of Haverhill was it possible to find available such material for municipal office."[1]

Financial Results

The results in the field of finance are similar to those in cities of Iowa and Texas. Marked economies have been effected. While many figures have been quoted

[1] George M. Nichols, in *Twentieth-Century Magazine*, December, 1910.

COMMISSION GOVERNMENT

to show the relative saving under the new administration, the subject is sufficiently complex to require a careful inspection of the entire financial situation. Such an examination was made by Harvey S. Chase & Co., the well-known accountants of Boston. After a detailed study of receipts and expenditures in the offices of mayor, auditor, treasurer, city clerk, license commission, police department, health department, overseers of the poor, park department, and all other divisions of municipal administration examined, the firm reported as follows, stating that they had given to the examination and preparation of the report an amount of labor and expense far in excess of the compensation agreed upon: —

"Schedule IV makes the fact evident that the running expenses of the city in 1909 have been kept inside of the $12 tax limit. Such a result has not been achieved in Haverhill for many years past. The present administration deserves much commendation for its foresight and vigilance in supervising the city's expenditures, and in holding down the totals to the limits indicated. Comparing this result with what has happened in previous years, when borrowing money for various classes of running expenses was the rule rather than the exception, the achievement appears to be a notable one, which should be highly encouraging to those citizens of Haverhill who favored the recent change in the form of municipal government." The report recommends further improvements in the methods of bookkeeping.

The monthly pamphlet record of receipts and expenditures published by the city is most useful to the average citizen in showing him in detail how his money has been spent and the actual cash receipts.

About twice as much street paving has been done with the same amount of money as formerly.

City Solicitor Nichols, commenting, at Lowell, on the improved conditions at Haverhill, said: "You will ask, How did this happen? Did you have a crowd of grafters who were robbing you? I have never seen anything that I could actually put my finger on, in the way of stealing. It was not stolen, it just went, just as any man's money will leak out of his business, and he will assign, if he does not attend to his business or if he has no sort of business management. The change has been brought about by personal supervision."

Gloucester reports similar improvement. The reduction in the city debt was $18,000, the first year, with all bills paid. The roads were never in better condition, though $6000 less was expended on them than formerly. Public buildings, too, have been cared for at less expense.

Many of these statements do not seem at first as significant as they appear after comparison with former conditions. There is room, however, for further improvement, and the ability to recognize this is one of the hopeful signs of administration under the new plan.

Lynn

Lynn, Mass., adopted in October, 1910, an improved commission form, containing recall, referendum, initiative, nonpartisan primaries, and very comprehensive publicity features. The mayor and four commissioners took office in January, 1911.

The mayor of Haverhill summarized the changes from the aldermanic plan to the new form, at the end of the first year of operation, in a statement which can be applied to many other commission cities: —

"A practical testing out of this new administrative method during the year has demonstrated beyond a question many general features of excellence over the old-time form. The elimination of the necessity for the concurrent vote of two boards, and of the possibility of a mayor's veto and reference, have contributed largely to the dispatch of business. The doing away with the numerous standing committees of the old-time city council with their powers of expenditure without reference to the council, their informality and often irregularity of procedure, closed one avenue of facile and ill-advised expenditure and has eliminated a fruitful source of dispute and litigation. The public meetings of the council, with its votes recorded by yea and nay, have insured to the city daylight methods of expenditure and the certainty that the municipal government as a whole, as well as the people at large, knows where the money has been spent. The placing of one of the aldermen at the head of each of the four departments, and the attitude of the municipal council in looking to him for his recommendation as to matters concerning his department, has led to the fixing of personal responsibility for official acts, impossible of attainment under the old system. This same division of affairs of the city into departments, each with its head, has further resulted in the possibility of personal, individual initiative on the parts of the heads of departments.". . .

"Finally, the fact that each head of a department must come to the municipal council for final authority to act, and that all expenditures under one department are submitted for approval of a majority of the other heads of departments, insures . . . a broad knowledge, on the part of the council, of the city's affairs as a whole.

"It is conceived that the successful management of city affairs is a question of business — the handling of the income and receipts of the city so as to secure to its inhabitants the greatest possible amount in public benefits which can be afforded from the resources which the city has at its command."[1]

[1] E. H. Moulton, mayor of Haverhill, in *Bulletin of the League of American Municipalities*, February, 1910.

CHAPTER IX

WEST VIRGINIA, TENNESSEE, AND THE SOUTH

HUNTINGTON, W. Va., a city of 35,000, on the banks of the Ohio, had suffered for many years from the worst sort of partisan politics. Democrats vied with Republicans to secure political success in local contests; policemen and firemen were drafted into service to help round up the votes, and gangs of "repeaters," convoyed by policemen or other city employees, visited the various precincts, voting as often as was deemed necessary for the success of the party.[1] These conditions are not confined to Huntington; but there municipal affairs were so badly demoralized that some of the younger and more vigorous political leaders on both sides cast about for a remedy. George I. Neal, a lawyer and a leading young Democrat, and Elliott Northcutt, a large clothing merchant and a Republican, got together with others and discussed various plans at some length. The commission form seemed to offer promise of abolishing the worst features of their council government; and it was finally decided to accept it, with the provision that there should be four commissioners instead of five, not more than two of whom should be from any one party. It was hoped to make the city administration bipartisan, and, by effectually abolishing the violent party feeling, make

[1] Statements of many citizens to writer. Conditions have since changed.

WEST VIRGINIA, TENNESSEE, THE SOUTH

possible a stable city government. Instead of a referendum to all the voters as a check on the acts of the commission, many favored a special referendum board, a separate body of citizens, elected from the various wards, which would have power to veto ordinances or recall officials. The plan was accepted, and the proposed charter was secured from the legislature; it took effect March 1, 1909. Four commissioners were elected to take the place of mayor and council, the vote being as follows: —

Switzer (Democrat)	2658
Chapman (Republican)	2555
Coon (Democrat)	2468
Pollock (Republican)	2440
Evans (Citizens)	2052
Dusenberry (Citizens)	1943
Mynes (Republican)	1462

The four candidates having the highest number of votes — two Democrats and two Republicans — were declared elected and took office in June, 1909. A Citizens' Board, as the other body is called, was elected at the same time, having 64 members, 16 from each of the four wards, of whom not more than 8 from a ward may belong to the same political party. These are the two unusual items in the Huntington commission charter — its bipartisan character and the Citizens' Board.

The attempt to divide the city administration equally extended to offices other than those of mayor and commissioners. Partisan rancor had been of such long standing that it was feared the usual commission plan, even with its checks, might fail to remove party strife; hence, it was determined to apportion all the offices.

COMMISSION GOVERNMENT

Of the commissioners, two are Republicans and two Democrats; the city treasurer is a Democrat; the chief of police is a Republican; the city engineer, a Democrat; the city attorney, a Republican; the city clerk, a Democrat. The police judge is a Democrat. Of the city physicians, one is a Republican, one a Democrat, and the third is a negro. Even the policemen are divided approximately half and half between the two parties. The commission plan of putting all the power necessary into the hands of a small board, a fact in itself discouraging to partisanship, when properly safeguarded, was supplemented by this method of the parties "starting even"; but the commission idea was depended on to carry the reform through.

No political party may nominate more than three persons for the Board of Commissioners, no two of whom shall be from the same ward; nor may more than eight members of the Citizens' Board be from the same ward. Not more than two commissioners, who belong to one party, can be elected. Each officer, elective or appointive, after swearing to faithfully discharge the duties of his office, is required to take oath also that he will not administer his office with the aim to benefit any political party. "The object and aim of this act," declares section 93 of the charter, "is to procure honest and efficient administration of the affairs of the city of Huntington, free from partisan distinction or control."

The Citizens' Board has the right of veto on any franchise or ordinance passed by the Board of Commissioners, and the right to hear charges against any commissioner. A majority vote of the Citizens' Board may veto an ordinance or franchise; a two-thirds vote

WEST VIRGINIA, TENNESSEE, THE SOUTH

removes a commissioner. The Citizens' Board has its president, its rules, and keeps the usual records, the city clerk acting as secretary. This, it should be noted, is only a veto-and-recall board, not a second chamber with coördinate power.

These provisions are a part of the plan adopted by Huntington to secure efficient local government. It must not be forgotten, however, that the main elements of the commission form are present. Under the old government there were 20 councilmen, 5 members from each of four wards. There were 12 Democrats and 8 Republicans. Each councilman received $8 a month, and the mayor $50 a month. Now four commissioners, elected at large, receive $1800 each, except the mayor, whose salary is $2100. The Board is given authority to pass ordinances and to appoint all officers except the members of the Citizens' Board, and "such other officers as the Board may create, with power to fix their salaries." The latter provision, however, is subject to veto by the Citizens' Board. Each commissioner is head of a department and gives as much time as is necessary. The Board meets every morning at nine o'clock, informally, to hear complaints and receive petitions and requests. A more formal meeting is held every Monday afternoon.

"The commission plan has removed politics from city elections," said the owner of the *Huntington Daily Advertiser*. "Although the wet-or-dry issue is still present in Huntington, the partisan rancor of the past has been abolished."

"The new plan has taken the city government out of politics," said a prominent dealer in clothing and women's furnishings, "and has done away with the bitter enmity between Republicans and Democrats."

"Politics have been almost entirely eliminated from our city administration," said one of the largest clothiers, a Republican; while an insurance man, a Democrat, summed up the results in these words: —

"The old council was unpaid and gave little time to the city business; now they are paid and give all of their time that is necessary, though not usually their entire time. Each man is the head of a department; every one knows who he is. The Board has enough authority to do all that is needed. Moreover, we divided the government between the parties, and that helped to start things right. Each person votes for four men — two Republicans and two Democrats, or two Democrats, a Republican, and a Prohibitionist, etc., besides sixteen members of the Citizens' Board. The commission is thus bound to contain members of differing politics, nationally."

There has not been a single charge of graft or improper conduct against the commissioners. The city has kept within its income at all times, having funds with which to meet outstanding obligations. The expenditure of a half million dollars during the next year (the fiscal year at Huntington begins July 1) for street paving, sewer, construction, and public buildings was viewed with equanimity by the citizens and voters. No danger of misuse of funds is even hinted at.

The term of the commissioners in Huntington is three years, all being elected at the same time. Besides the general referendum and the recall, in the hands of the citizens' board, all bond issues must be approved by a three-fifths majority of the voters. The usual publicity

WEST VIRGINIA, TENNESSEE, THE SOUTH

features are present. The Board of Commissioners, moreover, constitutes a civil service board, the mayor presiding and the city clerk being clerk ex-officio; it holds examinations at least once a year, to fill vacancies in the police and fire departments.

Bluefield, W. Va., has a similar type of commission government, secured from the legislature in March, 1909, but the four commissioners are called the "Board of Affairs" and hold office for four years, two being elected each second year. What is known in Huntington as the Citizens' Board is given the name of "Council" in Bluefield, and is smaller, consisting of four members elected from each of the nine wards. The "Council" (referendum board) has the right of veto on ordinance, franchise, or license "by a majority vote of all the members elected"; the right to demand facts and require reports from the Board of Affairs and the right to fill vacancies in the Board in certain contingencies.

The results in Bluefield are said to be similar to those secured in Huntington.

Charleston, the state capital, wished also to have the commission form, but the law was so amended as to make two coördinate bodies, the assent of both of which is necessary for the passage of ordinances. This is clearly a return to the discredited two-chambered council system. It violates one of the fundamental principles underlying the commission form, namely, the concentration of municipal authority in a single small elective body.

Parkersburg adopted the commission form March 21, 1911, and the officers elected on May 2 took office May 15, 1911. The charter includes provisions for the referendum, initiative, and recall.

COMMISSION GOVERNMENT

Memphis

In Memphis (Tenn.), the small board plan was put into operation on January 1, 1910, after a long struggle and much litigation. The new charter provides for a board of five, with terms of four years each, and salaries of $6000 a year for the mayor and $3000 for each of the commissioners. Besides the usual features, each commissioner has the right to nominate the officials and subordinates in his department, the board electing them. The board may remove any officer for misconduct. The chief of the police or fire departments may suspend or discharge a subordinate temporarily, but his act must be approved later by the commissioner in charge of that department, and final appeal lies to the whole board. The checks provided in the charter are publicity; a referendum on bond issues, upon petition of five hundred qualified voters; franchise regulations as provided in the state law; and a civil service commission of three, appointed by the board of commissioners and removable by them. Their term is three years, one being appointed each year; each member receives a salary of $300 a month.

The commission has been in operation in Memphis scarcely long enough to enable conclusions to be drawn as to its effectiveness. The members elected are representative business men.

Chattanooga voted in February, 1911, to adopt a commission charter and began operation May 8, 1911.

The charters of several other cities in Tennessee, sometimes included in the list of those having the commission form, possess certain features, such as election at large or a small council, while one or more of the other elements of the plan are lacking; in few or none of them does the commission exercise both administrative and ordinance powers; nor is each member the head of a department.[1]

Mississippi

"An act to provide for a commission form of government for cities and towns in the state of Mississippi, and for other purposes," approved March 21, 1908, specifies three or five commissioners, as each city shall decide, elected at large, one of whom shall be voted for as mayor. The number of commissioners, their salary, the time required of each, the bond to be given by each, and such other officers as it may be desired to elect in each city, are to be set forth in the petition requesting a vote on the commission form of government. This petition, if signed by 10 per cent or more of the voters, requires a special election to be held to vote on the question. If the vote is favorable, the secretary of state issues a charter to the city.

The usual broad powers are conferred upon the mayor and commissioners, and a compulsory referendum on all franchises is provided.

Hattiesburg and Clarksdale are the only cities in Mississippi, so far, to take advantage of the new law. In both cities the plan went into effect January 1, 1911; Clarksdale has three commissioners. Gulfport voted in the negative in March, 1910; in Biloxi, where the state

[1] Bristol, Clarkesville, Adams, Ashland City, and Etowah are some of the cities which have been included in the lists so published.

law was strongly urged by the Commercial Club, the plan has been defeated twice, the second time, in June, 1910, by a decreased majority.

Kentucky

The state of Kentucky passed a commission law in 1910, applying to cities of the second class.[1] The city of Lexington, whose Commercial Club strongly favored the plan and pressed it to final passage, defeated the proposition to adopt it in that city. Newport, however, adopted it. The Kentucky law provides for a board of five commissioners, elected at large, the mayor for four years and the commissioners for two years each. The only other elected officer is the police judge, who is chosen also for a four-year term, his election alternating with that of the mayor; that is, every two years four commissioners are elected for a two-year term, and either a mayor or a police judge for a four-year term. The mayor is paid $3600 a year; the commissioners, $3000 each. The mayor has the department of public affairs; the other departments are each assigned to a commissioner by the board. The mayor has no veto. There is a referendum upon a petition of 25 per cent; and voters may originate ordinances by the same percentage on petition, and approval of the ordinance by a majority vote at an election. There is no recall; but any commissioner can be removed by the other four commissioners, for cause. Nonpartisan primary and election ballots, after the Des Moines plan, are provided. On the whole, the Kentucky act may be classed among the "improved" commission laws, although the recall is absent.

[1] Acts of Kentucky, 1910, Chap. 50. Approved March 21, 1910.

Louisiana

Louisiana also, in 1910, passed a commission law, which applies to cities of 7500 population or over.[1] Cities of over 25,000 which shall adopt the plan are to be governed by a mayor and four councilmen; cities of less than 25,000 population, by a mayor and two councilmen. The mayor is given charge of public affairs and public education. There is also a department of public utilities. The term of office is four years, and salaries range from not over $1000 to each councilman and $1500 to the mayor, in cities of between 7500 and 10,000 population, to not more than $2500 to each councilman and $4000 to the mayor, in cities of 60,000 or over. Each candidate for office must announce himself as a candidate for a specific place in the council, that is, he must designate in advance what department he wishes to head. Provisions are included for the initiative, referendum, and recall, all of these being available on petition of 33 per cent of the voters. The act was approved July 7, 1910; and already Shreveport, with a population of 28,015, has voted and begun operation.

North and South Carolina

In South Carolina, an act approved February 21, 1910, applies to cities of between 20,000 and 50,000 population. It includes provisions for the referendum, recall, initiative, civil service commission, and *party primaries*. The city of Columbia is operating under the law.

High Point, N.C., under a special charter granted in 1909, has a true commission government, though

[1] Except New Orleans, Monroe, Lake Charles, and Baton Rouge. Acts, State of Louisiana, 1910, Act 302, Secs. 1, 2.

the number of commissioners is unusually large, there being nine, each in charge of a department.[1] The salaries are small, and each commissioner gives "as much time as is necessary" to his municipal duties. Charters were granted early in 1911 to Greensboro and Wilmington. These have five commissioners.

Alabama

The legislature of Alabama passed in 1911 three commission acts, one applying to cities of 100,000 population or more, under which Birmingham, the only city affected, immediately organized; a second, applying to cities of from 25,000 to 50,000 population, under which the city of Montgomery organized; and a third, approved April 8, 1911, authorizing the adoption of the commission form by any city not authorized by any other law.

The first of these acts provides for a commission of three, two of whom shall be appointed by the governor at first, the third being the present mayor who is to hold office until November, 1913. Thereafter, the commissioners are to be elected, one commissioner being elected each year for a term of three years. One of the commissioners is vested with judicial powers also.[2] The three departments are known as Public Justice; Streets, Parks, City and Public Property, and City and Public Improvements; Accounts, Finances, and Public Affairs. A referendum on franchises is permitted upon petition of 1000 legally qualified voters. Nominations for commissioners are to be made upon petition of at least 500 voters. A second election is provided, in case no can-

[1] For names of departments and discussion, see Chap. XVII, p. 200.
[2] Acts of Alabama, No. 163 (H. 112), Sec. 5.

WEST VIRGINIA, TENNESSEE, THE SOUTH

didate has a majority at the first. A recall election is to be held upon petition of 3000 voters. The salary of commissioners is $7000 each, per annum. The act was approved March 31, 1911.

The act which applies to cities of 25,000–50,000 provides for five commissioners, four appointed by the governor, together with the present mayor, all to hold office till October, 1915, after which all commissioners are to be elected for a term of four years. The departments are Public Affairs, Accounts and Finances, Justice, Streets and Parks, and Public Property and Public Improvements. A referendum on franchises upon petition of 1000 voters, and a "petition asking for the resignation of any commissioner of the city" signed by 1000 voters, are included, as well as a broad referendum on ordinances upon petition of 25 per cent of the voters, and nomination of each candidate upon petition of 100 voters. Other interesting provisions are noted in the tables in Part II. After operating under the commission form for four years, any city may return to the old form upon petition of 1000 voters, and a majority vote in favor of such return.

A city organized under the third act is to be governed by three commissioners, one elected each year for a term of three years. The recall is included and a preferential ballot, but no initiative, and a peculiar referendum on franchises.

Besides Texas, therefore, the states of West Virginia, Kentucky, Tennessee, Mississippi, Louisiana, North Carolina, South Carolina, and Alabama have passed state laws or granted special charters allowing cities to adopt the small-board plan.

CHAPTER X

COLORADO AND THE PACIFIC STATES: PREFERENTIAL VOTING

A STRIKING addition to the features usually incorporated in commission plans is the preferential ballot of Grand Junction, Col., a ballot on which the voter expresses several preferences or choices for officials. After providing for five commissioners,[1] vested with large powers, and checked by publicity features, referendum, initiative, and recall, the charter consolidates primary and election into one, providing, after the usual nominating petitions are filed, for a ballot of the form given on the following page.

The charter provides that the ballot shall be in substantially the preceding form "with the cross (X) omitted when there are four or more candidates for any office. (When there are three and not more candidates for any office, then the ballot shall give first and second choice only; when there are less than three candidates for any office, all distinguishing columns as to choice, and all reference to choice, may be omitted.)"

It will be noticed from an inspection of the ballot, that the voter may vote his first choice, his second choice, and one or more third choices, for each commissioner (there being five commissioners, of whom only three are shown on the sample form).

[1] An alternative proposition, providing for *three* commissioners, was voted down.

COLORADO AND THE PACIFIC STATES

PREFERENTIAL BALLOT OF GRAND JUNCTION

Commissioner of Public Affairs	First Choice	Second Choice	Third Choice
John Doe			X
James Foe	X		
Louis Hoe		X	
Dick Joe			X
Richard Roe			
Commissioner of Highways			
Mary Brown	X		
Harry Jones		X	
Fred Smith			
Commissioner of Water and Sewers			
Joe Black	X		
Robert White			

The following instructions [1] explain the method of using the ballot: —

"*Instructions.* — To vote for any person, make a cross (x) in ink in the square in the appropriate column according to your choice, at the right of the name voted for. Vote your first choice in the first

---

[1] Charter, Sec. 18.

column; vote your second choice in the second column; vote any other choice in the third column; vote only one first and only one second choice. Do not vote more than one choice for one person, as only one choice will count for any candidate by this ballot. Omit voting for one name for each office, if more than one candidate therefor. All distinguishing marks make the ballot void. If you wrongly mark, tear, or deface this ballot, return it, and obtain another."

As soon as the election is over and the polls are closed, the election judges, counting the ballots, enter the number of first-, second-, and third-choice votes for each candidate on the tally sheet. Any candidate receiving more than half the total number of first-choice votes for that office is declared elected. If, however, no one has a majority of first-choice votes, then the name of the candidate having the smallest number of first-choice votes is counted out, and the votes for him are not thereafter counted; but the second-choice votes for each of the remaining candidates are counted and added to the first-choice votes of the same candidate, and the one receiving a majority of first- and second-choice votes is declared elected. If still there is no majority, which will not often occur, the name of the candidate having the smallest number of first- and second-choice votes together is discarded; the third-choice votes for each of the remaining candidates are added, and thus a majority found.[1]

Some method of preferential voting enables the real sense of the community to be arrived at, without the time and expense of a primary. A nominating primary,

---

[1] See Charter, Sec. 22; also, text of this part of Grand Junction charter, on pp. 334 ff.

COLORADO AND THE PACIFIC STATES

which is a preliminary election, is the usual method employed for throwing out the third, fourth, and other choices; in the Des Moines and many other nominating methods only the two highest choices survive the primary, to come forward for election. The Grand Junction plan at one stroke does the entire act, assuming that the voters do not need an intermission of three or four weeks in which to change their minds after the nominating primary. Another method of counting the ballots, however, has been devised.[1] The nominating petition in Grand Junction requires 25 individual certificates, — that is, 25 separate petitions, each signed by one person, and sworn to before a notary public.[2] The departments, besides Public Affairs, Finance and Supplies, and Highways, are Water and Sewers, and Health and Civic Beauty. There is a civil service commission of three, unpaid, and to be appointed by the city council (commission) prior to January 1, 1913.[3] The charter was adopted by the city on September 14, 1909.

Colorado Springs has a commission of five, and other features similar to those of Grand Junction, but instead of a preferential ballot, there are two elections, similar to the usual primary and election.

California

The double election for commissioners is a distinguishing feature of the commission plan in use in Berkeley (Cal.). This differs from the method in use in Des Moines in that the first election is final for those can-

[1] See discussion under "Preferential Voting," p. 259.
[2] Charter, Secs. 8–13.   [3] Charter, Secs. 131, 132.

didates who receive a majority of the votes cast; for candidates not receiving such a majority, it serves as a primary, a second election being necessary. Berkeley began operating under the new form, July 1, 1909. Besides the mayor and four councilmen, an auditor is elected, and four school directors.

San Diego (Cal.) has a council of five, *and* a mayor who is not a member of the council. A treasurer is elected besides the council and mayor, and a board of education. Nonpartisan nominations on petition of 50 electors; a double initiative, a petition of 7 per cent requiring the submission of the proposed ordinance at a general election, a petition of 15 per cent, submission at a special election; a referendum upon a petition of 7 per cent; and a recall on a petition of 25 per cent, — are among the features of this charter. The new plan was installed May 3, 1909.

Oakland (Cal.)[1] elected July 6, 1910, a board of fifteen freeholders to frame a new charter. The board reported, October 3, 1910, a measure providing for all the substantial features of the commission plan, supplemented by most specific provisions for civil service board, nonpartisan primaries and elections, publicity, and extended regulations pertaining to franchises and to municipal contracts. An interesting section is that which proposes to let franchises to the highest bidder, that is, to the responsible bidder offering to pay the city the highest percentage of the annual gross receipts. Unusual and improved modifications of the recall, referendum, and initiative are included. An auditor is elected besides the mayor and four commissioners, as

[1] Population, 150,174, census of 1910.

well as six school directors. All are to serve for four-year terms, but the mayor alternates with the auditor, one being elected each two years; and two of the commissioners are elected every two years. Hence, a voter, every two years, has before him for consideration the choice of a mayor (or an auditor), two commissioners, and three school directors — six persons in all to vote for. The mayor's annual salary is $4200; the commissioners and the auditor each receive $3600. The new charter was ratified by the city, December 8, 1910, and adopted by the legislature, February 15, 1911. The officials elected under it will take office July 1, 1911.

A statement from the mayor of San Diego[1] reports that the establishment of a purchasing department has saved the city a considerable amount during the first year of its operation; overcharges were not allowed nor careless purchasing permitted. More streets have been graded and paved than during any similar term in the city's history. The water and sewer departments have abolished contract work, making excavations and laying pipe by day labor, at a substantial saving. The bonded indebtedness of the city has been reduced during the first year by $59,200, and the tax rate lowered from $1.48 to $1.30 per $100 valuation. Street lighting rates have been reduced from $84 per year to $60 per year, which will save the city about $8000 per year. Eleven hundred new water meters were installed, — a significant item, — and 41 miles of new water pipe were laid, during the first 12 months.

[1] See also paper presented at the annual meeting of the League of American Municipalities, at St. Paul, August, 1910, by Mr. Grant Conard, mayor of San Diego.

COMMISSION GOVERNMENT

In Berkeley, the commissioner of public supplies is purchasing agent, and his department has proved to be most important. The city closed the first fiscal year under the new form with surplus of about $33,000, besides $8750 on hand in the cash basis fund.[1] The cost of arc lights was reduced. The city ordinances were compiled, after being revised.

Modesto, San Luis Obispo, Santa Cruz, Vallejo, Monterey, and Pomona have ratified commission charters since December 1, 1910, and the same have been adopted by the legislature.[2]

Washington and Oregon

Tacoma (Wash.) adopted a charter very similar to that of Berkeley, including the double election, and an additional elective fiscal officer, called, in Tacoma, the controller. Both charters include nonpartisan elections, the referendum, initiative, and recall; that of Tacoma includes also a civil service commission. In the latter city each chief of a department (councilman) has the right to appoint and remove his subordinates, except that the mayor's appointees, in his department, are subject to confirmation by the council. Administrative sessions are held daily. The plan went into effect in May, 1910. In 1911, the mayor and two commissioners were recalled.

Spokane (Wash.) adopted,[1] December 28, 1910, an improved type of commission, including the preferential ballot of Grand Junction. The officials took office March 14, 1911.

---

[1] See First Annual Report of the Mayor and Councilmen of the City of Berkeley, for year ending June 30, 1910, p. 8.

[2] Riverside (Cal.) has a partial form of commission government, discussed on p. 287.

Baker (Ore.) adopted a commission in October, 1910. There are three commissioners; a petition of not less than twenty-five individual certificates puts the name of the candidate on the election ballot, there being no primary or nominating election.[1] It will be recalled that the referendum and initiative are permitted to cities by the constitution of Oregon.[2]

New Mexico

The territorial legislature of New Mexico enacted, March 18, 1909, a law allowing any city of over 3000 population "to be governed by a mayor and not less than two commissioners nor more than four commissioners, all elected at large," which, "when elected, shall organize and divide the government of the city into departments ... and each department shall be presided over by either the mayor or a member of the commission." Close examination, however, shows that this commission may elect a superintendent of city affairs, virtually a business manager for the municipality. This is not a commission government, in the usual sense. A final section of the act, however, authorizes voters to adopt the commission form.

Roswell (N. Mex.) has a city supervisor who manages the city affairs, the mayor acting in that capacity at present. There is little resemblance to the commission plan, however, since the city elects, besides the mayor, clerk, and treasurer, ten councilmen, two from each of the five wards. The mayor-supervisor has large powers,

---

[1] For detailed provisions, see Tables 1 to 12, Part II.
[2] Art. IV, § 1 a.

COMMISSION GOVERNMENT

and the government is said to be efficient, for a city of about 10,000 population.

LEGISLATION DURING 1911

Alabama

The three acts passed by the legislature of Alabama during 1911 have been already described.

California

In California, the statute relating to the government of cities of the fifth class (3000–10,000 population) was amended so as to permit the submission to the voters of the questions whether the city administration should be divided into five departments with one member of the existing Board of Trustees, five in number, as a commissioner in charge of each department; and whether the officers heretofore elective should be appointed by the board. The officers formerly elected are recorder, treasurer, assessor, and marshall (besides a board of education and library trustees). A similar provision was made to apply to cities of the sixth class.

A separate and comprehensive act providing for the exercise of the recall, initiative, and referendum in cities was passed by the legislature of California in March, 1911, in addition to the general acts permitting the use of these methods of control in state matters.[1]

Idaho

Idaho adopted in 1911 (approved March 13) a commission law permitting cities of 3000 population or over,

[1] Acts of California, 1911, Chap. 185.

COLORADO AND THE PACIFIC STATES

upon presentation of a petition of 25 per cent, and adoption by popular vote, to be governed by a council of five, partially renewable every two years. The mayor and two councilmen alternate at elections with the mayor and the two other councilmen. The recall and the initiative are included, but no provision is made for a referendum in the act.

New Jersey

The general act passed by the legislature of New Jersey [1] draws a line between cities of 10,000 population or over, and those of less size, providing five commissioners in the former, and three in the latter. The number may be increased from three to five, or decreased from five to three, by an ordinance passed by the commission. Nonpartisan primaries and elections, the recall, initiative, and referendum are all included. A city, after operating six years under the commission, may resume its former charter upon a petition of 25 per cent, and a majority vote of the electors.[2]

Montana

The Montana Act [3] makes a similar difference in the number of commissioners, cities of 25,000 population or more being allowed a board of five, — a mayor and four councilmen, — while those of less population are to have a mayor and two councilmen. Nonpartisan primaries and elections, a civil service commission of three members and the recall, initiative, and referendum are features found in the law.[2]

[1] Laws of 1911, Chap. 221, approved April 25, 1911.
[2] For more detailed provisions of this and other acts, see Tables 1 to 12, in Part II.   [3] Laws of 1911, Chap. 57, approved Feb. 28, 1911.

COMMISSION GOVERNMENT

Utah

Chapter 125 of the Laws of Utah, 1911, approved March 20, 1911, provides that all cities of the first and second classes *shall* be governed by a commission, thus leaving no discretion to each city as to adoption of the plan. In cities of the first class, a mayor and four commissioners, and in cities of the second class, a mayor and two commissioners, are constituted the governing body. All are elected at large; a city auditor is also elected in cities of both classes. The terms of mayor and commissioners are four years each, the mayor and two commissioners alternating every second year with the auditor and the other two commissioners, in cities of the first class. In cities of the second class, the terms of mayor and auditor are two years each, while the commissioners serve for four years; the mayor, auditor, and one or the other of the commissioners are elected every two years. There appears to be neither referendum, initiative, recall, nor primary election.

Washington

In addition to the special charters granted previously to Tacoma and Spokane, the legislature of Washington passed[1] an act permitting cities of between 2500 and 20,000 population to adopt and install a form of government providing for a "city commission" of three members, with terms of three years each. They are to be nominated at nonpartisan primaries, upon petition of 100 voters and the referendum and initiative may be invoked by a petition of 25, the recall, 35 per cent.

[1] Approved March 7, 1911.

COLORADO AND THE PACIFIC STATES

Wisconsin

The Wisconsin Act was amended in 1911,[1] as already noted, so as to include the recall and initiative, to make the terms of all three members of the council six years each, and certain other changes, including a small reduction in the table of salaries of councilmen. In cities of 10,000 or more population, the mayor and other members of the council are to devote their entire time to their municipal duties.

Wyoming

The Wyoming Act[2] includes recall and initiative provisions available upon a petition of twenty-five per cent, while to use the referendum the unusually high percentage of thirty-five is required, except that a referendum or franchise is permitted on a petition of ten per cent. To adopt the form of government proposed — that by a mayor and two commissioners — a petition of fifteen per cent of the electors is a prerequisite to the holding of an election at which the voters adopt or reject the plan. Nonpartisan primaries are included; no primary is held if there are but two candidates for mayor or but four candidates for commissioners. The act applies to cities incorporated under special charter, and of over 10,000 population at the preceding census; to cities of the first class, and to cities and towns of not less than 7000 population.[3]

[1] Laws of 1911, Chap. 287.
[2] Approved Feb. 21, 1911.
[3] In South Dakota, Kansas, and other states, amendments of greater or less importance were adopted in 1911, some of which have already been noted, others being either of minor significance or not yet obtainable. North Dakota added the recall, initiative, and broad referendum.

CHAPTER XI

SUMMARY OF COMMISSION CITIES

THE growth of the commission form has been traced from its beginning in Galveston, up through Houston and Des Moines, to a general adoption by cities of widely separated sections, and of varying size and conditions. The existence of unsatisfactory city governments in American municipalities is brought out with great clearness as the reason for the change in the new form. Waste, extravagance, incompetence, civic bankruptcy, lax methods of conducting city business, have been encountered, even where no charge of corruption has been made. The rapid spread of the idea indicates how bad the conditions must have been to lead to such swift acceptance of promised relief. In each community, general interest has been followed by discussion, agitation, and final adoption. No more democratic movement has existed in recent years. Business and professional men have led the demand for a new system of government, which has been opposed by office-holders under the old régime, by public utility corporations in some cases reported and frequently by liquor interests. The right to try the new form has been obtained only after a hard struggle, requiring sometimes two or three elections to win.

The results of the commission form have been recorded in cities presenting an unusual situation, as Galveston during the first years and Chelsea, Mass., and cities operating under ordinary conditions, which include the vast majority of cases. It is now in order to summarize these results in the various fields of municipal activity — in city finance; in the police, fire, and health departments; in the care of streets and alleys, sidewalks, bridges, sewerage, and the whole engineering field; in municipal service and franchises, including water, lighting, and local transportation; and in other departments.

Finance

It is in the field of municipal finance that the most definite effects are evident. Floating debts were retired without a bond issue, in Houston and Galveston; bonds long outstanding were paid without increase of taxes, in Leavenworth, Galveston, and elsewhere; back taxes were vigorously recovered, and current taxes promptly collected, in the Texas cities. All city income has been carefully looked after; interest required on municipal funds on deposit in banks, yielded, in Galveston, $136,451.30 in a little over nine years;[1] Houston, $40,000 in five years; Cedar Rapids, more than $1000 a year, and other cities, varying amounts. A decrease in the cost of running the departments, coupled with an increase in revenue, has made possible extended improvements without bond issues. Offices have been consolidated where practicable, the assessor with that of the collector of taxes in Galveston; Houston saved $2000 a year by combining the offices of

[1] This amount includes interest on taxes (see p. 14), which, however, represents also a saving to the city.

comptroller and secretary, and $2000 a year more by appointing a bank cashier as city treasurer, at a nominal salary of $600. In these two cities, which have had the commission plan longest, the results have most significance.

Modern bookkeeping methods have been inaugurated in Des Moines, Cedar Rapids, and other cities; a purchasing department has been installed in Houston and San Diego, which exercises a watchful care over all supplies. Other commission cities have done the same. So it is with other improvements. It would be impossible in a list of over a hundred municipalities to record here the detailed information on all of these points, even if it had been secured. Laborers' wages and bills for supplies have been paid promptly in Houston, Des Moines, Galveston, Cedar Rapids, Leavenworth, and Haverhill; discounts for cash have been utilized. Better work from municipal employees has been the rule, as a result of the active supervision exercised by each commissioner in his department. Individual responsibility to the commissioner; the commissioners' responsibility to the board; and the responsibility of the board to the voters, enforced by means of publicity, referendum, recall, civil service rules, etc., is the chain in which no link is missing. There used to be a gap between the head of the department and the council; and another between council and voters, the connection of each councilman being only with that small section called a ward, and then only at election time, — after election there was no referendum to prevent bad ordinances from going into effect, no initiative to compel the enactment of needed city regulations, no recall to oust an incompetent or corrupt alderman. But supply the missing links; establish an unbroken line of responsibility, and see how every official and employee watches the city's interests; how money is saved in countless small ways and some large ones; how the cost of brick for paving is less in Houston than formerly; how defective brick or wood blocks are rejected in Des Moines and Cedar Rapids; how even the tax rate sometimes goes lower,[1] though municipal improvements increase in number and size. Make all the allowance necessary for lack of exact comparative data under the old system; for the overemphasis laid by commissioners on their own achievements; for the enthusiasm of citizens unaccustomed to reasonably efficient city government. There still remains a large residue of gain, a marked improvement over the aldermanic régime, substantial progress. And the most convincing thing that the visitor encounters is not always large items; a small economy like the reduction of the cost of prescriptions at the city dispensary in Houston, from thirty-five cents each to eight cents, is frequently very significant of the great change which has occurred under the commissions and the new spirit that pervades the whole.

Protection of Life and Property: Law Enforcement

In the police department, most difficult to handle in its dealing with crime, its task of law enforcement and protection of property, the commissions show good results, though not so many, nor so marked, as in the field of finance. Fewer burglaries in Des Moines,

[1] Great significance, however, is not necessarily attached to this feature by the writer.

because better policemen; gambling repressed in Galveston, Houston, and Des Moines, pool rooms shut and slot machines thrown out; saloons closed promptly at the hour required, in Houston, Des Moines, Cedar Rapids, and elsewhere; the redlight district abolished in Des Moines under the first commission, and not merely scattered into other sections of the city. Sometimes more arrests appear for petty crimes, due to greater activity of the police force; but the real repression of crime and vice, while not so complete as it might be, is more sincerely attempted and more nearly accomplished than formerly. Under the commission plan, a forceful and courageous commissioner like Hamery of Des Moines has enough power to carry out his reforms, responsible, of course, to the board and to the voters. Public sentiment which has hitherto been difficult to ascertain on questions of police reforms, at least can be expressed more clearly and promptly than before. Formerly, when several issues were involved, the man who wanted more street improvements had to vote for a candidate who perhaps also favored an ultra-liberal policy as to vice. Now, an election on measures (the referendum) may be had separately, and a bad candidate retired (by the recall) while his dereliction is present in the mind of the public.

Fire and Health Departments

In the fire department, conditions have usually been so good that the improvement under the board system has been much less than in other lines of municipal activity. An increase in completeness of equipment is reported from some cities.

SUMMARY OF COMMISSION CITIES

In the department of health, a decided advance is in evidence in both Galveston and Houston — sewerage systems having been extended; unsanitary fruit stands and other obstructions removed from sidewalks; garbage collected and burned, at Houston; quarantine regulations enforced at Galveston; an epidemic suppressed at Cedar Rapids; creeks oiled at Dallas and cisterns screened at Galveston, to prevent mosquitoes.

In the exercise of engineering functions the commission cities have shown marked results. Cleaner streets in Houston, Galveston, Leavenworth, Des Moines, and Huntington, W. Va.; more and better paving laid than formerly, in Galveston, Leavenworth, Haverhill, and San Diego; street improvements made promptly in Kansas City (Kan.), Haverhill, and Cedar Rapids; the whole engineering department more effective, in Austin. In this field it is easier to determine results, though care should be taken not to try to compare items which are not comparable.

In water, light, street railway service, etc., conditions are generally better; meters are being installed in Houston, San Diego, Dallas, and elsewhere, to reduce waste of water. The cost of lighting was reduced in Berkeley, Des Moines, Houston, and San Diego. Street car service has been improved in several cities, though not yet in Des Moines.

Franchises are hedged about with more specific provisions in the commission cities, but these provisions often occur in noncommission charters. Only in so far as the granting of franchises, and the rates and character of the service supplied by public utility corporations, are better regulated by a small responsible board than

COMMISSION GOVERNMENT

by a large and irresponsible council, is the commission plan to be credited with the good conditions which may exist. Much additional information is needed on this point.

Partisanship, in the sense of adherence to national party lines, has been greatly reduced in every city from which reports have been received, in many cases being almost entirely eliminated. Local politics, however, remain.

Finally, in the beginning of a wise foresight for the future growth of the city, as shown by the purchase of the island at Cedar Rapids for a city hall and park, and by the employment of an expert to plan drives and parkways and general improvements; by the commencement of a "city plan" in Dallas, and by proposed "civic centers" elsewhere, has the commission form shown its real merit. In the cities where it has been tried, its introduction has been followed by financial, engineering, moral, or other civic improvement over conditions existing previously under the aldermanic system. The reasons for the results noted are to be understood from a study of the principles underlying the commission form.

CHAPTER XII

THE CITY BUSINESS MANAGER — STAUNTON, VA.

INSTEAD of the commission form, several cities have installed a municipal business manager, whose duties are exercised subject to the control of the council, and whose functions, while mainly financial, are also of a general directive nature. One of the first cities to inaugurate this method was Staunton, Va.

When the city of Staunton cast about for a plan under which the efficiency of its municipal government might be increased, the council committee, after study and much correspondence, decided that the Galveston-Des Moines plan promised most and ought to be adopted. Commission government — a municipal "board of directors" — had greatly improved conditions in Galveston, Houston, and were under discussion in Dallas, Des Moines, Cedar Rapids, and other cities. Why not Staunton?

But the constitution of Virginia prescribes rigidly the form of city government for all municipalities of the first class. Staunton has more than 12,000 population, and, therefore, is a city of the first class. Such a city, according to the constitution, must have a mayor and a council of two chambers. Since they could not legally abolish mayor and council for a board of commissioners, and an amendment to the constitution was not considered feasible, those who favored a change worked out, after much thought, a plan for the creation of the office of "city manager." Authority to appoint new officers was specifically given in the city charter, and after much discussion and some opposition, the new plan was adopted, early in 1908.

Retaining the mayor and council the ordinance[1] created the office of general manager for the city of Staunton, to whom was given "entire charge and control of all the executive work of the city in its various departments, and entire charge and control of the heads of departments and employees of the city." His duties are to make all contracts for labor and supplies, and "in general perform all the administrative and executive work now performed by the general standing committee of the council, except the finance, ordinance, school, and auditing committees." Besides, "the general manager shall discharge other duties as may from time to time be required of him by the council."

These other duties consist in hearing all complaints of citizens; of advising and assisting the Council in making up the yearly budget of expenditures; and of overseeing all the work of the various departments. Under his direction are superintendents of (*a*) streets; (*b*) electric lighting; (*c*) waterworks; (*d*) the city park; (*e*) an overseer of the poor. The general manager does not directly look after all the details of these departments, but through their superintendents supervises and directs.

To his municipal duties the manager devotes his entire time. He is appointed by the council for the term

[1] Passed January 13, 1908.

THE CITY BUSINESS MANAGER

of one year; and is required to give a bond for $5000 before entering upon his office. His salary was $2000 a year, but has been raised to $2500.

What have been the results of this change of government?

In the first place, all of the business activities of the city have been brought together under a single head, closely coördinating the work of the different branches. In former days, when the waterworks department wanted to haul pipe from a freight car or yard to the street where the trenches waited for the laying of the mains, it had to hire its teams, even though city horses and wagons stood idle in the stalls; for these horses and wagons belonged to the street department, not to the water department; and there was no one to see that one branch of the city's working force helped another, in municipal affairs the policy seeming to be "let not thy right hand know what thy left hand doeth." Now, the city manager knows what work is going on in each division of the city work, and when the water department is ready for the pipe, the teams of the street department are on hand, and the pipe is delivered promptly. So all parts of the machine are made to work together.

In the second place, there is one purchasing agent for all city supplies — a single head whose duty it is to know market prices, buy as cheaply as possible, and get good quality. Formerly each council committee looked after the purchases for the department under its supervision, and there was no one whose business it was to look sharply at the items of cost. The saving in this respect has been great. Cylinder oil, which used to cost the city 79 cents a gallon, is bought now for about 50 cents. No drop in the market price accounts for so much difference. Granolithic paving, for which the city used to pay from $1.75 to $2.25 a square yard, is now done for less than $1. Waterpipe costs less than formerly. Old boilers and junk are sold, instead of being allowed to rust away; and in many ways it is apparent that the municipality has a business head. While impossible to prove absolutely, in the absence of accurate data on the expenditures under the former system, it is fairly certain that in the first year of operation the $3500 or $4000 which the manager's office cost, was more than saved by close buying, more careful use of city property, and the utilization of the waste time of city employees; and the saving has since continued.

The city's books are open to inspection at any time. The manager's assistant will tell you any evening at the close of business just how the city stands financially, in each fund. Bills are collected promptly every month, and paid promptly. The council controls all expenditures. The city manager's proposed outlays are first authorized by the council, whenever the items amount to over $100. After the amounts have been expended, the bills are audited by the council's auditing committee. In this way the manager's expense items are subject to initial authorization and to auditing — checks more than sufficient. But though the council is responsible for all expenditures, it depends to a great extent on its general manager for practical advice as to how much to spend in each department and the best way to spend it.

THE CITY BUSINESS MANAGER

At the beginning of the fiscal year the general manager submits his estimates to the finance committee, showing in detail the needs of the various departments, together with his recommendations. From this report the finance committee makes its recommendation to the council of the amount of taxes to be levied for the fiscal year. The general manager has no authority to fix the rate of taxation or to contract loans on account of the city, but this is all left in the hands of the finance committee and the council, who are the representatives of the people. The ordinance committee, with the assistance of the city attorney, draws up all of the ordinances and puts them in proper legal form to be presented to the council. The council adopts the ordinances, fixes the rate of taxation, and formulates the policy, and the mayor and general manager see that they are carried out. The mayor has entire charge of the police and fire departments. The general manager, however, does all of the purchasing for these departments on a requisition from the chiefs. The finance, ordinance, and auditing committees are retained, as their duties require very little time and attention, and serve as a check on the general manager.

Mr. Charles E. Ashburner, a civil engineer of Richmond, was until recently the city manager. He has one assistant, who keeps the minutes of the committee meetings — for the council committees meet regularly with the business manager — and attends carefully to the records, bookkeeping, notices to citizens, etc. The day at the office is a full one — complaints, requests for information, bills to examine and charge to the right accounts, and file; a council committee meeting or two;

engineering work to superintend (for the business manager is also city engineer); contracts to draw, supplies to inspect, letters, reports of employees: these are all part of the day's work. The management of the business of a municipal corporation takes thought and care and prompt action, as does that of any private company.

In Roswell, New Mexico, the city supervisor, who is appointed by the council, as already noted, is really a city manager, having control and supervision of streets, sidewalks, and improvements, besides being municipal purchasing agent.

A form of government under which an elective commission of five appoint a municipal manager has been proposed for Lockport, N.Y.

It will be of interest to observe to what extent this idea finds favor in new charters. The city manager is equivalent to a single commissioner, in charge of finances and general oversight. Whether there may not well be a manager for each of the several departments, health and police and parks, for example, and whether the city is as purely a financial proposition as many believe, can be determined only after more cities have had experience with a municipal business manager.

PART II

ANALYSIS AND COMPARISON OF COMMISSION CHARTERS AND LAWS

PART II

ANALYSIS AND COMPARISON OF COMMISSION CHARTERS AND LAWS

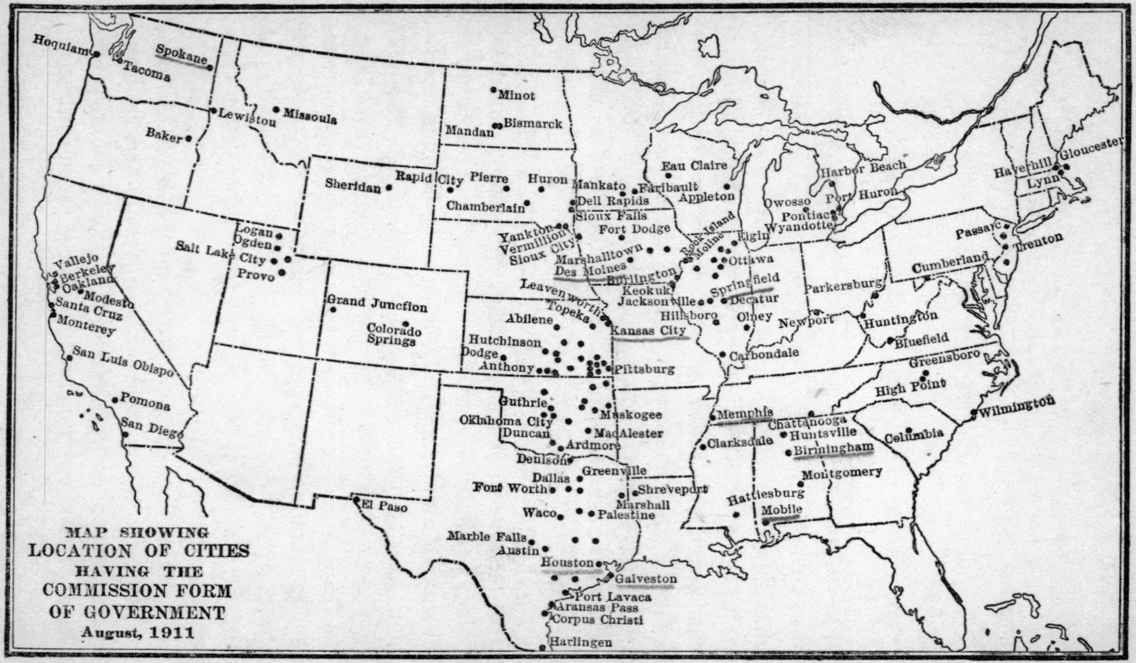

MAP SHOWING
LOCATION OF CITIES
HAVING THE
COMMISSION FORM
OF GOVERNMENT
August, 1911

CHAPTER XIII

COMMISSION GOVERNMENT: ESSENTIAL FEATURES

The broad characteristics of administrative commissions in general, including those in the fields of business and social institutions, it is not the purpose of this volume to consider. The executive committee of the fraternal order, the board of deacons of a church, the trustees of charitable organizations, the boards of directors of industrial concerns, are examples of the small group whose members direct and administer the business of the larger unit. Nor is it possible here to discuss the many governmental commissions created during recent years — temporary legislative or investigating committees, or more permanent boards of control, commissioners of the sinking funds, and public service commissions — which have become important arms of government. We are to deal only with commissions in cities, and, even then, with a particular type of municipal commission, the fundamental part of what has come to be known as the "commission form," and the adoption of which in Galveston, Des Moines, and other centers has been described in Part I.

The term "commission government" used at times in referring to the many boards of state or federal jurisdiction, has an entirely different meaning from "commission government in cities." In the former instance, many boards exercise portions of the governmental power of the larger political unit, a certain field being assigned to each. In the latter, a single commission wields undivided authority in the municipality. This distinction should be borne in mind throughout the discussion, the term being used exclusively in the latter sense. In a field so new, comparison of the forms to which the name "commission government" has been applied, is likely to prove especially helpful in gaining a clear conception of the term itself and the elements involved. In the laws under which these cities are organized let us note the features in common and those in which they differ; determine the relation of the various items, and so far as is possible ascertain the effect of each on the success or failure of the plan in producing good city government.

Essential Features of the Commission Form

Of the features of the commission plan some may be said to be both characteristic and important, while others are either not typical or are not fundamental enough to merit extended consideration.

Whether this small governing body is called a board of commissioners or a council is not essential. The qualifications of the members are also relatively unimportant. The names of the departments into which the city's activities are divided, the time given by each commissioner to his municipal duties, the term of office, and the salaries paid, while of greater moment, are hardly to be classed as vital, though many of these items will be discussed in connection with other phases of the subject.

The fundamental features of commission government

ESSENTIAL FEATURES

group themselves naturally under two broad heads: the powers, duties, and form of organization of the Commission; and the methods provided for its control by the people. Under these heads, the more particular elements which stand out clearly are the size of the board, its method of election, its powers, the division of duties among its members, and the "checks" or methods of control placed in the hands of the voters, whereby power is offset by responsibility. The characteristics of the commission form based on the charters and general acts adopted so far by American cities, are: (1) the small number of officers constituting the governing body; (2) their election by the whole body of voters, instead of by wards; (3) the exercise of administrative oversight and broad appointing power, as well as legislative authority, by the board; (4) the assignment of each commissioner to be the head of a definite department, for the conduct of which he is responsible to the commission, and to the people; and (5) the "checks" designed to assure direct popular control. These "checks" may be few or many, ranging from the simple publicity in the Galveston plan, and a referendum on bond issues only, already provided by state law, to the referendum on all ordinances, the initiative, recall, nonpartisan primaries and elections, a civil service commission, and various specific prohibitions, as in the more recent charters of Des Moines, and other municipalities.

These features, present in substantially all of the commission cities, may be regarded as the basic elements of the plan. They are manifestations of the two broad principles underlying all of the "commission forms" of city government; namely, greater authority in a small governing body, and greater ease in locating responsibility and exercising control, by the voters. These are sometimes referred to as "concentration of power and concentration of responsibility." Each of the elements of the commission plan merits attention as it appears in its varying forms in the different charters and comparison as to its value, for purposes of municipal government, with the corresponding element in the usual mayor-and-council system.

Charters or General Acts

Any comparative study of the cities which are employing the commission form should note at the beginning the distinction between special charters and general acts. Not quite half of the sevenscore municipalities which have the commission form operate under a special charter granted by the legislature, as Galveston, Houston, and most of the larger Texas cities, Haverhill, Gloucester, and Lynn (Mass.), and Huntington and Bluefield (W. Va.). In the states where a large degree of "home-rule" is permitted to cities, as in California, Oklahoma, Colorado, and Michigan, each city is organized under a special charter framed by a committee of its own citizens, adopted by a majority vote of the electors, and approved by legislature or governor. In other states, such as Iowa, Kansas, North Dakota, South Dakota, Wisconsin, and Illinois, commission cities are organized under a general law, applicable to all or to certain classes of cities. The cities where special charters are the rule (whether legislative or "home-made"), and those governed under a general statute, are shown in the following table: —

ESSENTIAL FEATURES

TABLE 1. LIST OF COMMISSION CITIES

A. *Under Special Charters*

CITY	POPULATION, 1910	DATE PASSED BY LEGISLATURE, OR SUBMITTED BY CHARTER COMMITTEE	DATE BEGINNING OPERATION (a)
Texas —		Legislature	
Galveston	36,981	Apr. 19, 1901 (b)	Sept. 18, 1901
Houston	78,800	Mar. 18, 1905	July 5, 1905
Dallas	92,104	Apr. 13, 1907 (c)	June 1, 1907
Fort Worth	73,312	Feb. 26, 1907 (d)	May 7, 1907
El Paso	39,279	Feb. 25, 1907	Apr. 1907
Denison	13,632	Mar. 21, 1907 (e)	Apr. 1907
Greenville	8,850	Mar. 15, 1907 (f)	Apr. 1907
Austin	29,860	Feb. 3, 1909 (g)	Apr. 19, 1909
Waco	26,425	Feb. 3, 1909 (g)	Apr. 1909 (h)
Palestine	10,482	Mar. 19, 1909	Apr. 1909
Corpus Christi	8,222	Mar. 15, 1909	Apr. 1909
Marshall	11,452	Feb. 12, 1909	Apr. 1909
Idaho —			
Lewiston	6,043	Mar. 13, 1907	July 1907
Massachusetts —			
Haverhill	44,115	June 3, 1908	Jan. 1909
Gloucester	24,398	June 11, 1908	Jan. 1909
Lynn	89,336	June 10, 1910	Jan. 1911
Tennessee —			
Memphis	131,105	Apr. 27, 1909	Jan. 1910
Chattanooga	44,604	Feb. 3, 1911	May 1, 1911

(a) Date when commission (council) took office.
(b) Amended March 30, 1903.
(c) Minor amendments, March 24 and May 7, 1909.
(d) Minor amendments, March 10, 1909.
(e) Minor amendments, February 24, 1909.
(f) Amended March 22, April 28, and May 10, 1909.
(g) Minor amendments, March 24, 1909.
(h) Commissioners took office 1909; mayor, 1910.

COMMISSION GOVERNMENT

TABLE I — *Continued*

A. *Under Special Charters*

City	Population, 1910	Date passed by Legislature, or submitted by Charter Committee	Date beginning Operation
North Carolina —			
High Point	9,525	Feb. 27, 1909	May 1909
Greensboro	15,895	Feb. 7, 1911 (*i*)	May 9, 1911
Wilmington	25,748	Mar. 3, 1911	May 6, 1911
West Virginia —			
Huntington	31,151	Mar. 1, 1909	June 1909
Bluefield	11,188	Mar. 3, 1909	June 1909
Parkersburg	17,842	Mar. 21, 1911 (*i*)	May 15, 1911
Oklahoma —		Charter Com.	
Ardmore	8,618	Sept. 22, 1908 (*j*)	Apr. 27, 1909 (*k*)
Enid	13,799	July 14, 1909 (*j*)	Dec. 20, 1909
Tulsa	18,182	July 3, 1908 (*j*)	Feb. 1909
McAlester	12,954	Apr. 2, 1910 (*j*)	Oct. 4, 1910
Muskogee	25,278	July 2, 1910 (*j*)	Apr. 4, 1911
El Reno	7,872	July 14, 1910 (*i*)	Apr. 1911
Bartlesville	6,181	Aug. 1910 (*i*)	Oct. 31, 1910
Sapulpa	8,283	Jan. 17, 1910 (*j*)	1910
Miami	2,907	1910 (*j*)	1910
Wagoner	4,018	Oct. 4, 1910 (*j*)	May 1911
Duncan	2,477	June 27, 1910 (*j*)	Nov. 1910
Purcell	2,740	1910	Jan. 1, 1911
Guthrie	11,654	Jan. 30, 1911 (*i*)	May 1911 (*i*)
Oklahoma City	64,205	Mar. 9, 1911 (*i*)	May 9, 1911 (*l*)
Colorado —			
Colorado Springs	29,078	Mar. 20, 1909 (*m*)	July 27, 1909
Grand Junction	7,754	Aug. 6, 1909 (*m*)	Nov. 9, 1909

(*i*) Date adopted by city.   (*j*) Date submitted by board of freeholders.
(*k*) Date of first election.
(*l*) Date of election of commissioners. Operation not yet begun, since validity of election is denied, and matter is in litigation.
(*m*) Date framed by charter convention.

ESSENTIAL FEATURES

TABLE I — *Continued*
A. *Under Special Charters*

City	Population, 1910	Date passed by Legislature, or submitted by Charter Committee	Date beginning Operation
California —			
Berkeley	40,434	Mar. 4, 1909 (*n*)	July 1, 1909
San Diego	39,578	Jan. 26, 1909 (*n*)	May 3, 1909
Oakland	150,174	Dec. 1910 (*o*)	July 1, 1911
Modesto	4,034	July 8, 1910 (*p*)	July 1, 1911
San Luis Obispo	5,157	July 11, 1910 (*p*)	May 15, 1911
Santa Cruz	11,146	Jan. 31, 1911 (*q*)	July 3, 1911
Vallejo	11,340	Feb. 21, 1911 (*q*)	July 1, 1911
Monterey	4,923	Dec. 12, 1910 (*q*)	July 1, 1911
Pomona	10,207	1911	July 1911
Washington —			
Tacoma	82,972	Aug. 5, 1909 (*p*)	May 1910
Spokane	104,402	Dec. 28, 1910 (*q*)	Apr. 1911
Oregon —			
Baker	6,742	Oct. 3, 1910 (*q*)	Dec. 6, 1910
Minnesota —			
Mankato	10,365	Feb. 4, 1910 (*p*)	Apr. 1910
Faribault	9,001	Feb. 7, 1911 (*q*)	Apr. 12, 1911
Maryland —			
Cumberland	21,836	Jan. 1910 (*r*)	June 6, 1910
Michigan —			
Port Huron	18,863	Nov. 5. 1910 (*q*)	Jan. 2, 1911
Pontiac	14,532	Jan. 30, 1911 (*q*)	Apr. 10, 1911
Harbor Beach	1,556	Mar. 7, 1910 (*s*)	Apr. 17, 1910
Wyandotte	8,287	Mar. 2, 1911 (*q*)	Apr. 10, 1911

(*n*) Date of approval by legislature, after submission by board of freeholders and adoption by the voters of the city.   (*o*) Date of first election.
(*p*) Date submitted by board of freeholders.   (*q*) Date adopted by city.
(*r*) Passed by legislature.   (*s*) Date approved by governor

COMMISSION GOVERNMENT

TABLE I — *Continued*

B. *Under General Acts*

City	Population, 1910	Date adopted by City	Date beginning Operation
Iowa —			
Des Moines	86,368	June 20, 1907	Apr. 6, 1908
Cedar Rapids	32,811	Dec. 2, 1907	Apr. 6, 1908
Keokuk	14,008	July 2, 1909	Apr. 11, 1910
Burlington	24,324	Nov. 29, 1909	Apr. 11, 1910
Sioux City	47,828	Feb. 15, 1910	Apr. 11, 1910
Marshalltown	13,374	July 15, 1910	Apr. 1, 1911
Fort Dodge	15,543	Aug. 16, 1910	Apr. 1, 1911
Kansas — Cities of first class (*a*)			
Leavenworth	19,363	1908	Apr. 1908
Wichita	52,450	Feb. 2, 1909	Apr. 6, 1909
Hutchinson	16,364	1909	Apr. 1909
Topeka	43,684	Nov. 2, 1909	Apr. 1910
Kansas City	82,331	July 14, 1909	Apr. 1910
Kansas — Cities of second class (*b*)			
Independence	10,480	Dec. 8, 1908	Apr. 22, 1909
Coffeyville	12,687	Sept. 14, 1909	Apr. 18, 1910
Parsons	12,463	Oct. 26, 1909	Apr. 18, 1910
Pittsburg	14,755	Feb. 21, 1910	Apr. 18, 1910
Iola	9,032	Mar. 10, 1910	Apr. 18, 1910
Wellington	7,034	Mar. 8, 1910	Apr. 18, 1910
Emporia	9,058	Mar. 1910	Apr. 6, 1910
Marion	1,841	Mar. 3, 1910	Apr. 18, 1910
Cherryvale	4,304	1910	May 1, 1911
Abilene	4,118	Mar. 1910	Apr. 18, 1910

(*a*) Applies to cities of over 15,000 population.
(*b*) Applies to cities of from 2000 to 15,000 population.

ESSENTIAL FEATURES

TABLE 1 — *Continued*
B. *Under General Acts*

City	Population, 1910	Date adopted by City	Date beginning Operation
Kansas — Cities of second class			
Newton	7,682	Mar. 1910	Apr. 18, 1910
Girard	2,446	Mar. 1910	Apr. 18, 1910
Dodge City	3,214	Nov. 1910	Apr. 9, 1911
Neodesha	2,872	Mar. 17, 1910	May 5, 1911
Anthony	2,669	Feb. 2, 1909	Apr. 22, 1909
Caldwell	2,205	Mar. 8, 1909	Apr. 22, 1909
Eureka	2,333	Apr. 4, 1910	Apr. 13, 1910
Council Grove	2,545	Feb. 6, 1911	Apr. 14, 1911
South Dakota —			
Rapid City	3,854	1910	May 2, 1910
Sioux Falls	14,094	Sept. 29, 1908	May 1, 1909
Yankton	3,787	1910	1910
Pierre	3,656	Mar. 1910	May 2, 1910
Dell Rapids	1,367	Mar. 1910	May 2, 1910
Huron	5,791	Feb. 1, 1910	May 2, 1910
Chamberlain	1,275	Mar. 29, 1910	May 2, 1910
Vermillion	2,187	1910	1910
Aberdeen	10,753	Feb. 28, 1911	May 1911
North Dakota —			
Bismarck	5,443	Mar. 1909	Apr. 1909
Mandan	3,873	Oct. 2, 1907	Dec. 2, 1907
Minot	6,188	Apr. 21, 1909	July 19, 1909
Wisconsin —			
Eau Claire	18,310	Feb. 15, 1910	Apr. 1910
Appleton	16,773	Feb. 6, 1911	Apr. 1911
New Mexico —			

TABLE I — *Continued*

B. *Under General Acts*

City	Population, 1910	Date adopted by City	Date beginning Operation
Mississippi —			
Hattiesburg	11,733	1910	Jan. 1, 1911
Clarksdale	4,079	Dec. 30, 1910 (c)	Jan. 1, 1911
Kentucky —			
Newport	30,309	Nov. 7, 1910	Jan. 1912
Louisiana —			
Shreveport	28,015	Sept. 15, 1910	Nov. 15, 1910
South Carolina			
Columbia	26,319	Feb. 22, 1910 (c)	May 11, 1910
Texas —			
Kenedy	1,147	Feb. 26, 1910	Mar. 2, 1910
Aransas Pass	1,197	1910	Apr. 1910
Harlingen	(d)	Apr. 5, 1910	Apr. 1910
Lyford	(d)	1910	Aug. 29, 1910
Barry	(d)	1910	Aug. 1910
Port Lavaca	1,699	1910	Aug. 11, 1909
Marble Falls	1,061	1910	Apr. 16, 1910
Elkhart	(d)	Nov. 8, 1910	Nov. 1910
Terrell	7,070	Dec. 21, 1910	Apr. 1911
McAllen	(d)	Feb. 18, 1911	Feb. 20, 1911
Abilene		April 1911	May 1911
San Benito	(d)	June 1911	June 1911
Illinois —			
Springfield	51,678	Jan. 1911	Apr. 1911
Moline	24,199	Feb. 3, 1911	Apr. 1911

(c) Date act passed by legislature.

(d) Population figures not available from Bureau of the Census, since village is not incorporated.

ESSENTIAL FEATURES

TABLE I — *Continued*

B. *Under General Acts*

City	Population, 1910	Date adopted by City	Date beginning Operation
Illinois —			
Rock Island	24,335	Jan. 1911	Apr. 1911
Rochelle	2,732	Jan. 1911	Apr. 1911
Pekin	9,897	Feb. 6, 1911	Apr. 1911
Jacksonville	15,326	Jan. 31, 1911	Apr. 1911
Hillsboro	3,424	Feb. 13, 1911	Apr. 1911
Decatur	31,140	Jan. 17, 1911	Apr. 1911
Elgin	25,978	Jan. 21, 1911	Apr. 1911
Dixon	7,216	Jan. 17, 1911	Apr. 1911
Ottawa	9,535	Jan. 17, 1911	Apr. 1911
Kewanee	9,307	Jan. 1911	Apr. 1911
Carbondale	5,411	Feb. 1911	Apr. 1911
Spring Valley	7,835	Feb. 1911	Apr. 1911
Clinton	5,165	Feb. 28, 1911	Apr. 1911
Alabama — (*e*)			
Montgomery	38,136	Apr. 6, 1911 (*f*)	Apr. 10, 1911
Birmingham	132,685	Mar. 31, 1911 (*f*)	Apr. 10, 1911
Mobile	51,521	June 5, 1911	
Huntsville	7,611	June 19, 1911	
California — (*g*)			
Idaho — (*h*)			
Montana —			
Missoula	12,869	May 18, 1911	1911

(*e*) Three general acts apply in Alabama: see pp. 98, 99.
(*f*) Act passed by legislature.
(*g*) General act (amendment) passed April 10, 1911.
(*h*) Applies to cities of 3000 and over.

COMMISSION GOVERNMENT

TABLE I — *Continued*
B. *Under General Acts*

City	Population, 1910	Date adopted by City	Date beginning Operation
New Jersey —			
Trenton	96,815	June 20, 1911	1911
Hawthorne	3,400	July 19, 1911	1911
Passaic	54,773	July 25, 1911	1911
Margate City	129	July 25, 1911	1911
Utah —			
Logan	7,522	(*i*)	
Murray	4,057	(*i*)	
Ogden	25,580	(*i*)	
Provo	8,925	(*i*)	
Salt Lake City	92,777	(*i*)	
Washington — (*j*)			
Hoquiam	8,171	June 5, 1911	1911
Wyoming — (*k*)			
Sheridan	8,400	August, 1911	Mar. 1, 1912

(*i*) Act applies without adoption by city.   (*j*) Applies to cities of 2500–20,000.
(*k*) Act approved Feb. 21, 1911.

This list[1] does not include four cities in New York, — Buffalo, Mt. Vernon, Beacon, and Saratoga Springs, — which have voted favorably, but are not yet authorized by the legislature to organize under the commission plan; nor the many partial and incomplete forms found in a number of instances[2]; nor such unusual types as Washington, D.C., and Chelsea, Mass.[2]

[1] Total, 151 cities. The foregoing table is revised to August 15, 1911, but the continued adoption of the plan by new cities makes any list soon incomplete.

[2] Riverside (Cal.), Boise (Ida.), St. Joseph (Mo.), Taunton (Mass.), Beaumont (Tex.), and several other cities have incomplete forms. See "Unusual and Partial Forms of Commission Government," pp. 283 ff.

CHAPTER XIV

THE SMALL BOARD

THE first important feature of the commission laws and charters is the *small governing body*. The following table arranges the cities and states according to the number of commissioners (or councilmen) provided:—

TABLE 2. NUMBER OF COMMISSIONERS (*a*)

A. Charters

CITIES WITH THREE COMMISSIONERS	POPULATION, 1910	CITIES WITH FOUR COMMISSIONERS	POPULATION, 1910	CITIES WITH FIVE COMMISSIONERS	POPULATION, 1910
Denison, Tex.	13,632	Palestine, Tex.	10,482	Galveston, Tex.	36,981
Greenville, "	8,850			Houston, "	78,800
Marshall, "	11,452	Huntington, W. Va.	31,161	Dallas, "	92,104
				El Paso, "	39,279
McAlester, Okla.	12,954	Bluefield, "	11,188	Austin, "	29,860
Bartlesville, "	6,181			Waco, "	25,425
Miami, "	2,907	Ardmore, Okla.	8,618	Corpus Christi,"	8,222
Duncan, "	2,477	Enid, "	13,799		
Guthrie, "	11,654	Sapulpa "	8,283	Haverhill, Mass.	44,115
				Gloucester, "	24,398
Vallejo, Cal.	11,340			Lynn, "	89,336
Baker, Ore.	6,742			Memphis, Tenn.	131,105
				Chattanooga, "	44,604
Pontiac, Mich.	14,532			Wilmington, N.C.	25,748
				Parkersburg, W. Va.	17,842
				Muskogee, Okla.	25,278
				Tulsa, "	18,181

(*a*) Including mayor.

COMMISSION GOVERNMENT

TABLE 2 — *Continued*

A. *Charters*

Cities with Five Commissioners	Population, 1910	Cities with Six Commissioners	Population, 1910	Cities with Seven Commissioners	Population, 1910
Colorado Springs, Col.	29,078	Fort Worth, Tex.	93,312	Lewiston, Ida.	6043
Grand Junction, "	7,754	San Diego, (*b*) Cal.	39,578		
Berkeley, Cal.	44,034				
Oakland, "	150,174				
Modesto, "	4,034				
San Luis Obispo, "	5,157				
Monterey, "	4,923				
				Cities with Nine Commissioners	
Tacoma, Wash.	82,972				
Spokane, "	104,402				
Mankato, Minn.	10,365				
Cumberland, Md.	21,839			High Point, N. C.	9525
Port Huron, Mich.	18,863				
Harbor Beach, Mich.	1,556				
Wyandotte, "	8,278				

(*b*) Including mayor, who is not a member of council.

Of the cities operating under special charters, we find 30, out of the 51 listed, provide for five commissioners, while six have four commissioners, and eleven have three. In only four cities are there more than five members, and in not one of these has the board as many as ten. Four state acts provide for five commissioners in all cities; Wisconsin, Washington, and Wyoming, for three; while in Iowa, Kansas, Louisiana, Texas, Montana, New Jersey,

THE SMALL BOARD

TABLE 2 — *Continued*

B. *General Acts*

Three Commissioners	Four Commissioners	Five Commissioners
Iowa — cities of 7000–25,000 Kansas — cities of second class South Dakota (*e*) Wisconsin (*a*) Louisiana — cities of 7500–25,000 Texas — cities of less than 10,000 Mississippi (*b*) New Mexico (*b*) Alabama — cities of 100,000 and over Alabama (general) Montana — cities of less than 25,000 New Jersey — cities of less than 10,000 (*d*) Utah — cities of second class Washington Wyoming	New Mexico (*b*)	Iowa — cities of over 25,000 Kansas — cities of first class South Dakota (*e*) North Dakota Kentucky (*c*) Louisiana — cities of over 25,000 South Carolina Illinois Mississippi (*b*) New Mexico (*b*) Alabama — cities of 25,000–50,000 Montana — cities of 25,000 or more New Jersey — cities of 10,000 and over (*d*) Utah — cities of first class

(*a*) Applies to cities of second, third, and fourth classes.

(*b*) The Mississippi law provides for three or five commissioners; that of New Mexico, three *to* five.   (*c*) Law applies to cities of second class.

(*d*) But the commission may increase the number of members from three to five, or decrease the number from five to three.

(*e*) A recent amendment (1911) permits city to have three commissioners if desired.

and Utah, the larger cities have five, the smaller three, commissioners. In Alabama, cities of over 100,000 population (Birmingham) are to have three commissioners, cities of 25,000 to 50,000 population, five commissioners, and other cities, three commissioners. In Mississippi, New Mexico, and South Dakota an option is given. In most instances preference is shown for an odd number; but in Huntington and Bluefield the desire to have the two large parties evenly represented in the board led to the choice of four as a number evenly divisible. A little over half of the total number of commission cities, August 15, 1911, are governed, or are to be governed, by five commissioners. In place of the usual council, consisting sometimes of two bodies and containing from ten to fifty or more members, there is thus substituted a single small board usually of five or three members.

Reasons for a Small Board

The number of members which should constitute a municipal commission depends upon two principal considerations: (1) the natural numerical limit to an efficient working board; and (2) the number which can well be elected by the voters of a city at any one time.

Natural Limit of Efficiency

The number of members of the municipal governing body should be within the natural limit of efficiency for an executive board. The greater the number of members, the less the responsibility of each. In large boards of directors and committees it is frequently the fact that many members are absent. The point at which the individual ceases to consider important his membership in a group varies in different bodies, but may be said, from experience in many fields, to be for active managing boards at or below seven, certainly below ten. That the work of city governing is of this actively administrative and managerial nature has been recognized by the commission cities. The larger number sometimes found in the boards of directors of corporations is due to another principle, namely, that of stock representation. In the corporation, a small number of directors usually perform the real duties of the board.

The Short Ballot

The second consideration is very important. Our American ballots are overloaded with the names of candidates; there are so many offices to be filled that it is impossible for any one but a politician to inform himself as to the merits of each of the aspirants for the many places; and men vote the straight party ticket, a cross at the head of a column which contains a few familiar names affording relief from considering the long list below.

An easy and logical remedy is to reduce the number of names on the ballot. Why should not five men represent a city more ably than twenty? Is it not the character of their action, rather than the number of men who act, which determines whether a governing body is truly representative? In the past, it has been assumed that merely to allow the people to vote for their officers was to insure democratic government, and the more men they voted for, the more democratic the government. It is now recognized that democracy, or government in accordance with the will of the people, can be best secured by affording the people the means of more fully expressing their will, either in the control of their officials or in the passage of measures. One method of control of officials is to permit the people to elect representatives at any time that a real need arises, instead of only at

COMMISSION GOVERNMENT

stated intervals. The "recall" is merely this privilege of electing a new official sooner than usual. Another method is to allow the people to vote directly on measures as well as on men; heretofore, the two have been bound together, and the only way to secure needed laws has been to vote for the men who stand for such measures but who also stand for others possibly undesirable. The "short ballot" is another such method, much more important than is generally recognized and so simple that it should be instantly welcomed as an addition to the list of effective methods for securing good government. Its purpose is to reduce the number of elective officers to the smallest necessary number, small enough to enable the voters to know something of each candidate.

Present electoral methods in cities are open to valid objections, which have been set forth clearly as follows:[1] —

The usual ballot "submits to popular election offices which are too unimportant to attract or deserve public attention. It submits to popular election *so many* offices at one time that many of them are inevitably crowded out from proper public attention; and the business of making up the elaborate ticket makes the political machine an indispensable instrument in electoral action. Many officials, therefore, are elected without adequate public scrutiny, and owe their selection, not to the people,

---

[1] See "The Short Ballot Principle," and other publications of the Short Ballot Organization. The officers of this organization are President, Woodrow Wilson, Princeton, N.J.; Secretary and Treasurer, Richard S. Childs, 383 Fourth Avenue, New York City. The purpose of the organization is "to explain the Short Ballot Principle to the American People."

but to the makers of the party ticket, who thus acquire an influence that is capable of great abuse."

The "short ballot" method requires, "first, that only those offices should be elective which are important enough to attract (and deserve) public examination; and second, that very few offices should be filled by election at one time, so as to permit adequate and unconfused public examination of the candidates." The value of these propositions is so evident that acceptance follows their mere statement. While not covering the entire field of popular control — what single proposition ever did? — the short ballot method is of great moment, and its adoption by many of our foremost publicists and citizens is evidence of its soundness. It is one of the important features of the commission form in cities.

Prompt Action

Not only are better men likely to be elected when the number chosen is few, but after election it is also easier to hold the few responsible. Citizens know the men who compose the board as a whole, and the individual heads of departments are few enough to be also known. Moreover, action by a small board is likely to be more promptly taken than by a large council: and the need of action by governmental bodies rather than the fear of such action is felt more and more as government exercises business functions. Three illustrations may be cited from Cedar Rapids. A well-known real estate agent, a former member of the city council, wished approval of the plat of a new subdivision. He secured it from the commission in one day. Under the old plan it would have required six months; at least, that was the time taken to get through a previous plat. A local telephone company wished permission to put its wires underground and to make certain reconstructions. The franchise for this was introduced under the old régime in May of one year and was reported out by the committee in March of the next year. The Douglas Starch Works wished recently to have an unimportant street vacated. Application was made to the commission and approved the same day. It should be remembered that the ordinance granting the vacation is subject to referendum, so that had the commission given away an important street, the act could have been vetoed by the people. Similar incidents have occurred in other cities. The commission is small enough to act promptly.

The small council or commission is thus better, both from the viewpoint of the voters, who must select and afterwards hold responsible for needed action, and from that of the board itself, which must act.

Other Elective Officers

This small board comprises, in most cases, all the elective officials chosen in the city. Other officers, such as city engineer, assessor, and treasurer, elected under the aldermanic plan, are appointed by the commission. Elective officers, other than the commissioners, are usually school directors or boards of education, or library trustees, who are generally put in a class by themselves at elections. The charter of Gloucester, for example, specifically provides that no other city officers shall be elected at the city election, "except as aforesaid," the phrase referring to three school directors elected annu-

THE SMALL BOARD

ally. Twenty-seven cities out of fifty-one tabulated under "Special Charters," on pp. 152–156, elect no other officials than the commissioners (not counting boards of education or library officials), and few of the general acts provide for other elective officials, save that of Kentucky, where a police judge also is elected, and Mississippi, where the local petition for the commission form may provide for other elective officers.

In the list of cities under special charters, at least twelve elect one additional official; two cities elect two additional; El Paso and Santa Cruz elect three; and Waco (Tex.), McAlester (Okla.), Colorado Springs, and Pontiac, Harbor Beach, and Wyandotte (Mich.), elect more than three. Huntington and Bluefield, in this respect, are in a class by themselves, since they each elect a fairly numerous citizens' board as a veto-and-recall body, the members being elected by wards.

Fort Worth, Greenville, and Marshall (Tex.) elect an assessor-and-collector of taxes (and previous to April, 1911, a corporation counsel); Memphis, a tax assessor; Berkeley, Oakland, Vallejo, and Tulsa, an auditor; San Diego, a treasurer; Tacoma, a controller; San Luis Obispo, a city clerk; and Chattanooga a city judge. Mankato (Minn.) elects a judge and a special judge of the municipal court; and Port Huron (Mich.) a police justice and an assistant police justice. El Paso elects also a judge of the corporation court, a treasurer, and an assessor-and-collector; Santa Cruz, an auditing commission of three; Waco, besides the commissioners, judge, and assessor as elected in El Paso, elects a city attorney, a city secretary, and a board of water commissioners. McAlester elects a municipal judge and a board of inspection of three members, whose duty is to audit the city's accounts. Colorado Springs continues to elect a park commission; and the three cities of Michigan elect additional officials as noted on p. 156.

In these exceptions — less than thirty cities out of a total of one hundred and fifty — can be traced apparently two ideas: first, that of providing a fiscal or financial officer independent of the commissioners and therefore, according to the theory, a check upon its financial acts; and second, in fewer cases, that of the separate election of judicial officers. The desire of having a controller, or auditor, or treasurer, or, in four Southern cities, an assessor or collector, elected separately and therefore not appointed or removable by the commissioners, is based upon the theory that five commissioners are likely to become a unit in action, and so be able to conceal the true financial status of the city or their misuse of funds. It does not appear why four or five commissioners and an auditor are less likely to become such a unit than five commissioners, when all commissioners and the auditor are selected by the same authority and all work together. How easy for the auditor to join the others — no more difficult than for the commissioner of finance! Are the people likely to elect a more honest controller than an honest finance commissioner? Why not elect an inspector to watch the controller; and an examiner of accounts to check up the inspector — and where are we to stop? The theory is wrong — a relic of the old sort of checks and balances. Pick the commissioners carefully, elect as good men as possible, and hold them responsible directly to the people — that is, the voters. If a check of the other sort is desired, depend upon some one not connected with the city administration — either a state auditing official for the city or, better, a bureau of municipal research or some similar active citizen's body, unofficial, but equipped to interpret municipal statistics.

Complete or Partial Renewal of Commission

Closely connected with the number elected is the question whether all the commissioners shall be chosen at the same time. It has been argued that to vote one year for two members of the board, and the next year for the other three members, each, say, for a two-year term, is desirable, since it tends to still further concentrate attention on the fewer officials chosen at any one election. On the other hand, it has been urged that too frequent elections, and the corresponding short terms in office, have the same effect on the voter as too many candidates for office; that it detracts from the importance of the individual election. From this point of view it appears as well to elect five men all at once for a two- or four-year term, as is done in South Carolina, as to vote for one commissioner each year for a term of five years, as in North Dakota. In South Carolina a mayor and two commissioners are elected for a four-year term, and two years later the other two commissioners for a four-year term. The election of only part of the commissioners at one time prevents the people from treating their administrative board as a unit, and voting on all of them at the same time: and under most commission charters, the board is rightly regarded as a unit. The power to retire the whole board at once is favored by many. On the other hand, continuity of administration argues against such a course, the replacement of one or two members of the commission causing less break in the management of city business than when all the directing heads are new. Much may be said also in favor of dividing municipal functions into two classes, placing finances, the engineering work, and perhaps parks in one class, and police, health and morals, and the general directive duties in another. The voters may then elect the first three commissioners one year, concentrating public attention upon the physical and financial aspects of the administration; and two years later (supposing a four-year term for commissioners) choose a mayor and a commissioner of police and health, at which election the voters would give their attention to the general policy and the sanitary and moral needs of the city. Which of these considerations are most weighty can be determined only by trial. The variety of provisions on this point in the different commission laws should soon yield sufficient experience to enable definite conclusions to be drawn as to the relative merits of each plan.

The following table summarizes the various provisions as to whether or not all members are elected at one time, what other elective officials there are besides the commissioners (councilmen), and the length of term of the mayor and other commissioners:[1]

[1] The data in this table and those following are not complete in a few instances where provisions exist outside of the commission charters and acts.

THE SMALL BOARD

TABLE 3. TERMS OF COMMISSIONERS AND OTHER PROVISIONS
A. Charters

City	Name of Commission	Number of Com'rs (a)	Number Elected at One Time	Other Elective Officials	Term of Mayor-Com'r (yrs.)	Term of Other Com'rs (yrs.)
Texas —						
Galveston	Bd. of Com'rs	5	All		2	2
Houston	City Council	5	All		2	2
Dallas	Bd. of Com'rs	5	All	(b)	2	2
Fort Worth	Bd. of Com'rs	6	All	(c)	2	2
El Paso	City Council	5	All	(d)	2	2
Denison	City Council	3	(e)		2	2
Greenville	City Council	3	All	(c)	2	2
Austin	City Council	5	All	(f)	2	2
Waco	Bd. of Com'rs	5	(g)	(h)	2	2
Palestine	City Council	4	All		2	2
Corpus Christi	City Council	5	All		2	2
Marshall	Bd. of Com'rs	3	(i)	(j)	2	2

(a) Including mayor.

(b) A board of education, of seven members, elected each two years.

(c) An assessor-and-collector of taxes is also elected.

(d) El Paso elects also a judge of the corporation court, a treasurer, and an assessor-and-collector.

(e) Mayor and one commissioner elected for two years; the next year the other commissioner is elected for two years.

(f) School trustees.

(g) Mayor elected in 1910 for two-year term; other four commissioners elected in 1909, for two-year term; and so thereafter.

(h) Waco elects also a collector-and-assessor of taxes, a city secretary, city attorney, judge of the corporation court, and a board of five water commissioners.

(i) Chairman and city secretary are elected for two-year term; the next year the two other commissioners are elected for two-year term. The board consists of the chairman and two commissioners.

(j) Marshall elects one additional official, who acts as treasurer, assessor-and-collector, and as city secretary.

COMMISSION GOVERNMENT

TABLE 3 — *Continued*

A. Charters

CITY	NAME OF COMMISSION	NUMBER OF COM'RS	NUMBER ELECTED AT ONE TIME	OTHER ELECTIVE OFFICIALS	TERM OF MAYOR-COM'R (yrs.)	TERM OF OTHER COM'RS (yrs.)
Idaho —						
Lewiston	Mayor and Council	7	(k)		2	2
Massachusetts —						
Haverhill	Municipal Council	5	(l)	(m)	2	2
Gloucester	Municipal Council	5	All	(m)	1	1
Lynn	Municipal Council	5	(n)	(m)	2	2
Tennessee —						
Memphis	Bd. of Com'rs	5	All	(o)	4(p)	4(p)
Chattanooga	Bd. of Com'rs	5	All	(q)	4	4
N. Carolina —						
High Point	City Council	9	All		2	2
Wilmington	Council	5	All		2	2
W. Virginia —						
Huntington	Bd. of Com'rs	4	All	(r)	3	3
Bluefield	Bd. of Affairs	4	(s)	(t)	4	4
Parkersburg	Council	5	All		3	3

(k) Mayor and three councilmen are elected one year, three other councilmen the next year.

(l) Mayor, two aldermen, and two members of school committee, elected each even-numbered year; the other two aldermen, and two members of school committee, elected each odd-numbered year. (m) School committee.

(n) Mayor and two commissioners elected one year for a two-year term; the next year two other commissioners are elected for a two-year term.

(p) First administration holds from January 1, 1910, to November, 1911; thereafter term is four years. (o) Tax assessor.

(q) City Judge also elected. (r) "Citizens' Board."

(t) "Council," which is not the usual council, but is similar to the "Citizens' Board" in Huntington.

THE SMALL BOARD

TABLE 3 — *Continued*

A. *Charters*

City	Name of Commission	Number of Com'rs	Number elected at one time	Other Elective Officials	Term of Mayor-Com'r (yrs.)	Term of Other Com'rs (yrs.)
Oklahoma —						
Ardmore	Bd. of Com'rs	4	(s)	(u)	2	4
Enid	Bd. of Com'rs	4	All	(u)	2	2
Tulsa	Bd. of Com'rs	5	All	(v)	2	2
McAlester	City Council	3	(w)	(x)	3	3
Muskogee	Council	5	(y)		2	4
Bartlesville	Bd. of Com'rs	3	(w)		3	3
Sapulpa	Bd. of Com'rs	4	(s)		4	4
Duncan	Bd. of Com'rs	3	(w)	(u)	3	3
Guthrie	Bd. of Com'rs	3	One		6	6
Colorado —						
Colorado Springs	Council	5	(z)	(a)	4	4
Grand Junction	City Council	5	(z)		4	4
California —						
Berkeley	Council	5	(b)	(c)	2	4

(s) Two commissioners elected each second year for four-year terms.

(u) Board of education.

(v) Auditor also elected in Tulsa ; two-year term.

(w) One member is elected each year for a three-year term.

(x) Municipal judge and a board of inspection (three members) also elected.

(y) Mayor (two-year term) and two commissioners (four-year terms) elected; two years later, mayor and the two other commissioners.

(z) Mayor and two commissioners elected for four years ; two years later, the other two commissioners are elected for four years.

(a) Park commission and board of directors of public library are continued.

(b) Mayor and auditor are elected for two-year term. Two councilmen and two school directors elected every two years for a four-year term.

(c) Auditor and school directors.

COMMISSION GOVERNMENT

TABLE 3 — *Continued*

A. *Charters*

City	Name of Commission	Number of Com'rs	Number Erected at One Time	Other Elective Officials	Term of Mayor-Com'r (yrs.)	Term of Other Com'rs (yrs.)
California —						
San Diego	Common Council	6	(*d*)	(*e*)	2	4
Oakland	Council	5	(*f*)		4	4
Modesto	Council	5	(*g*)	(*h*)	4	4
San Luis Obispo	Council	5	(*i*)	(*j*)	2	4
Santa Cruz	Council	5	(*k*)	(*l*)	2	4
Vallejo	Council	3	(*m*)	(*n*)	4	4
Monterey	Council	5	(*k*)		2	4
Washington —						
Tacoma	Council	5	(*o*)	(*p*)	4	4
Spokane	Council	5	(*d*)		4	4

(*d*) Two members of the council are elected each two years for a term of four years; the other members, two years later, for four-year term. In San Diego, also a mayor every two years for a two-year term.

(*e*) Treasurer and board of education elected also.

(*f*) The mayor, two commissioners, and three school directors are elected each two years for a four-year term; two years later the auditor, two other commissioners, and three other school directors are elected for four years.

(*g*) Mayor and two commissioners elected for four years; two years later, the other two commissioners are elected for four years.

(*h*) Board of education.

(*i*) Term of mayor and city clerk is two years; two councilmen are elected every two years for four-year term.

(*j*) City clerk and four school directors.

(*k*) Mayor (two-year term) and two commissioners (four-year terms) elected; two years later, mayor and the two other commissioners.

(*l*) Auditing Committee of three, and Board of Education.

(*m*) Mayor is elected for four-year term; and one commissioner for two-year term; two years later other commissioner is elected for two-year term, and an auditor for a four-year term.

(*n*) Auditor and school directors.

(*o*) Mayor and two commissioners elected for four-year term; two years later, controller and two other commissioners elected for four-year term.

(*p*) Controller.

THE SMALL BOARD

TABLE 3 — *Continued*

A. *Charters*

CITY	NAME OF COMMISSION	NUMBER OF COM'RS	NUMBER ELECTED AT ONE TIME	OTHER ELECTIVE OFFICIALS	TERM OF MAYOR-COM'R (yrs.)	TERM OF OTHER COM'RS (yrs.)
Oregon — Baker	Bd. of Com'rs	3	(*q*)		4	4
Minnesota — Mankato	Council	5	All	(*r*)	2	2
Maryland — Cumberland	Mayor and City Council	5	All		2	2
Michigan —						
Port Huron	City Com'n	5	All	(*s*)	2	2
Pontiac	Commission	3	(*t*)	(*u*)	3	3
Harbor Beach	Council	5	All	(*v*)	1	1
Wyandotte	City Com'n	5	All	(*w*)	2	2

(*q*) Two elected for four-year term; two years later, the third elected for four-year term.
(*r*) Judge and special judge of the municipal court.
(*s*) Police justice and assistant police justice elected, one every second year, for four-year term.
(*t*) One member elected each year for a term of three years.
(*u*) Justice of the peace; also one constable and one supervisor are elected in each ward in April, annually.
(*v*) Two constables and two justices of the peace; the term of constables is one year; that of justices, four years, one being elected each second year.
(*w*) City clerk, city treasurer, justice of the peace, and four constables. Terms are two years, except that of justice of the peace, four years.

(*i*) Mayor elected for four years; two years later police judge elected for four years; all commissioners elected every two years.
(*j*) Mayor and two councilmen elected for four-year term; two years later, two other councilmen elected for four-year term.
(*k*) Three members alternate with two.
(*l*) Every two years a mayor and two councilmen are elected, the former for a two-year term, the latter, for four years.
(*m*) Mayor and two councilmen elected for two-year term, the next year, the the other two councilmen. In cities of less than 25,000 the mayor and one councilman alternate similarly with the other councilman.
(*n*) In cities of first class, mayor, and two commissioners alternate every two years with other two commissioners; an auditor is elected every two years; in cities of second class, mayor and auditor (two-year terms), and one or the other commissioner (four-year terms) are elected every two years.
(*o*) Auditor, city recorder, and city treasurer.

155

COMMISSION GOVERNMENT

TABLE 3 — *Continued*
B. *General Acts*

STATE	NAME OF BOARD	NUMBER OF COM'RS	NUMBER ELECTED AT ONE TIME	OTHER ELECTIVE OFFICIALS	TERM OF MAYOR COM'R (yrs.)	TERM OF OTHER COM'RS (yrs.)
Iowa	Council	5 (3)	All		2	2
Kansas — cities of first class	Bd. of Com'rs	5	All		2	2
Kansas — cities of second class	Bd. of Com'rs	3	1 (*a*)		3	3
South Dakota	Bd. of Com'rs	5 (3)	1 (*b*)	(*c*)	5	5
North Dakota	Bd. of Com'rs	5	1 (*b*)	(*c*)	5	5
Wisconsin	Council	3	(*d*)	(*e*)	6	6
Minnesota (*f*)	Council	(*g*)	(*g*)	(*g*)	(*g*)	(*g*)
Illinois	Council	5	All		4	4
New Mexico	Commission	3 or 5	All			
Mississippi	Commission	3 or 5	(*g*)	(*h*)	(*g*)	(*g*)
Kentucky	Bd. of Com'rs	5	3 (*i*)	(*i*)	4	2
Louisiana	Mayor and Council	5 (3)	All		4	4
South Carolina	City Council	5	(*j*)		4	4
Texas	Commission	3	All		2	2
Alabama—cities of 100,000 or over	Bd. of Com'rs	3	(*a*)		3	3
Alabama—cities of 25–50,000	Bd. of Com'rs	5	All		4	4
Alabama—(general)	Bd. of Com'rs	3	(*a*)		3	3
California	Bd. of Trustees	5	(*k*)	(*h*)	4	4
Idaho	Council	5	(*l*)		2	4
Montana	Council	5 (3)	(*m*)		2	2
New Jersey	Bd. of Com'rs	5 (3)	All		4	4
Utah	Bd. of Com'rs	5 (3)	(*n*)	(*g*)	4 (*g*)	4
Washington	City Com'n	3	(*a*)		3	3
Wyoming	Council	3	All		4	4

(*a*) Each year one commissioner is elected for a term of three years.
(*b*) Each year one commissioner (of five) is elected for a term of five years.
(*c*) Directors of board of education.
(*d*) Mayor or one commissioner elected every two years.
(*e*) Board of education continues to be elected or appointed as before.
(*f*) In Minnesota, each city frames its own commission charter.
(*g*) No provision in general act.
(*h*) At time of adoption of commission form, city may provide for other elective officers.

(*For other references, see page 155.*)

156

THE SMALL BOARD

From this table it is seen that nearly half of the commission cities elect all of their commissioners at one time.

Among those which do not, there is a variety of provisions. The mayor and one other commissioner alternate with the third commissioner in Marshall and Denison (Tex.), the term being two years, and the election of either a commissioner, or the mayor and a commissioner, occurring every year; while in Baker (Ore.), the same alternative scheme applies every second year, the term of office being four years.

A mayor and two commissioners (or aldermen) alternate at elections with the two other commissioners, in Haverhill, Lynn, and Pontiac (Mich.) (two-year terms, annual elections); and in Colorado Springs, Grand Junction, Modesto (Cal.), Oakland, Tacoma, and Spokane (four-year terms, and elections every two years).[1] The law of South Carolina provides for a similar alternation (four-year terms). In the Kentucky act, the mayor and two commissioners are to be elected, the former for a term of four years, the latter for two years, and two years later a police judge is to be elected for a four-year term, and the other two commissioners for two years. Another variation of the three-two alternating plan is found in the charters of Muskogee, Berkeley (Cal.), San Luis Obispo, Monterey, and Santa Cruz, where the election of a mayor, with a two-year term, and two commissioners with four-year terms, is followed two years later by the election of the mayor, again for two years, and of the other two commissioners for four-year terms.

[1] Elective officers other than the mayor and the other commissioners are given in the preceding table.

San Diego has a similar arrangement, but, having five commissioners besides a mayor, the alternation every two years is that of mayor and two commissioners with mayor and three commissioners. In Lewiston a mayor and three commissioners are elected one year; the other three commissioners the next year.

In Bluefield (W. Va.), Ardmore, and Sapulpa (Okla.), where there are four commissioners including the mayor, they alternate two and two, the term being four years, and the time between elections, two years.

One commissioner (of three) is elected each year for a three-year term in McAlester, Bartlesville, and Duncan (Okla.); and in the Kansas cities of the second class, under the recent general act of the state of Washington and under two acts in Alabama; while one commissioner is elected each year for a five-year term in North Dakota and South Dakota. In these states thirty cities are using this method of electing one commissioner each year for three or five years. In Wisconsin, under the act as amended in 1911, the mayor or a commissioner is elected every two years for a six-year term, which is also true of the charter of Guthrie (Okla.).

The states which passed commission acts in 1911 also exhibit a wide variation in the matter of partial renewal of the commission.

It is thus evident that all at once, or part at one election and part the next, or one of the commissioners elected every year for a term of as many years as there are commissioners, are the three broad methods of election in use in the commission cities; and that sixty cities or more are employing the first, and over thirty, the last, of these methods.

THE SMALL BOARD

Length of Term

The length of term of the commissioners is closely connected with the subject just preceding. From the table on pp. 151–156, a considerable difference is manifest in the term of office of the members of the board. In the early charters, particularly those of the Texas cities, including Galveston, Houston, and Dallas, and in the general laws of Iowa, and of the Kansas act applying to cities of the first class, the term was two years; but the more recent charters and acts, including California and Washington cities, and the laws of Louisiana, South Carolina, and Illinois, provide for a term of four years. The provision in South Dakota and North Dakota is for a five-year term, both for mayor and for the other commissioners.

In general it may be said that the length of term of the mayor is the same as that of the other commissioners, the only exceptions being in the charters of Ardmore, Muskogee, Berkeley, San Diego, San Luis Obispo, Santa Cruz, and Monterey, and in the laws of Kentucky and Idaho. Thirty charters provide for a two-year term for mayor; twenty-three charters, a two-year term for the other commissioners. Harbor Beach and Gloucester elect all the commissioners every year. Six cities—Huntington and Parkersburg (W. Va.), Bartlesville, McAlester, and Duncan (Okla.), and Pontiac (Mich.)—have three-year terms for all members of their board; while twelve charters, in the case of mayor, and nineteen in the case of the other members, grant a term of four years. The average term of the mayor in

COMMISSION GOVERNMENT

the fifty-one cities tabulated[1] on pp. 151-155 is a little more than two and a half years; that of the other commissioners, not quite three years (2.8+).

Of the general acts, five, those of Iowa, Kansas (first-class cities), Texas, Idaho, and Montana have a term of two years for mayor; four, of three years; nine, of four years; two, five years, and one — Wisconsin — six years. The mayor's average term under the state laws is slightly over three years.

The average term of the other commissioners (or councilmen or aldermen) under the general acts is 3.3+. Five states have a term of two years, four of three years, nine of four years, two of five years, and one — Wisconsin — of six years.

The average length of term of all the commissioners, including the mayor, in all the commission cities, regardless of whether under special or general act, is somewhat over three years.

Reasonably Long Terms Desirable

It is manifestly to the interest of the city to keep its officials long enough in office for them to acquire familiarity with their duties and knowledge of the best means of discharging them. There can scarcely be any doubt that the term of two years is too short a period for this purpose; in fact, the most conspicuous group of short-term cities, those of Texas, have reëlected their commissioners repeatedly, thus lengthening their terms in practice. Four of the commissioners of Galveston

[1] Out of a total of 60 commission cities under special charters, August 15, 1911.

THE SMALL BOARD

have held office for ten years;[1] two of Houston's small council, continuously since 1905; and other cities present similar instances, though of not so long duration. As frequent elections cease to be necessary as a "check" on officials, in the presence of other and more effective means of control, it may be possible to elect men for terms of four or even six years in most of our cities; and if officials show capacity, they may be reëlected several times.

[1] Reëlected in 1911 for a sixth term of two years.

CHAPTER XV

ELECTION AT LARGE: A REDEFINITION OF REPRESENTATION

A SECOND characteristic of all the forms of commission government in cities is the abolition of wards as election units. All the electors of the city vote for each commissioner, not merely those from a specified section. This is called voting "at large." Every commission charter, and similarly every state act, has this provision, either specifically stated or enforced in actual practice. This is true of the recent charters of Oakland and Spokane as well as those of the Texas cities, which were among the first to adopt the plan. "By the qualified voters of the whole city," is the provision in Huntington; the commissioners "may be residents of any part of the city," says the Haverhill charter; "all members of said commission shall be elected from the municipality at large, without regard to ward lines," runs the Mississippi law. This feature, in connection with the small board, is responsible for the inclusion of certain municipalities in some lists of commission cities. Boise, Idaho, for example, provides for a mayor and four councilmen "elected on a general ticket"; and a similar provision appears in the charters of other cities which have otherwise few elements of the commission form. Election at large, however, is a fundamental element common to all the types of commission government.

ELECTION AT LARGE

The elective principle is retained, but is simply applied to a larger unit. Some misapprehension appears still to exist on this point, the term "commission" suggesting to many the idea of an appointed body. It is true that the first commission of Galveston was partly appointed, three members of the five being named by the governor of Texas; but in 1903 the commission was changed to one entirely elective. The board is elective in all the commission charters since adopted, with the exception of Chelsea, Mass., which presents unusual features.[1] It is, therefore, proper to emphasize the presence of this basic principle of democracy in this new form of municipal government. The voters elect the commissioners (or councilmen), the only change in the election being that *all* the voters vote for *all* the commissioners.

Whether the city as a whole, or the ward, is the proper voting unit, depends upon which is the real unit of activity — for governmental as well as for commercial affairs. To this question there can scarcely fail to be but one answer. A merchant who resides in one ward, does business in the down-town district, and has barns or storerooms or warehouses in a third, clearly has an interest in the city as a whole. He votes for an alderman in his residence ward, but in all three wards is taxed; and in all three he needs fire and police protection, light and water service, sewer connections, and good pavements. While there are, in some cities, certain large natural divisions, such as the boroughs of Manhattan or Brooklyn, in Greater New York, the ward is purely an artificial unit, except in a few instances, and usually represents unduly small divisions of the municipality.

[1] See p. 282, "Unusual and Partial Forms of Commission Government."

COMMISSION GOVERNMENT

Ward elections, as at present conducted, mean really two things: first, election *from* the ward, that is, the candidate or candidates must reside in the ward from which they are elected; and second, election *by* the ward, that is, by the voters of the ward. It is conceivable that candidates might be nominated *from* the wards, but elected *by* the voters of the entire city; or that candidates nominated from any part of the city might be voted for by the voters of a ward. Under the aldermanic plan, the candidate must not only be a resident of the ward, but may be voted for only by the voters of that ward. This double provision, for such it is, has two effects: first, to limit aldermanic office to residents of the ward, no matter if there are more capable candidates outside; and, second, to render it unnecessary for the candidate to be known by the entire city. There can scarcely be a question that this system overemphasizes the ward,— the parts of the city,— rather than the whole.

The commission plan provides usually for both nomination and election at large of the candidate.[1] He may be a resident of any section of the city; and he is chosen by the entire body of voters. As a result, it is possible to elect men better known and of broader outlook and larger capacity, no matter in what ward they reside. The alderman represents and cares for the interests of his ward, — those who elected and may reëlect him; the commissioner represents and must care for all the wards — all the voters who elected and may reëlect him. He is, therefore, free to act in behalf of the entire city.

---

[1] Exceptions are High Point, N.C., and Muskogee, Okla., where election is at large, but candidates must be chosen from a certain district or ward. See table and notes, pp. 251–252.

ELECTION AT LARGE

This has been clearly evidenced in Houston, Galveston, Des Moines, and other municipalities. It has been objected that men formerly ward aldermen have been selected as commissioners. This is true, but inspection shows that it is the best of the ward aldermen who are so elected.

Again, under the ward system of representation, the ward receives attention, not in proportion to its needs, but to the ability of its representatives to "trade" and arrange "deals" with fellow members. The pernicious system of logrolling results.

"To secure one more electric light in my ward, it was necessary to agree to vote for one more arc in each of the other seven wards," said a former councilman; "the city installed and paid for eight arc lamps when only one was needed." So with sewer extensions, street paving and grading and water mains. Nearly every city under the aldermanic system offers flagrant examples of this vicious method of "part representation." The commission form changes this to representation of the city as a whole.

The danger of having most or all of the commissioners elected from the same ward or section, and hence careless of the needs of other sections, has not materialized in actual experience. Des Moines, divided by the Des Moines River into East and West sides, elected for its first commission two from one side and three from the other; and there has been no attempt discernible on the part of the West Side councilmen to unduly favor their part of the city. They are accountable to the entire city, and therefore act for the entire city. In Cedar Rapids, similarly divided by the Cedar River, of the first councilmen (commissioners) chosen, only one was from the West Side, but he states that he has had no difficulty in securing adequate provision for the needs of that section. Bohemian-Americans, constituting probably a fourth of the population of Cedar Rapids, had not a member of their nationality on the first board of commissioners, yet persons of Bohemian parentage have been appointed to places in the city government on their merits, and their section of the city has received its share of appropriations for paving, water mains, street lighting, etc. One of the first things done by the new commission in Cedar Rapids was to extend sewerage and water connections to a large Bohemian Catholic church, which had never been able to secure these facilities under the former council. Nor has there been ward favoritism in Houston, Galveston, Huntington, Leavenworth, Wichita, Lewiston, or Dallas, so far as can be learned. The simple fact that every voter in the city is a constituent of each commissioner tends to correct any danger from possible overrepresentation of any one section or element of the community.

Should Commissioners give their Entire Time?

The members of this small board are required, in many cities, to give their entire time to their official duties, though usage on this point varies, and there is a marked difference of opinion. Sentiment in Galveston strongly favors part time, in the belief that very able men can be secured as commissioners, if they are required to devote only a small share of their attention to the city's business. On the other hand, Houston,

ELECTION AT LARGE

Des Moines, and other cities require their council members (commissioners) to devote the entire working day.

The commissioner becomes more experienced and valuable the more time he gives to the work and the longer he is a commissioner. Since an able man cannot afford to leave his business and devote all of his time to city affairs if he is likely to be retired at the end of two or four years, the tendency is strongly in the direction of longer terms. As a result of this, and the advent of the commission plan generally throughout the country, a new and valuable field of governmental service may be established, as in Germany, that may tend to make municipal commissionerships a profession.

Most small cities do not need the services of five, or even three, men for seven or eight hours each day. In such cities, part time is now the rule, and is probably best. The present council system offers an extreme example of service for part time only, night sessions being usual and meetings occurring often only once a month. Much more attention may well be required of the municipal director and still not all the day be occupied in public business.

If, in the larger city, the election of some of the best business men to its governing board becomes increasingly possible, it may well be provided that some members be elected at a low salary to give part time, and others at a high salary to give all their time, that point to be settled at the time of nomination. If the voters prefer that Mr. A, a most capable financier or manufacturer, give part of his time at $3000 a year, rather than have Mr. B, a less capable man, at $6000 a year, give all of his time, let them so indicate on the nominating ballot. If they wish one commissioner to give a part of his time and another, for instance, the mayor, to devote all of his time, the primary or election ballots might so designate, and the salary to be paid. Besides the names of candidates, columns for "time required" and "salary," opposite each name would appear on the ballot, in that case. This plan would not shut out the first-class business man, whose experience would be most helpful to the city, but who cannot afford, for three or five thousand dollars a year, or even for a higher salary, to neglect his own business and devote all of his time to the city's affairs.

The time requirements in commission cities at present are as follows: —

ELECTION AT LARGE

TABLE 4. TIME REQUIRED OF COMMISSIONERS

A. Charters

ENTIRE TIME	PART TIME	NOT SPECIFIED
Houston, (a) Tex.	Galveston, (b) Tex.	Austin, Tex.
Dallas, Tex.	Denison, (c) Tex.	Waco, Tex.
Ft. Worth, Tex.	Marshall, (d) Tex.	Palestine, Tex.
El Paso, (e) Tex.	Corpus Christi, Tex.	Haverhill, Mass.
Greenville, Tex.	Lewiston, (c) (f) Idaho	Gloucester, Mass.
Tulsa, Okla.	High Point, (c) N.C.	Memphis, Tenn.
McAlester, Okla.	Huntington, (f) W.Va.	Enid, Okla.
Purcell, (g) Okla.	Bluefield, (h) W.Va.	Bartlesville, Okla.
Grand Junction, Col.	Ardmore, (i) Okla.	Berkeley, Cal.
Spokane, Wash.	Muskogee, (j) Okla.	San Diego, Cal.
Baker, Ore.	Sapulpa, (k) Okla.	Oakland, Cal.
Pontiac, Mich.	Duncan, (c) Okla.	Modesto, Cal.
	Guthrie, (c) Okla.	
	Col. Springs, (i) Col.	
	Tacoma, (i) Wash.	
	Mankato, (i) Minn.	
	Cumberland, (b) Md.	
	Clarksdale, Miss.	

(a) All the commissioners, including the mayor, give their entire time.

(b) Mayor, 6 hours a day. No provision as to other commissioners.

(c) As much time as necessary, or as public interests may require.

(d) Mayor ("chairman"), entire time; other commissioners, as much time as necessary.

(e) Mayor gives entire time; each of the four aldermen, not less than six hours a day.

(f) No provision in law, but only part time in practice.

(g) Mayor and financial secretary give entire time.

(h) Public office and stated hours.

(i) "Ample time."

(j) Such time "as may be required for the efficient discharge of such duties."

(k) Such time as "may be necessary for the full and complete discharge of said office." In Colorado Springs, the mayor gives, in practice, all of his time, and the other four commissioners, most of their time.

TABLE 4 — *Continued*

B. *General Acts*

Entire Time	Part Time	Not Specified
Kansas — Cities of first class (*a*)	Illinois (*b*)	Kansas — Cities of second class
Iowa (*c*)	South Dakota (*d*)	Mississippi (*e*)
New Mexico (*f*)	North Dakota (*d*)	Kentucky (*g*)
Wisconsin (*j*)		Louisiana (*h*)
		South Carolina (*g*)
		Texas (*i*)

(*a*) "In cities having from 30,000 to 60,000 population the mayor shall devote at least 6 hours per day"; and in cities of over 60,000 population, "the mayor and other commissioners shall devote *all* their time to the duties of their office and the affairs of the city."

(*b*) "Such time to the duties of their respective offices as a faithful discharge thereof may require"; in cities of 20,000 population and over, the mayor and commissioners shall devote at least 6 hours a day. — Sec. 30.

(*c*) No provision in law; but in most cities of Iowa, councilmen (commissioners) are reported to give practically their entire time.

(*d*) No provision in law; but in most cities of South and North Dakota, the councilmen (commissioners) give only part time.

(*e*) The time required of each commissioner must be specified in the petition requesting the adoption of the commission form.

(*f*) Shall not be otherwise employed.

(*g*) Regular office hours.

(*h*) Office at city hall.

(*i*) Regular meeting once a month for one day; applies to cities of 10,000 population or less.

(*j*) In cities of 10,000 population or more. See Laws of 1911, chapter 287.

Salaries

The salaries paid to the commissioners are much higher than those of former councilmen and usually greater than that of the former mayor. This is but reasonable when all of their time, or a considerable portion of it, is required. Frequent meetings and constant supervision of municipal affairs are necessary, even in many of the smaller cities which do not require the entire attention of their commissioners. The salaries paid are as follows: —

TABLE 5. SALARIES OF COMMISSIONERS (a)

A. Charters

CITY	POPULATION, 1910	MAYOR-COMMISSIONER (PER ANNUM)	OTHER COMMISSIONERS (PER ANNUM)
Texas —			
Galveston	36,981	$ 2000	$ 1200
Houston	78,800	4000	2400
Dallas	92,104	4000	3000
Fort Worth	73,312	3600	3000
El Paso	39,279	3000	1800
Denison	13,632	1800	1500
Greenville	8,850	1200	1200
Austin	29,860	2500	2000
Waco	26,425	2400	1000
Palestine	10,482	750	500
Corpus Christi	8,222	1800	500
Marshall	11,452	1800 (b)	300 (c)
Idaho —			
Lewiston	6,043	300	200 (d)(e)

(a) Or councilmen, or aldermen.   (b) Known as "chairman."
(c) City secretary receives $ 1500 annually.
(d) "Not to exceed" this amount.
(e) Three dollars per meeting actually attended, but not over $ 200 per year. Salaries of mayor and other commissioners are subject to increase by vote of electors.

COMMISSION GOVERNMENT

TABLE 5 — *Continued*

A. *Charters*

City	Population, 1910	Mayor-Commissioner (per Annum)	Other Commissioners (per Annum)
Massachusetts —			
Haverhill	44,115	2500	1800
Gloucester	24,398	1200 (*f*)	1000 (*f*)
Lynn	89,336	3500	3000
Tennessee —			
Memphis	131,105	6000	3000
Chattanooga	44,604	3000	2250
North Carolina —			$2 per meeting (*g*)
High Point	9,525	500	
Wilmington	25,748	800–1900 (*h*)	800–1900 (*h*)
West Virginia —			
Huntington	31,161	2100 (*i*)	1800 (*i*)
Bluefield	11,188	1500 (*j*)	1500 (*j*)
Parkersburg	17,842	3000	2000
Oklahoma —			
Ardmore	8,618	1500 (*k*)	600 (*k*)
Enid	13,799	1500 (*l*)	1500 (*l*)
Tulsa	18,182	1500	1200
McAlester	12,954	2500	2500 (*m*)

(*f*) Limit is $1800 for mayor and $1500 for councilmen.

(*g*) Not over two meetings per month.

(*h*) Within these limits, council fixes salary of its members.

(*i*) Limit is $2500, subject to veto of citizens' board.

(*j*) Limit is $2000, after city has population of 30,000.

(*k*) For first year's services, salary of mayor is to be $1800, and each other commissioner $900.

(*l*) When city attains population of 20,000, salary shall be $2000; 25,000 population, $2500; 30,000 population, $3000; and 40,000 population, $3500. Thereafter, no increase.

(*m*) Members of board of inspection (three), whose duty is to have city accounts examined, receive salary of $50 per year.

ELECTION AT LARGE

TABLE 5 — *Continued*

A. Charters

City	Population, 1910	Mayor-Commissioner (per Annum)	Other Commissioners (per Annum)
Oklahoma —			
Muskogee	25,278	3000	2500
Bartlesville	6,181	2000 (*n*)	2000 (*n*)
Sapulpa	8,283	2000 (*o*)	1800 (*o*)
Duncan	2,477	600 (*p*)	480 (*p*)
Guthrie	11,654	1800 (*q*)	1500 (*q*)
Colorado —			
Colorado Springs	29,078	3600 (*r*)	2000
Grand Junction	7,754	1500 (*s*)	1200 (*s*)
California —			
Berkeley	40,434	2400	1800
San Diego	39,578	2000	2000
Oakland	150,174	4200	3600
Modesto	4,034	none (*t*)	none (*t*)
San Luis Obispo	5,157	600	500
Santa Cruz	11,146	1200	900
Vallejo	11,340	2400	1800
Monterey	4,923	250 (*u*)	200 (*u*)

(*n*) Increase of salary may be submitted to voters by means of the initiative.

(*o*) Salaries range from $2000 for mayor, while population is less than 25,000, to $5000 when city has 100,000 population; and for commissioners, similarly, from $1800 to $3000.

(*p*) Until city has 4000 population; thereafter, $900 for mayor and $720 for other commissioners.

(*q*) Provision is made for higher salaries after population of city is 20,000.

(*r*) Half will be charged to department of water and waterworks, the head of which is the mayor.

(*s*) Two commissioners — the mayor-commissioner and the commissioner of water and sewers — receive $125 a month; the three other commissioners, $100 a month. — Sec. 35.

(*t*) No compensation unless the electors (by ordinance proposed under the initiative) otherwise provide. — Sec. 16.

(*u*) Unless the voters by initiative ordinance shall otherwise provide.

COMMISSION GOVERNMENT

TABLE 5 — *Continued*

A. *Charters*

City	Population, 1910	Mayor-Commissioner (per Annum)	Other Commissioners (per Annum)
Washington —			
Tacoma	82,972	4000	3600 (*v*)
Spokane	104,402	5000	5000
Oregon —			
Baker	6,742	2500	2000
Minnesota —			
Mankato	10,365	900	600
Mississippi —			
Hattiesburg	11,733	2000	1800
Clarksdale	4,079	600 (*w*)	600 (*w*)
Maryland —			
Cumberland	21,839	1500	1200
Michigan —			
Port Huron	18,863	2000	1200
Pontiac	14,532	2000	2000
Harbor Beach	1,556	(*x*)	(*x*)
Wyandotte	8,287	250	250

(*v*) Salary of controller, who is also elected, is $ 2400.
(*w*) Not to exceed $ 50 per month. — Charter, Sec. 2.
(*x*) No salary paid.

TABLE 5 — *Continued*

B. *General Acts*

STATE	POPULATION	MAYOR-COMMISSIONER (PER ANNUM)	OTHER COMMISSIONERS (a) (PER ANNUM)
Iowa — Cities of	7,000–10,000	$600	$450
	10,000–15,000	1200	900
	15,000–25,000	1500	1200
	25,000–40,000	2500	1800
	40,000–60,000	3000	2500
	60,000 and over	3500	3000
Kansas — Cities of first class (b)	15,000–20,000	1800	1000
	20,000–30,000	2000	600
	30,000–40,000	2000	1500
	40,000–60,000	2500	1800
	60,000 and over	4000	3000
Kansas — Cities of second class	2,000–5,000	300	250
	5,000–7,000	700	500
	7,000–10,000	1000	900
	10,000–15,000	1200	1000
South Dakota	under 2,000	25	25
	2,000–10,000	(c)	(c)
	10,000 and over	1200	600
North Dakota		(d)	(d)

(*a*) Or councilmen.

(*b*) "Not to exceed" these amounts.

(*c*) Twenty-five dollars per annum in cities of 2000 or under, and $50 per annum additional for each additional one thousand, or major portion thereof, of population, in cities having over 2000 population. Amendments passed in 1911 raised salary limit to $2000 for mayor and $1500 for commissioners, provided electors so vote. See laws of 1911, chapter 97, § 4.

(*d*) No salaries are fixed in the laws of North Dakota, Mississippi, or Minnesota. North Dakota provides for "such compensation as may be provided by law."

COMMISSION GOVERNMENT

Table 5 — *Continued*

B. General Acts

State	Population	Mayor-Commissioner (per Annum)	Other Commissioners (per Annum)
Wisconsin (e)	under 2,500	500	400
	2,500– 3,500	600	500
	3,500– 5,000	1000	750
	5,000– 7,500	1200	1000
	7,500–10,000	1500	1200
	10,000–15,000	2500	2000
	15,000–20,000	3000	2500
	20,000–30,000	3500	3000
	30,000–40,000	4000	3500
	40,000 and over	5000	4500
Illinois (g)	under 2,000	50	40
	2,000– 5,000	250	100
	5,000– 10,000	600	400
	10,000– 15,000	1200	900
	15,000– 20,000	2000	1700
	20,000– 30,000	2500	2000
	30,000– 40,000	3500	3000
	40,000– 60,000	4000	3500
	60,000– 80,000	4500	4000
	80,000–100,000	5000	4500
	100,000–200,000	6000	5500
New Mexico		1800	1400
Minnesota		(f)	(f)
Mississippi		(f)	(f)

(e) As amended in 1911.

(f) No salaries are fixed in the laws of North Dakota, Mississippi, or Minnesota. North Dakota provides for "such compensation as may be provided by law."

(g) "Not to exceed" these amounts.

TABLE 5 — *Continued*

B. *General Acts*

STATE	POPULATION	MAYOR-COMMISSIONER (PER ANNUM)	OTHER COMMISSIONERS (PER ANNUM)
Kentucky	second class	3600	3000
Louisiana (g)	7,500–10,000	1500	1000
	10,000–15,000	2000	1500
	15,000–25,000	2500	2000
	25,000–40,000	3000	2000
	40,000–60,000	3500	2400
	60,000 and over	4000	2500
South Carolina	20,000–50,000 (h)	2500	2000
Texas (i)	under 10,000 (h)	$5 a day (j)	$5 a day (j)
Alabama — Cities of	100,000 or over	7000	7000
Alabama — Cities of	25–50,000	4500	3000
Alabama — general (k)	7,500–15,000	1500	1500
	15,000–50,000	$100 for each 1000 population	
	over 50,000	1000 for each 10,000 population	
California	Cities of 5th and 6th classes	(l)	(l)

(g) "Not to exceed" these amounts.
(h) State laws for commission government applies to cities of this size.
(i) General act.
(j) For each regular meeting, one day in each month.
(k) Applies to cities other than those covered by the preceding acts.
(l) No compensation, except while acting as board of equalization.

COMMISSION GOVERNMENT

TABLE 5 — *Continued*

B. General Acts

STATE	POPULATION	MAYOR-COMMISSIONER (PER ANNUM)	OTHER COMMISSIONERS (PER ANNUM)
Idaho	3,000– 7,000	300	150
	7,000–10,000	600	450
	10,000–15,000	1200	900
	15,000–25,000	1800	1200
	25,000–40,000	3000	2000
Montana	Cities of 3d class, less than 3000	600	500
	— Over 3000	1000	900
	Cities of 2d class	1650	1500
	Cities of 1st class, less than 30,000	3000	2500
	— 30,000–50,000	4000	3000
	— 50,000 or more	4500	3500
New Jersey (*m*)	less than 500	75	50
	500– 1,000	250	200
	1,000– 2,500	500	350
	2,500– 5,000	750	500
	5,000– 10,000	1000	750
	10,000– 20,000	1500	1200
	20,000– 40,000	1800	1500
	40,000– 90,000	2500	2000
	90,000–200,000	3500	3000
	over 200,000	5500	5000

(*m*) Separate graduated scale, somewhat higher, for cities of fourth class.

TABLE 5 — *Continued*

B. *General Acts*

STATE	POPULATION	MAYOR-COMMISSIONER (PER ANNUM)	OTHER COMMISSIONERS (PER ANNUM)
Utah	Cities of 2d class, less than 20,000	500–1500	600–2000
	— Over 20,000	4200	3600
	Cities of 1st class	4200	3600
Washington	2,500– 5,000	500	250
	5,000– 8,000	1200	1000
	8,000–14,000	2000	1800
	14,000–20,000	2500	2000
Wyoming	(*n*)	2400	2000

(*n*) Applies to cities under special charter, and of over 10,000 population; to cities of first class; and to cities and towns of not less than 7000 population.

Qualifications of Commissioners

The qualifications for commissioners range from the provisions of the Texas cities, requiring each member of the governing board to be (1) a citizen of the United States, (2) a qualified voter, (3) a resident of the city for a certain number of years, (4) in some cases twenty-five years of age, (5) a property owner, (6) not in arrears for taxes, and (7) in one instance, not a stockholder or director of any public service corporation having a city contract or franchise, to that of Grand Junction, Col., where the only provision in the charter is that the commissioner shall be a qualified elector. In the limited space here available, it is not practicable to discuss the subject in detail, nor is it of great relative importance.

COMMISSION GOVERNMENT

Restrictions

The holding of more than one office, or of any office the compensation of which has been increased during the commissioner's term, is usually prohibited. The most definite and drastic restriction, and one found in the majority of commission charters, prohibits a commissioner or councilman from having any financial interest in city contracts. The receiving of free transportation, tickets, or any gifts of substantial value from public service or other corporations, is often prohibited, also; and, lastly, the giving of a bond is frequently required. But none of the foregoing qualifications are essential, or peculiar to the commission charters as distinguished from other forms of charters.

CHAPTER XVI

CONCENTRATION OF MUNICIPAL AUTHORITY

INTO the hands of this small board elected at large is gathered the municipal authority formerly scattered among mayor, council, and the various independent administrative boards and departments. There has been no increase in the powers of the city, but a concentration of these powers in the hands of one small group.

At the same time, the form of municipal organization is changed, so that each member of the group is head of a department, and definitely related to all of the smaller units of the department. With the increased authority of the remodeled council (commission) and the changed governmental organization have been coupled many "checks" intended to make effective the will of the people, among others the referendum and the recall. These third, fourth, and fifth elements, as they have been numbered here for convenience, — the centering of power in a single small group, the assignment of one member as head of each department, and the checks provided to assure popular control — are so basic in their nature, that though they do not at first seem of unusual moment, they prove upon examination to include the first and second features, already presented, and to contain the essence of two broad principles, both contained in the term "responsible authority. This implies at once power and accountability — the capacity to accomplish and the possibility of a penalty for a failure to accomplish. Election at large is really a kind of "check" beforehand, — a method of insuring the choice of men who will represent the city as a whole, rather than a multiplicity of parts. Provision for a small board is another prior restriction, in order that voters may choose a few officials intelligently rather than select a larger number without thought. These are methods of enforcing responsibility by determining in advance the conditions of choosing public servants. The prior checks having been already considered, it will be in order in a later chapter to discuss those methods of control which are enforceable *after* election. First, however, should be presented the positive side of government, — the powers bestowed upon the body which is to pass laws and administer them in behalf of the people. How authority is exercised in cities under the mayor-and-council plan, and how under the newer commission system, may well be contrasted. Here may possibly be found some explanation of the success of the latter.

In the United States, the state legislature confers upon cities by charter the right to exercise certain specified functions. These "powers," or, more correctly, fields of activity, include the right to levy taxes, borrow money, issue bonds, establish markets, hospitals, libraries, and schools, lay out and pave streets, enact building regulations, grant franchises, and, in many cases, acquire and operate waterworks and other public utilities. At some time in the future, the state may recognize more clearly a proper general municipal field, and it may not be necessary to specify in such detail

CONCENTRATION OF AUTHORITY

what cities may do, nor to go to the legislature for every new small grant of municipal power. Home rule for cities, however, is not the theme of this discourse, nor does the field of activity of the city under the ordinary council differ from that under the commission. In this respect, it is well to sharply distinguish these "powers" of the city — that is, the fields in which it may act — from the "powers" of the governing body — that is, the authority which it may exercise within the fields of activity permitted to the city. The legislative power of the council means its right to make laws (ordinances) on those subjects which the state allows the city to control. Administrative power means the right to enforce or carry out those laws or regulations, and the laws passed by the legislature. The commission-council exercises not only the usual ordinance-making power, but also appoints the officers and oversees the administrative departments of the city. It *decides* (by ordinance) what shall be done, appoints the men to do it (the subordinate officials and employees), and sees that it is *done*. The board exercises close administrative control over all the departments by being itself the administrative head of the government, although it subdivides the work among its members, in order the more effectively to do its work.

The powers of the commission may be considered first in general, and then under the heads of ordinance power, appointing power (considered broadly), and administrative authority, remembering always that this discussion does not deal with what power the city has, or should have, but how much of the power of the city is exercised by the commission, and in what manner.

COMMISSION GOVERNMENT

General Powers

Under most charters the board is given either the general powers formerly exercised by mayor and council and by all the executive departments, or only the powers of mayor and council are so transferred. In the latter case, it is provided that each commissioner shall also be head of a department, thus in effect accomplishing the same concentration of legislative and administrative authority.

The "Board of Commissioners," runs the Galveston charter, "shall constitute the municipal government of the city,"[1] shall be held to be the successors of the mayor and alderman, and "shall have and exercise all the rights, powers and duties of the mayor and board of aldermen of cities, as may be conferred by the constitution and laws of this state, and shall have and exercise all the rights, powers and duties conferred . . . by the terms of this act."[2] Houston, while retaining the old name of "City Council" provides that "the administration of the business affairs of the city of Houston shall be conducted by a mayor and four aldermen, who together shall be known and designated as the City Council,"[3] who are given "full power and authority, except as herein otherwise provided, to exercise all powers conferred upon the city. . . . "[4]

Under the Iowa law, the council (of five) possesses "all executive, legislative and judicial powers and duties now had, possessed and exercised by the mayor, city council, solicitor, assessor, treasurer, auditor, city en-

[1] Charter, Sec. 5.
[2] Charter, Sec. 6.
[3] Charter, Art. V, Sec. 1.
[4] Charter, Art. VII, Sec. 1.

CONCENTRATION OF AUTHORITY

gineer, and other executive and administrative officers, in cities of the first and second class, and in cities under special charter," and also all the powers of the "board of public works, park commissioners, board of police and fire commissioners, board of waterworks trustees, and board of library trustees," in all cities where these boards now exist or may be hereafter created.[1] "The board of commissioners," runs the Kansas law for cities of the first class, "shall constitute the municipal government of such city and shall be the successors of the mayor and council"; and "said board of commissioners shall have and exercise all such rights, powers, and duties as are conferred upon it by this act, and such other powers, rights and duties as are now, or shall be hereafter conferred by the laws of the state of Kansas upon the mayors and councils of the cities of the first class, not in conflict with the provisions of this act."[2] The South Carolina law grants to the board all legislative, executive, and judicial powers and duties conferred upon the city.

Though differing in wording, other charters and state laws similarly confer broad powers upon the small governing board. It should be noted that not only the authority exercised by the former mayor and council is conferred by the Galveston and other charters upon the board of commissioners, but additional powers, as set forth in the charter or general act. This additional authority lies not so much in the field of making and passing ordinances, which is the usual legislative function of council-and-mayor, and which has been retained

[1] Act as amended in 1909, Sec. 1056–a 25. Corresponds to Sec. VII of law of 1907. [2] Art. IV, Sec. 23.

under the commission form, as in the appointment of city officers, and in close *administrative* control.

Appointing Power

Under the commission form, subordinate officers formerly elected are appointed usually by the commission-council, which possesses also a broad power of control after appointment. The term "appointing power" as here used, includes the right (1) to appoint and remove all, or practically all, of the subordinate officers and employees of the city; (2) to create new offices and discontinue them; and, (3) to fix salaries (except of the commissioners, to prescribe their duties, and to transfer officers, or change their duties.

The Board of Commissioners of Galveston is given authority to appoint, by majority vote of all the members, all officers and subordinates in all departments of the city and to remove any officer or employee, with or without cause.[1] The police and fire commissioner is allowed to recommend or nominate persons for appointment in the police and fire departments, while the Board as a whole has the power of final selection. The Iowa law ("Des Moines plan") provides that "the council shall at its first meeting or as soon as practicable thereafter, elect by majority vote the following officers: a city clerk, solicitor, assessor, treasurer, auditor, civil engineer, city physician, marshall, chief of fire department, market master, street commissioner, three library trustees, and such other officers and assistants as shall be provided for by ordinance and necessary to the proper

[1] Charter, Secs. 19, 21, 29.

CONCENTRATION OF AUTHORITY

and efficient conduct of the affairs of the city. . . . Any officer or assistant elected or appointed by the council may be removed from office at any time by vote of a majority of the members of the council, except as otherwise provided in this act."[1] Similar broad powers of appointment and removal are given to the council-commission under the Kansas law (both for first- and second-class cities), the laws of Wisconsin, North Dakota, South Carolina, and Mississippi; and the charters of Lewiston, Bluefield, Haverhill, and Gloucester, Berkeley, San Diego, and other cities.

Nomination by the mayor, subject to confirmation by the rest of the board, is the rule in Houston, Dallas, Waco, and Palestine (Tex.), cities of the "strong-mayor type." In Memphis, each commissioner nominates the subordinates in his department, the board electing them; a substantially similar provision exists in the charter of Grand Junction, Col. In Colorado Springs each commissioner recommends the officers in his department, while the mayor appoints; day laborers and unskilled workmen in each department are employed and discharged by the commissioner in charge of that department. In Tacoma, each chief of a department appoints and removes in his own department, except that the mayor's appointments in his own department are subject to confirmation by the council as a whole. Removal in Houston and Denison is by the *mayor or* by the council, which places the mayor in a position of great power, since he can remove without the action of the council. In Palestine (Tex.), the head of a department may remove with the consent of the mayor. The

[1] Act as amended in 1909, Sec. 1050–a 26.

power to temporarily suspend any subordinate in his department is given at Galveston to the chief of the police and fire department; while in Fort Worth the police and fire commissioner has the right to employ policemen and firemen and to discharge them at his discretion, provided only his action does not conflict with the regulations of the Board of Commissioners.[1]

The power to create new offices, to appoint their incumbents, and to discontinue or abolish such offices at will, are provisions which add greatly to the efficiency of a city government. They are found in nearly all the commission plans, as are also provisions granting power to the Board to fix the salaries, prescribe and alter the duties, and assign further duties. These enable the Board to shift officers and subordinates into more suitable places and to transfer duties when necessary, thus insuring a large degree of elasticity.

Administrative Control

Close administrative oversight by the ordinance-making body is provided by giving such power specifically, in many instances, to the commission *as a whole*, and by making each commissioner head of a department which he directs individually. The ordinance-making body directs, either collectively or as individuals, — frequently in both capacities, — the carrying out of the provisions of the ordinances.

The Board of Commissioners, under the Galveston, Fort Worth, and other Texas charters is "vested with the power and charged with the duty of making all laws

[1] Galveston charter, Sec. 17; Fort Worth charter, Chap. III, Sec. 1.

CONCENTRATION OF AUTHORITY

and ordinances," and is also given control and supervision over all the departments of said city, "and to that end shall have power to make and enforce such rules and regulations as they may see fit and proper for . . . the organization, management and operation of all the departments of said city, and whatever agencies may be created for the administration of its affairs."[1] The city council of Denison, Tex., composed of a mayor and two aldermen, is required to "see that prompt and efficient service is performed and discharged in every department."[2]

"Said commissioners," provides the Dallas charter, "shall perform all of the executive duties of the respective departments to which they may be assigned, as above provided, but said board, *as a whole*, shall have supervision of, and be responsible for, the administration of each of said departments."[3] Substantially the same provision occurs in the charter of Austin, Tex.[4]

The state laws under which Iowa cities and Kansas cities of the first class operate, grant, as already noted, executive and judicial, as well as legislative, powers to the council. The Wisconsin law provides: "A city so reorganized shall be governed by its council, consisting of the mayor and councilmen . . . and such council shall have all the powers and perform the duties had and exercised by the mayor and council and the general administrative and executive officers, boards and commissions of such city, whether its former organization existed under general or special law."[5]

---

[1] Galveston charter, Sec. 12.　　[2] Charter, Art. VII, Sec. 1.
[3] Charter, Art. III, Sec. 8.　　[4] Charter, Art. II, Sec. 5.
[5] Session laws of Wisconsin, 1909, Chap. 448, Sec. 925 m–308.

COMMISSION GOVERNMENT

The term "administrative power" as applied should be qualified as of a broadly directive and managerial character, since the details of execution, and even some of the immediate directing and inspection, is done by officials subordinate to the commissioners — fire and police chiefs, waterworks superintendent, city engineer, foremen of street-cleaning gangs, etc. It is true that administrative control of a kind is provided under the usual mayor-and-aldermen type of city government; but it is of a loose and indefinite character, and whatever intelligent correlation of council and departments exists, is secured by unofficial conferences, not provided for nor recognized by the law. Under the commission form the need for a close relation of council and departments is frankly acknowledged, and effective means provided to that end by giving the new small-council specific authority over the administrative activities of the city, and by making each councilman actually head of a department.

Financial Powers

In connection with its other duties, the commission is given authority to levy taxes, to vote appropriations, and, in general, a broad control of the finances of the municipality. In making up the annual budget of expenditures, each commissioner is required to submit, usually to the mayor, thirty or sixty days before the time of making up the budget, estimates of the amounts which will be needed during the ensuing year to properly run his department, and the revenues which his department can probably be counted on to yield. The

CONCENTRATION OF AUTHORITY

mayor submits all the estimates so made to the board as a whole, which determines the amount to be expended, the tax rate, and the appropriation for each department. Extravagant expenditure is prevented by the provision, in many charters, that the total amount appropriated in the budget shall not exceed the estimated income. Many charters provide that after the appropriations are once fixed they cannot be increased, unless the income estimated has been exceeded by the actual receipts. Sometimes, as in Memphis, the board is allowed to spend more in one department than at first estimated if the amount be taken from other departments, the total expenditure not exceeding that at first agreed upon.

In Colorado Springs, Lewiston, Boise (not a commission city, though sometimes so classed), and elsewhere, the mayor may veto separate items in appropriation measures. Careful auditing of the accounts of the department is provided for in many charters, some requiring an annual examination of the city's accounts, and authorizing the mayor to appoint experts to make such examination.

The board of commissioners frequently sits as a board to equalize the assessment of taxes; and sometimes acts as a civil service commission, as in Huntington and Bluefield.

Summary of Powers

The powers of the commission, therefore, are much greater than those of the usual city council, including, as they do, close administrative oversight, as well as legislative authority, the appointment of subordinate

COMMISSION GOVERNMENT

executive officers, and the exercise of such financial and incidental powers as are necessary. Yet such concentration of control has proved most successful in the field of business, where similar problems of organization have to be met, and efficient collective action taken in behalf of a large group of interested members of the corporation.

Consider the method of governing the American railroad or manufacturing company. A body of stockholders elects annually a board of directors. This board of directors frequently includes many, if not all, of the executive officers of the company, — the president, vice president, secretary, general manager, treasurer, — besides some members who are not engaged in the active work of superintending the operations of the company. The board of directors elects the officers, decides who shall be president, who shall keep the funds, and who shall be the active manager. The board determines the policy to be followed during the ensuing year, — what new tracks shall be built, what new rolling stock must be purchased, whether rates shall be increased or lowered; if a manufacturing company, what methods shall be employed in reducing the cost of production, marketing products, and meeting competition. As the year advances, the board looks sharply after the outcome of plans; it sees that a certain amount of work is done by a given time; it insists upon securing results as outlined. Each of the executive members of the board takes charge of a certain field of work. The board, collectively and through its individual members, is exercising administrative control; it has determined the policy of the company, that is, acted in a legislative

CONCENTRATION OF AUTHORITY

capacity; and has selected its chiefs of divisions by virtue of its appointive power. The strong, virile, successful business corporation *combines* the "powers" which it has been so carefully attempted to keep apart in our logical theories of government. The commission plan has drawn straight from American business experience its essential elements of success, discarding, so far as city government is concerned, the theory of strict separation of powers, since the main functions of cities are similar to those of business corporations.

Suppose the functions of the city to be taken over by a Consolidated Insurance, Protective, and General Utilities Company. In order to prevent robbery and maintain order, the company establishes an organized body of watchmen and patrolmen, who guard the citizen's life and property, by day and by night. To supply fire protection, it installs a waterworks system, establishes engine houses, and supplies equipment. To safeguard health it enforces quarantine regulations and maintains a hospital; it provides a sewerage system; it collects garbage and burns it. For purposes of business service and easy intercourse it furnishes paved streets, sidewalks, and bridges. It supplies additional means of public convenience. For the services rendered, this General Utilities Company charges each citizen an annual sum based on the total cost of the service, plus a profit. It is to the interest of the company to keep running expense low by wise management and to secure as large a revenue as practicable. This is accomplished by having some one definitely accountable for each part of the work of reducing costs or increasing income. The board of directors, responsible to the stockholders, holds the

COMMISSION GOVERNMENT

officers and division chiefs answerable for results; these, in turn, pass on the requirements to superintendents, foremen, bosses, who have under them clerks, stenographers, messengers, mechanics, pipemen, electricians, and day laborers. Each is bound to do the share of the work specifically assigned to him, and if he does not, another fills his place. Responsibility for the whole, and for each part, is definitely fixed; and power goes with responsibility.

Turn now to the city. The municipal government is the general protective corporation, guarding the lives, property, and health of the citizens and providing necessary facilities. In the past this has been poorly done because under the old régime the voting stockholders in the municipal corporation have not been able to hold their managing board (the council) clearly responsible; nor has the council had adequate control over municipal officials and employees. The difficulty has been, first, that each member of this committee of representatives is chosen by a certain local group of stockholders (voters), and hence is answerable to a different constituency. The council, therefore, tends to be anything but a unit. Moreover, being too large for efficient work, and therefore compelled to act through loosely organized committees and subcommittees, it frequently falls under the control of a small coterie of members, who are responsible only to the local boss. In addition, when the people have elected their representatives, they have no effective means of recalling them, under the usual city charter, until the next election, two or four years later; nor can the voters express their opinion on the measures passed by their representatives unless a referendum is provided.

CONCENTRATION OF AUTHORITY

Then, in addition to the gap between voters and council, there has been lack of correlation between council and executive departments. The heads of these departments are frequently elected by the voters, not appointed by the council, and not removable by the council, in which case they are largely independent of its authority. The council may, with some justification, lay the burden of bad municipal conditions at the door of the departments, disclaiming responsibility for the acts of those over whom it has no adequate control. We are now discovering that it is only a feeble sort of administrative oversight which the council exercises, and that the actual enforcement of ordinances lies often with the departments, between the heads of which and the council there has been provided by law no close connection.

The absence of a strong guiding hand above is felt in the departments; the doubt as to whether department or council is responsible for failures makes employees less careful and diligent. There does not seem, however, to be the marked break in the chain of responsibility within the departments that there is between voters and council, or between council and departments.

The fact that the mayor, the head of the executive department, has a veto on the acts of the council, tends to further confuse the voter in his search for a responsible head of the government. The mayor may blame the council for bad conditions, the council accuse the departments, and the department heads assert that mayor and council are at fault; while the bewildered citizen does not know whom to charge with existing evils.

The commission form closes the gap between council and departments by making each member of the commis-

COMMISSION GOVERNMENT

sion-council chief of a department, and in charge of its activities; it connects voters and council, by giving the former the right to approve or reverse policies of the latter (by the referendum), to insist on new plans of action (by the initiative), and, if necessary, to replace councilmen (by the recall). The council is made smaller (a commission), and the members, elected by all the voters and responsible to the same broad constituency, are more likely to act with the others for the interests of the entire city. The powers of the council are enlarged to include not only the right to determine policies, but also to see that these policies are carried out by officials and subordinates which it has chosen. Adequate power is coupled with easily enforced responsibility.

CHAPTER XVII

EACH COMMISSIONER IN CHARGE OF A DEPARTMENT

CLOSELY connected with the concentration of large power in the hands of the commission as a whole, and its exercise of a broad administrative oversight as already considered, is the assignment of each commissioner to be head of a definite department, for the conduct of which he is responsible to the commission, and to some extent directly to the people. The two features seem to go together — collective responsibility on the part of the board for the efficient general administration of city affairs, and individual responsibility of the separate members as heads of administrative divisions. "The three commissioners," provides the charter of Clarksdale, Miss., "shall in their collective capacity be vested with all the powers and charged with all the duties conferred . . . but *each commissioner shall supervise and control* . . . the departments . . . assigned to him." "The work of the municipality shall be divided into departments with one of the commissioners at the head of each department," is the simple wording of the Mississippi general act.[1] The charter of Fort Worth, after the same general provisions as those of Galveston, adds the words, "it being the purpose of this act to charge each commissioner in control of a department with its management, and to fix directly upon him the responsibility for its proper conduct."[2]

[1] Laws of Miss., 1908, Chapter 100, Sec. 11.
[2] Charter, Chapter 2, Sec. 16.

COMMISSION GOVERNMENT

Division into Departments

The departments into which the city's business is divided — usually five in number, though sometimes four or three as already noted — are similar in many of the charters. General municipal oversight, finances, police and fire, and streets, — the first usually in the hands of the chairman of the board, who retains the title of mayor, — are well-marked divisions, to each of which a commissioner is assigned in most of the commission cities. The fifth department varies in name and in the field of its duties, these being naturally of a residual nature, — those activities not comprised under any of the other four, — frequently including waterworks and sewerage, and sometimes parks.

Galveston has a mayor-president, and commissioners of finance and revenue; police and fire; streets and public property; waterworks and sewerage. The charters of Dallas and Fort Worth and the laws of North Dakota and South Dakota have the same divisions. Houston divides its municipal administration into finance and revenue; police and fire; streets, bridges, and public grounds; and water, light, and health; besides the mayor, who has general oversight.[1] The Iowa law places the mayor in charge of public affairs, while the other departments are accounts and finance, public safety; streets and public improvements; parks and public property. The recent charter of Tacoma, well drawn on the whole, places the mayor in charge of public affairs, health, and sanitation; and provides, also, for the departments of finance; public safety; public works,

[1] The divisions have been changed somewhat (1911), the mayor exercising certain duties formerly assigned to other commissioners.

COMMISSIONERS OF DEPARTMENTS

streets, improvements, and property; and light and water. The Kentucky law, passed in 1910, and applying as yet only to cities of the second class, provides for departments of public affairs (in charge of the mayor); public finance; public safety; public works; and public property.

San Diego, Cal., separates the police from the fire department, allotting its five commissioners — not including the mayor — to finance, ways and means; police, health, and morals; public streets and buildings; fire and sewers; and water. The new charter of Oakland, Cal.,[1] gives the mayor, besides general oversight, the supervision of public utility companies, assigning to him the department of public affairs; while the other departments are revenue and finance; public health and safety; public works; and streets.

Where there are only three commissioners, duties are consolidated. In the Kansas law for cities of the second class, the mayor is given charge of police, fire, and health, and the other two members have finance and revenue, and streets and public utilities, respectively. High Point, N.C., with a commission of nine, has, besides the mayor, commissioners of finance and revenue; police and fire; streets and cemeteries; waterworks and sewerage; public buildings and property; lights and lighting; a purchasing commissioner; and an auditing commissioner. The commission charter proposed for Sacramento provides for a department of education. A recent tendency seems to be manifest in some quarters to put health and police control in charge of the same commissioner, an experiment worth trying.

[1] Adopted in December, 1910, and approved by the legislature in 1911.

COMMISSION GOVERNMENT

Assignment of Commissioners

The authority which designates what department each commissioner is to head varies but little under different charters. Usually the commission, as a body, assigns to its several members their respective fields of activity, except that of the mayor, who is elected to his specific place. In Galveston, the Board of Commissioners determines by majority vote what division of the work each of its members shall take, except the mayor, the four other commissioners having been elected with no designation of department. Each voter in Galveston knows, as a matter of fact, what position each candidate will almost certainly occupy, though not specified by law. This is true of the Iowa law; of the Kansas law for both first and second class cities; of the charters of Memphis, Colorado Springs, Tacoma, and many other cities. But all of the commissioners of Greenville (Tex.), Lynn (Mass.), and five other cities, are elected by the voters to head particular departments. In Houston, Fort Worth, and High Point, N.C., the mayor, as chief commissioner, decides what department each commissioner shall take, which is also the case in South Carolina; and in San Diego, Colorado Springs, Tacoma, Modesto, and Oakland, the mayor makes the assignments if the council cannot agree. Under the Huntington and Bluefield charters, the candidate receiving the highest vote becomes mayor, and assigns the departments, including his own. The board has power to reassign the departments in Wisconsin, South Carolina (although in the latter case the Mayor assigns), in Memphis, Tacoma, and elsewhere.

The following table summarizes the designating authority in the various cities and states:—

COMMISSIONERS OF DEPARTMENTS

TABLE 6. WHO ASSIGNS DEPARTMENTS OF COMMISSIONERS

A. Charters

MAYOR-COMMISSIONER ELECTED TO SPECIFIC PLACE	OTHER COMMISSIONERS ELECTED TO SPECIFIC DEPARTMENTS	OTHER COMMISSIONERS ASSIGNED BY THE COMMISSION	OTHER COMMISSIONERS ASSIGNED BY THE MAYOR
Galveston, Tex. Houston, " Dallas, " Fort Worth, " El Paso, " Denison, " Greenville, " Austin, " Waco, " Palestine, " Corpus Christi Marshall, (a) " Lewiston, Ida. Haverhill, Mass. Gloucester, " Lynn, " Memphis, Tenn. Chattanooga, " High Point, N.C. Wilmington, (b) N.C. Huntington, (c) W.Va. Bluefield, (c) W. Va. Parkersburg, "	Greenville, Tex. Lynn, Mass. Bartlesville, Okla. Duncan, (d) Okla. Grand Jct., Col. Baker, Ore. Guthrie, Okla.	Galveston, Tex. Dallas, " Denison, " Austin, " Waco, (e) " Palestine, " Corpus Christi, Tex. Marshall, (e) " Lewiston, Ida. Haverhill, Mass. Gloucester, " Memphis, Tenn. Chattanooga, " Wilmington, N.C. Parkersburg, W. Va. Ardmore, Okla. Enid, " Tulsa, " McAlester, " Muskogee, " Sapulpa, "	Houston, (f) Tex. Fort Worth, " El Paso, Tex. High Point, N.C. Huntington, W. Va. Bluefield, "

(a) Known as "chairman of the commission."

(b) Candidate receiving highest number of votes becomes mayor.

(c) Person receiving highest vote is mayor, and designates what department he and the other commissioners are to head.

(d) Mayor or one commissioner elected each year; only one official to vote for, at each election, not counting board of education.

(e) No statement in charter as to designating authority.

(f) Confirmed by the council.

COMMISSION GOVERNMENT

TABLE 6 — *Continued*
A. Charters

Mayor-Commissioner Elected to Specific Place	Other Commissioners Elected to Specific Departments	Other Commissioners Assigned by the Commission	Other Commissioners Assigned by the Mayor
Ardmore, Okla. Enid, " Tulsa, " McAlester, " Muskogee, " Bartlesville, (*g*) Okla. Sapulpa, " Duncan, " Guthrie, " Colorado Springs, Col. Grand Junction Berkeley, Cal. San Diego, " Oakland, " Modesto, " San Luis Obispo " Vallejo, " Monterey, " Tacoma, Wash. Spokane, (*h*) " Baker, Ore. Mankato, Minn. Cumberland, Md. Port Huron, Mich. Pontiac, " Harbor Beach, Mich. Wyandotte, "		Col. Springs, (*i*)(*j*) Col. Berkeley, Cal. San Diego, (*i*)(*j*) Cal. Oakland, (*i*)(*j*) Cal. Modesto, (*i*)(*j*) Cal. San Luis Obispo, (*i*)(*j*) Cal. Vallejo, (*i*)(*j*) Cal. Monterey, (*i*)(*j*) Cal. Tacoma, (*i*)(*j*) Wash. Spokane, (*i*) Wash. Mankato, (*i*) Minn. Cumberland, Md. Port Huron, Mich. Pontiac, Mich. Harbor Beach, Mich. Wyandotte, Mich.	

(*g*) Commissioner of public affairs is ex-officio mayor.

(*h*) One of the commissioners is elected president by the council, and thereby becomes mayor.

(*i*) Assignment of departments, except that of the mayor, may be changed by council.

(*j*) If council is unable to agree upon designation, mayor designates.

COMMISSIONERS OF DEPARTMENTS

TABLE 6 — *Continued*
B. *General Acts*

MAYOR-COM-MISSIONER ELECTED TO SPECIFIC PLACE	OTHER COMMISSIONERS ELECTED TO SPECIFIC DEPARTMENTS	OTHER COMMISSIONERS ASSIGNED BY THE COMMISSION	OTHER COMMISSIONERS ASSIGNED BY THE MAYOR
Iowa	Louisiana	Iowa	South Carolina
Kansas — cities of first class		Kansas — cities of first class	
Kansas — cities of second class		Kansas — cities of second class	
South Dakota		South Dakota	
North Dakota		North Dakota	
Wisconsin		Wisconsin	
Minnesota (*a*)		(*d*)(*e*)	
Illinois		Minnesota (*a*)	
New Mexico (*b*)		Illinois	
Mississippi		New Mexico (*b*)	
Kentucky		Mississippi (*f*)	
Louisiana		Kentucky	
South Carolina		Texas (*g*)	
Texas			
Alabama—cities of 100,000 or over (*c*)		Alabama—cities of 100,000 or over	
Alabama—cities of 25–50,000		Alabama—cities of 25–50,000	
Montana		Montana	
New Jersey		New Jersey	
Wyoming		Utah (*h*)	
		Wyoming	

(*a*) General law permits cities to frame charter, including these provisions. See laws of 1909, Chap. 170, Secs. 1–3.   (*b*) Inferred; not specifically stated.

(*c*) First commissioners consisted of the existing mayor, who became president of board of commissioners, and two other commissioners, appointed by the governor; but hereafter all are to be elected.

(*d*) Council "*may* designate one of its members as head" of each department created.   (*e*) Council may reassign departments.

(*f*) Charter of Clarksdale, Miss., framed under the state law, provides for election of mayor, and assignment (inferred but not stated) of departments by the commission.   (*g*) No statement as to designating authority.

(*h*) All five members of board of commissioners are assigned by the commission.

203

COMMISSION GOVERNMENT

Duties of Departments

The activities included under each of these departments may be inferred in a general way from the titles. The detailed distribution of offices and duties is not always set forth in each particular law or charter, while in Des Moines, Cedar Rapids, and other municipalities of Iowa, their enumeration is left to the commission-council, to be made by ordinance.

The subchiefs who look after the details of the administrative work are, in the department of water, lighting, and sewerage, for example, a superintendent of waterworks, a superintendent of lighting, and inspectors of electricity and of plumbing. The commissioner of streets and public improvements has foremen in charge of paving, street cleaning, sidewalk construction, grading — differing in number and duties with the size of the city and the amount of work to be done. Under the commissioner of finance are usually the assessor and collector of taxes, the treasurer, and the auditor, with their necessary assistants and clerks. The commissioners have thus only the larger aspects of the city's work to deal with, each being the manager of a division, and together constituting a managing board. The duties of the subordinate officers mentioned are those which usually pertain to such offices.

The Mayor

The position of mayor, under the commission form, is considerably different from that under the aldermanic system. The title used in Galveston is mayor-president; in Marshall, Tex., chairman of the board; in North

COMMISSIONERS OF DEPARTMENTS

Dakota, president of the board. In Grand Junction one of the commissioners is designated commissioner of public affairs, and is *ex-officio* mayor. Elsewhere, the name mayor has generally been retained without change. He is generally voted for separately on the municipal ballot,[1] but in nearly all cases is a member of the commission, and presides at its meetings, usually with the right to vote on all questions. He signs ordinances, contracts, and warrants on the treasury, and performs other ministerial acts. He also has certain emergency powers, such as the right to summon special policemen in times of riot or epidemic. He may call special meetings of the commission or council, and frequently presents the budget to that body. The mayor is still "the chief executive officer" of the city, in which capacity he is made the head of a department of public affairs, as in Des Moines, having oversight of municipal matters as a whole. In this department is frequently placed the corporation counsel (city attorney), the city clerk or city secretary, and sometimes one or more additional officers. In Colorado Springs, the mayor is commissioner of water and water works; in Memphis, of public affairs and health; in Tacoma, public affairs, health, and sanitation.

The mayor, under most commission plans, is one of the council, voting, but having lost the veto power so usual under the aldermanic form. In the so-called "strong-mayor type" of commission government, he has, however, both vote and veto, as in Houston, Dallas, Denison, Greenville, and Corpus Christi, Tex.; and in

[1] The recently enacted law of New Jersey (April 25, 1911) provides, however, that the commissioners shall choose one of their members to preside, and he shall be designated "Mayor."

Lewiston, Ida. In these cities he occupies the unusual position of being able to veto an ordinance passed by the board, and then, as a member of the board, to vote not to overrule his own veto. As it generally requires a two thirds or a four fifths vote to override a veto, the mayor and one commissioner can control. In High Point, N.C., the mayor has only a veto. In San Diego, he is not a member of the board of five, but possesses the veto power. In Colorado Springs he votes and also has the right to disapprove appropriation items. In several cities he has a vote only in case of a tie on the board. Usually, however, the veto power has been transferred to the voters as a whole, by means of the referendum. In Huntington, W. Va., as already explained, a Citizens' Board of sixty-four members is given the right of veto on ordinances. A smaller but similar board exists in Bluefield.

Broadly considered, the mayor, under the commission form of government, has been merged in the commission-council. As one of the governing board, he has equal voting power; but by virtue of his title, his emergency authority, and his general oversight of public affairs, his position is somewhat more influential than that of the other commissioners; his salary is often slightly higher than that paid to the other commissioners.[1] He acts as an integral part of the ordinance-making body, and the other members share his former administrative control. It should be pointed out, however, that the relation of the mayor to the other commissioners may vary from that of nearly equal authority, as in the majority of commission cities, to that of almost complete

[1] See table of salaries, pp. 171 ff.

domination by the mayor, as in Houston. The relation also of each commissioner, including the mayor, to the commission as a body, may vary from the board where each member is practically supreme in his own department, both in appointments and in the dictation of policy, to that in which the members take a large interest in one another's departments, the commission as a whole refusing to assent to plans or to confirm appointments, unless approved by a majority of all the commissioners. The problem is the same as that which confronts the business house, — how to insure a broad and general unity of action by the group without impairing the individual initiative of each officer; and no uniform rule as to what these relations should be will apply to all cases.

Unity and Simplicity of Organization

The simple form of city government under the commission plan is one reason for the success attained in many cities. This involves the close and direct connection of each part of the governmental machinery with every other part, that is, unity of organization, as well as fewer parts. In both respects the aldermanic form is unsatisfactory; it is neither a unit in action nor easily understood. A striking example of the faults of the usual city government—not worse, however, than that of many other cities—is shown by the chart on p. 208 of the governmental organization of Buffalo, N.Y.

From the chart it will be observed that the voters elect by wards a Board of Aldermen of twenty-five members which organize with the usual committees, and elect at large a Board of Councilmen, of nine members. The two bodies together constitute the Common Coun-

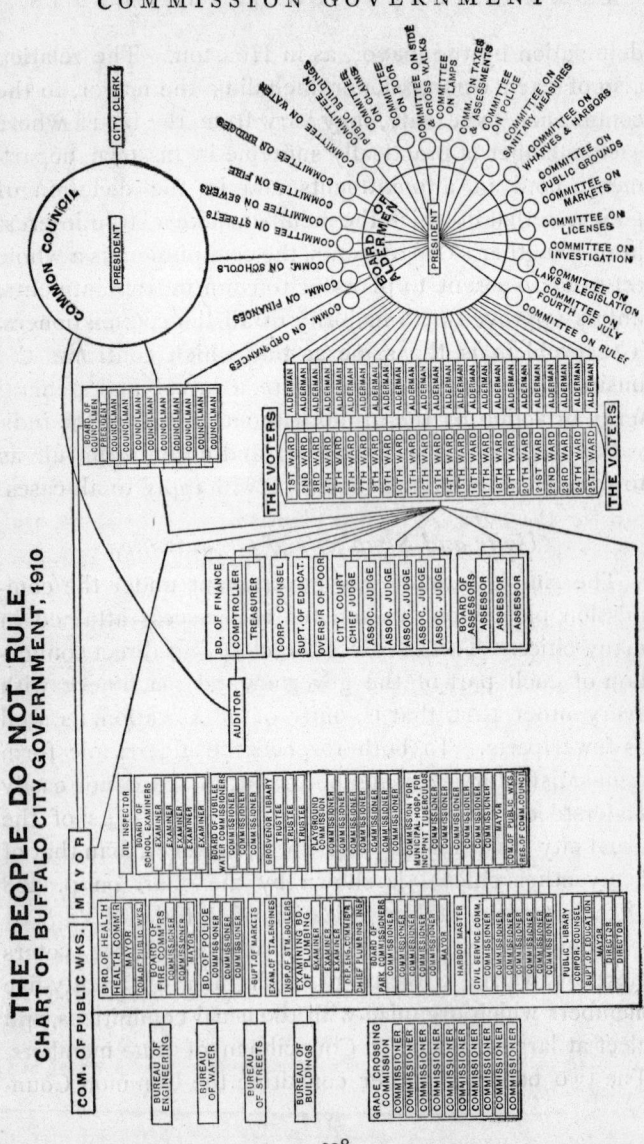

COMMISSION GOVERNMENT

THE PEOPLE DO NOT RULE
CHART OF BUFFALO CITY GOVERNMENT, 1910

208

COMMISSIONERS OF DEPARTMENTS

cil. At the same time, the voters choose a mayor, a treasurer, controller, corporation counsel, superintendent of education, overseer of the poor, a board of assessors, and a city court of six judges. They also elect a commissioner of public works, over whom the council has no direct control and who is an official of large powers. The commissioner of public works appoints the chiefs of the four bureaus under him, — engineering, water, streets, and buildings. The mayor appoints a board of health, a harbor master, an oil inspector, and a long list of other officers. The Board of Aldermen and the Board of Councilmen act together as one body (the Common Council) for the passage of ordinances, which must also be approved by the mayor, and for the budget; for the election of a city clerk, and a president of the council; and to ratify the appointment of the auditor by the controller.[1]

Not only is this complex system confusing to the voter, but action under it is slow and difficult. To secure such simple repairs as a new hinge on a fire station door requires a long process. The chief of the fire station first makes requisition upon the chief of the fire department; the latter forwards the requisition to the board of fire commissioners. These recommend the new hinge and forward the requisition to the Board of Aldermen. The Board of Aldermen act, the requisition is printed in their minutes, and is forwarded to the Board of Councilmen. The Board of Councilmen approve the

[1] The charts on pp. 208 and 211 are based on those of the Commission Government Association of Buffalo, and are believed to be substantially correct, although certain special boards, such as the sea wall commission, have been omitted from this discussion, since relatively unimportant, and tending to confuse the reader.

requisition for the new hinge, and it is printed in their minutes and forwarded to the mayor. The mayor approves, and the requisition is sent to the commissioner of public works. The latter forwards it to the superintendent of buildings; the superintendent hands it over to an assistant, who instructs a foreman to purchase the hinge and send men to put it on. And this is the process for a simple matter of repairs. Here are checks and balances enough, and of the most intricate sort!

A glance at the chart for the same city under the commission form (p. 211) shows how simple is the municipal organization proposed. It is not only easily understood by the voters, who have only five men to elect, besides a city court in Buffalo, but it is also prompt in action. The requisition for a new hinge, sent by the head of the fire station to the chief of the fire department, is referred to the councilman in charge of the department of public safety. The latter recommends the repairs, the council of five approve the recommendation, and the matter is settled. The head of the department of parks and public buildings sends an order to his superintendent of buildings to have the hinge put on. Hundreds of such business details are easily disposed of. Ease and promptness in action depend not only on the small number of men who constitute the council but also upon simplicity of organization.

How the "Boss" is Eliminated

The concentration of power in the hands of the small board, and the definite relating of the board and each member to the work of administration, not only directly increases municipal efficiency, but it also destroys the

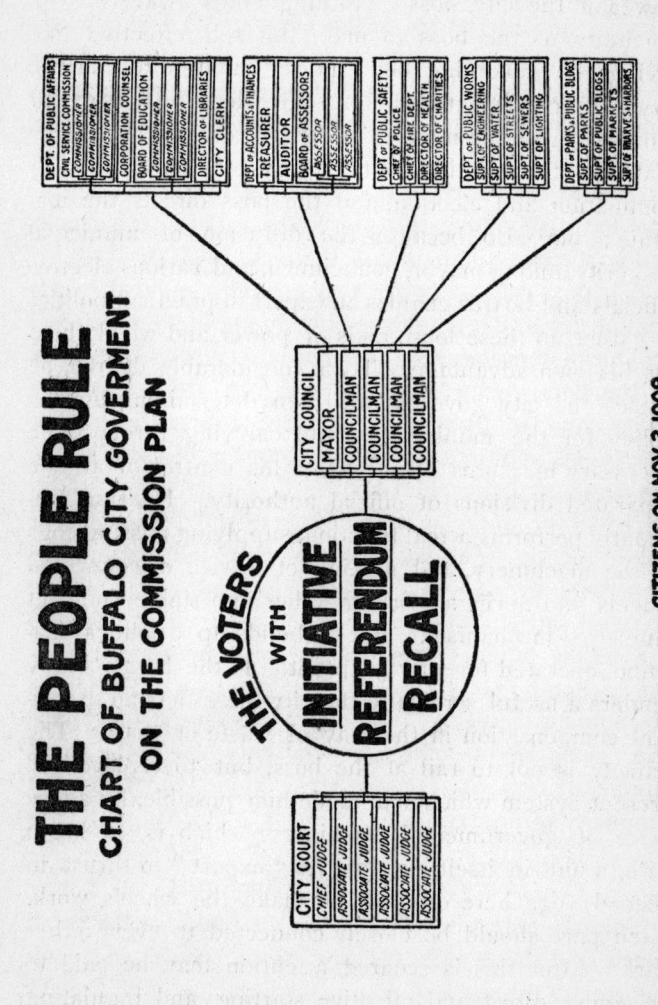

COMMISSIONERS OF DEPARTMENTS

THE PEOPLE RULE
CHART OF BUFFALO CITY GOVERNMENT ON THE COMMISSION PLAN

THE VOTERS WITH INITIATIVE REFERENDUM RECALL

CITY COURT
- CHIEF JUDGE
- ASSOCIATE JUDGE
- ASSOCIATE JUDGE
- ASSOCIATE JUDGE
- ASSOCIATE JUDGE

CITY COUNCIL
- MAYOR
- COUNCILMAN
- COUNCILMAN
- COUNCILMAN
- COUNCILMAN

DEPT. OF PUBLIC AFFAIRS
- CIVIL SERVICE COMMISSION
  - COMMISSIONER
  - COMMISSIONER
  - COMMISSIONER
- BOARD OF EDUCATION
  - COMMISSIONER
  - COMMISSIONER
  - COMMISSIONER
- DIRECTOR OF LIBRARIES
- CITY CLERK

DEPT. OF ACCOUNTS & FINANCES
- TREASURER
- AUDITOR
- BOARD OF ASSESSORS
  - ASSESSOR
  - ASSESSOR

DEPT. OF PUBLIC SAFETY
- CHIEF OF POLICE
- CHIEF OF FIRE DEPT.
- DIRECTOR OF HEALTH
- DIRECTOR OF CHARITIES

DEPT. OF PUBLIC WORKS
- SUPT. OF ENGINEERING
- SUPT. OF WATER
- SUPT. OF STREETS
- SUPT. OF SEWERS
- SUPT. OF LIGHTING

DEPT. OF PARKS & PUBLIC BLDGS.
- SUPT. OF PARKS
- SUPT. OF PUBLIC BLDGS.
- SUPT. OF MARKETS
- SUPT. OF WHARVES & HARBORS

CITIZENS ON NOV. 2, 1909
VOTED THAT THE CITY OF BUFFALO ASK THE STATE LEGISLATURE TO ENACT A CHARTER FOR BUFFALO ON THE COMMISSION PLAN

power of the city boss. Nothing takes away the opportunity of the boss to make himself effective like giving the governing body power enough to run the city's affairs without his help. Why does the boss exist? Partly because the number of elective officers is so large that a political machine is necessary to look after their nomination and election, and the boss directs the machine; but also because the diffusion of municipal authority among mayor, councilmen, and various elective officials and boards enables an expert in practical politics to gather up these loose ends of power and wield them for his own advantage. To a considerable degree, he unifies the city government, often determining upon a policy for the municipality and carrying through the necessary measures by means of his control of all the separated divisions of official authority. He thus frequently performs a real function, supplying missing cogs in the machinery, and making otherwise disconnected wheels and springs work together in a single compact municipal mechanism. But he builds up a political machine, operated for private profit. If the boss actually renders a useful service to the city, he exacts an exorbitant compensation in the way of waste or graft. The remedy is not to rail at the boss, but to replace the present system which has made him possible, by a new piece of governmental machinery, which is, to begin with, a unit in itself, needing no " expert " to thrust in needed cogs here or there to make the wheels work. Each part should be closely connected to every other part. After this is secured, attention may be paid to providing direct and effective starting and regulating levers, so that control may be easy and sure. Under

COMMISSIONERS OF DEPARTMENTS

the commission form, these controlling levers of the city's governmental apparatus are the referendum, the recall, the initiative, and similar improved appliances which are being included in so many of the recently constructed municipal charters. If the referendum is a brake, the initiative is a starting lever, and the recall a device to throw a defective belt off the pulley or a wheel out of gear, in order to replace it with another. This brings us to the consideration of these devices.

CHAPTER XVIII

"CHECKS": PUBLICITY

THE principle underlying the means provided in the aldermanic system for holding officials responsible for the exercise of their authority differs greatly from that under the commission plan. In the former, one chamber of the council is supposed to check the other, the mayor to check both; and the danger of too frequent or too prompt action is prevented by giving only a limited amount of power to each. It did not occur to those who devised this method that the time might come when government would *need to* act promptly, vigorously, and often. What they wished to prevent was easy governmental action. With the development of modern conditions, under which the municipality finds itself a vast business corporation, with the duty of supplying highways, pavements, water, lights, health, fire and police protection, parks, libraries, and other conveniences, the necessity for ease in accomplishing such results is greatly increased. The old "checks and balances," as applied to cities, have broken down, not even proving adequate to prevent misuse of power. As a positive theory of government has taken the place of the old negative idea, the necessity for new "checks" has become evident — checks which, while supplying powerful correctives whenever needed, will permit a larger freedom of action on the part of the representatives of the people. "Make the machinery hard to run and it will do little harm when we go away and leave it," theorized some of the early dabblers in the mechanics of government. "Make the machinery easy to run and also easy to control, but never expect it to run without attention," reason the modern municipal inventors who have rediscovered and applied old and fundamental political principles. Instead of depending upon one set of officials to check another set, the ultimate means of control have been placed in the hands of the people — that is, of the voters. "The healthful kernel of this new movement," says Professor L. S. Rowe, "is that it rests on an abiding faith in the efficacy of public control. It places responsibility for good government exactly where it belongs, namely, on the people themselves."[1]

In addition to the very general means of control already discussed, such as the election *at large* of a *small* governing body, and the organization of that body in such a way as to make the administration a unit, the more specific means provided in the commission laws and charters include (*a*) publicity of proceedings, of ordinances, particularly of franchises, and of all facts relating to municipal conditions; (*b*) the referendum; (*c*) the initiative; (*d*) the recall; (*e*) non-partisan primary and election methods; (*f*) a civil service commission; and (*g*) other provisions. These will be considered in the above order.

Publicity

The publicity features of the commission plan embrace (1) provisos that all meetings of the board shall be open to the public, and that the minutes shall consti-

[1] "Problems of City Government," p. 190.

COMMISSION GOVERNMENT

tute a public record; (2) regulations as to passing of ordinances; (3) publication of ordinances and proceedings; and (4) the frequent issue of financial and other statements. The following charter provisions illustrate: —

(1) In Galveston, where publicity is almost the only legal "check," "all *legislative* sessions of said board, whether regular or called, shall be open to the public." In Fort Worth, "all *official* sessions are open to the public." These seem to permit unofficial conference, sometimes necessary in matters which demand action before being made generally known. In Dallas, El Paso, and Palestine, "all sessions of said board, whether regular or called, shall be open to the public." In Houston, the commission shall "sit with open doors," which wording is followed in the charters of Greenville, Denison, and Corpus Christi. Marshall adds "except by unanimous vote" of the commissioners; and Colorado Springs "at all legislative sessions."[1] The Iowa law provides that all meetings "at which any person not a city officer is admitted, shall be open to the public." In Lewiston "all deliberations and proceedings must be public." The substance of these provisions is but slightly varied in the laws of Kansas, Wisconsin, North Dakota, South Dakota, South Carolina, and Kentucky, and the charters of Memphis, Huntington, Gloucester, Tacoma, and other cities.

That the minutes shall be open to public inspection is provided in the charters, among others, of Houston, Denison, Corpus Christi, Greenville, Huntington, and Bluefield. In Colorado Springs the journal of proceed-

[1] Charter, Sec. 12.

"CHECKS": PUBLICITY

ings "shall be a public record." In High Point, N.C., the journal "shall be public."

(2) Provisions regulating procedure in meetings of the board are found in many instances. Without attempting to treat them exhaustively, it may be noted that the yeas and nays must be recorded on the vote for all ordinances; sometimes on every vote of any sort. Recording the yeas and nays is required when requested by at least one member in Tacoma, and Galveston, for example, and by the law of North Dakota. The roll must be called when the vote is not unanimous, in Huntington and Bluefield. "All votes of the members of the municipal council shall be by yeas and nays, *when that is practicable*, and shall be entered upon the records," says the Haverhill charter. Many of these provisions are recognized at once as present in many charters not of the commission form, and are here given merely to set forth more clearly the actual auxiliary publicity checks in the commission charters. Provisions that each resolution shall be confined to one topic, that no resolution can be passed on the same day as introduced, and that all motions must be made in writing, are found in many instances. In some cases, an affirmative vote of the majority of commissioners *elected* is necessary to pass an ordinance.

Daily administrative sessions are compulsory under the charter of Tacoma. In Houston and other cities the board is "continuously in executive session," which means it may meet at any time, as the public business demands.

(3) Frequent publication of ordinances in local newspapers is usually provided, often within ten days after passage.

(4) Monthly (as in Cedar Rapids and Des Moines) or quarterly statements of finances or proceedings, in pamphlet form for free distribution to newspapers or to citizens, or both, is frequently added, to enable all to know what is being done by the board, and the status of the municipal funds. An annual statement, also, of the financial condition and of the work of the departments for the year is usually required.

These are the provisions intended to insure public knowledge of the work of the municipal board of directors. Each feature is useful to a greater or less degree, particularly the frequent meetings of the governing body, and the published monthly statements. The value of published statements varies greatly, with the frequency of their publication and the care with which they are prepared. Monthly or quarterly reports are shorter and more timely than annual statements, more interesting, and more quickly read. A simply arranged, clearly printed statement is also much more likely to receive attention from the citizen than a complex report, printed in small type, with its information unclassified. The reports should be so prepared as to invite and facilitate inspection. The gentle art of presenting financial and other facts so that the average citizen can grasp the salient points easily and instantly is worthy of attention from municipal officials. A glance through the pages of the annual report of Houston, with its illustrating maps clearly printed though small enough to handle easily, or that of Des Moines, in large type and with comparative tables of expenditures, will demonstrate their superiority over the old type of report.

Sessions of the commission have been already de-

"CHECKS": PUBLICITY

scribed under the separate cities. One needs only to attend a number of these meetings to realize the great change from those of the old city council. With fewer councilmen, election by the entire city, and enough power to meet all requirements, members are characterized by a spirit of directness, energy, and real dignity. Galveston, Houston, and Dallas, Des Moines, Cedar Rapids, and Memphis are essentially similar in this respect. The usual council chamber, with its high desk for the mayor and its circle of large chairs for the aldermen, has been replaced by a plain table with five men around it, the mayor-commissioner presiding at one end, a city map on the wall, papers and working memoranda spread out on the table, and a telephone at hand. This change is an indication of the decrease in officialism and a greatly increased efficiency. The council meeting under the new plan reveals an altered attitude toward municipal government on the part of both the governing body and the citizens generally.

CHAPTER XIX

REFERENDUM AND INITIATIVE

AMONG the most direct and valuable "checks" on municipal legislation are the referendum and the initiative. The referendum, broadly considered, is the power reserved to the voters to approve or reject by vote any act passed by their legislative body, — the right of popular veto, directly expressed. The initiative is the power of the voters to propose ordinances, laws, or amendments, usually upon petition; it is the positive side of the referendum. The referendum may be either compulsory or conditional in its use by the electorate, and advisory or mandatory in its operation upon the legislature. The referendum is compulsory when a law, to be valid, *must* be submitted for popular approval or rejection, and conditional when a law is submitted only upon petition of a specified number or percentage of voters. Under the mandatory referendum and initiative, the direct vote of the people is conclusive in the enactment of legislation. Under the advisory system, the voters instruct their representatives by direct ballot, but the representatives are not *legally* bound to follow the wishes of their constituents so expressed.

Methods of "direct legislation" have been used to a greater or less extent since the beginning of American government; the referendum or initiative are at present

REFERENDUM AND INITIATIVE

provided, in some form, by the constitutions or laws of Oregon, Oklahoma, Texas, South Dakota, Wisconsin, Nevada, Montana, Missouri, and other states. The referendum and the initiative are found in a large majority of commission cities, incorporated in the charters granted, or as a part of the state law permitting the commission form; in some states, as in Oklahoma, the constitution operates to specifically permit the use of these direct legislative methods, without additional state sanction.

In cities, the referendum may apply to all ordinances, in which case it usually includes franchises and bond issues; or it may apply only to franchises, the people not being permitted to reject other ordinances; or it may apply only to bond issues, and not to franchises or general ordinances. In many cases, as in Waco, Lewiston, and Colorado Springs, a referendum on bond issues is compulsory, a great variety of provisions obtaining; in others, it is conditioned upon the proper petition, as in Memphis, Houston, Fort Worth, and elsewhere. In Colorado Springs, all franchises must be submitted to the taxpaying voters. The signatures of only taxpaying voters are allowed in many Texas cities. In Huntington and Bluefield, W. Va., the referendum is not to the voters as a whole, but to a citizens' referendum board.

Passage or rejection by a majority of the voters, of an ordinance referred to them, is binding upon the council, making the franchise or other ordinance valid or invalid. A simple majority usually decides the matter; although occasionally a three fifths or two thirds vote is required to approve. The initiative is optional with the voters, being enforceable only upon presentation of a petition signed by the requisite number, requesting the submission of a certain ordinance. When once approved by the electors, the ordinance usually goes into effect without action by the council.

The value of the referendum and the initiative, as means of expressing the will of the electorate, depends in cities, as in the state, upon ease of application, and this in turn depends to a large degree upon the number of signatures required for the petitions. To secure an initiatory petition signed by over 50 per cent of the voters, for example, is virtually equivalent to an election, provided each voter who signs the petition is in favor of the proposed ordinance. To require the signatures of only one per cent, on the other hand, would be to make it possible to submit questions for public expression of opinion for which there was no demand, and to needlessly burden the voters. Somewhere between 10 and 30 per cent would seem to be a reasonable mean, high enough to indicate a real demand for action and yet not so high as to prevent use. A given number of signatures is required in some cities instead of a percentage of the whole vote. In Houston, franchises must be submitted to the electorate on petition of five hundred voters, and a specific number is similarly provided in Fort Worth, El Paso, Greenville, Waco, Lewiston, and High Point. The disadvantage of this method is that as the population and voters increase, the number of signatures becomes relatively less, requiring frequent amendment to restore the former proportion. As a rule, therefore, a percentage basis is employed, and the following is a summary of the percentages required: —

REFERENDUM AND INITIATIVE

TABLE 7. REFERENDUM: PERCENTAGES REQUIRED FOR PETITION

A. Charters

City	Ordinances	Franchises (a)	Bond Issues (a)
Texas —			
Galveston	—	—	(b)
Houston	—	500 voters (c)	(d) (e)
Dallas	15	500 voters	(f)
Fort Worth	500 voters	(g)	(e)
El Paso	—	400 voters (h) (i)	(f)
Denison	—	Compulsory (h)	(f) (e)
Greenville	—	100 voters (h) (c)	(j) (k)
Austin	25 (l)	Compulsory (e)	—
Waco	20	500 voters	—
Palestine	—	25 (h)	(e)
Corpus Christi	—	25 (c) (h)	(f)
Marshall	25	—	—
Idaho —			
Lewiston	—	300 voters	(m)

(a) Only the most important items are here tabulated, and the notes indicate some of the principal variations. The subject is too complex for complete tabulation in small space, and the table presents only the larger aspects of the provisions on this subject in commission charters. This applies to other tables as well.   (b) State law provides for referendum on bond issues.

(c) All franchises for over 30 years *must* be submitted to voters; and others *may* be so submitted by council.

(d) Compulsory referendum to taxpaying voters for all bond issues of over $100,000 in any one year. — Art. IV, Sec. 1.

(e) Compulsory referendum to taxpaying voters on purchase of public utilities by city.

(f) Referendum on bond issues compulsory, except refunding bond issues, etc.

(g) Referendum provisions as to all ordinances apply specifically to franchise ordinances.   (h) Council may submit any franchise to voters.

(i) Referendum to taxpaying voters.

(j) Referendum compulsory on bond issues of over $2000 in any one year. — Art. IV, Sec. 1.

(k) No public utility belonging to city can be sold except upon vote of 60 per cent of electors, election to be called upon petition of 200 qualified voters.

(l) Within 90 days of next general municipal election only 15 per cent petition required.

(m) Referendum on bond issues compulsory; requires approval of two thirds of votes cast at election. — Sec. 162.

TABLE 7 — *Continued*

A. Charters

City	Ordinances	Franchises	Bond Issues
Massachusetts —			
Haverhill	25	—	—
Gloucester	25	Compulsory (*n*)	—
Lynn	25	—	—
Tennessee —			
Memphis	—	500 voters (*o*)	500 voters
Chattanooga	—	500 voters (*o*)	—
N. Carolina —			
High Point	500 voters	(*p*)	—
Wilmington	35	Compulsory	—
W. Virginia —			
Huntington	(*q*)	(*q*)	(*r*)
Bluefield	(*q*)	(*q*)	—
Parkersburg	20	—	—
Oklahoma —			
Ardmore	25	Compulsory (*s*)(*t*)	—
Enid	(*u*)	Compulsory (*u*)	(*v*) (*w*)

(*n*) Applies to "exclusive" franchise.

(*o*) As provided in Acts of 1905, Chap. 54, Sec. 29.

(*p*) All franchises for over 30 years *must* be submitted to voters; and others *may* be so submitted by council.

(*q*) Right of veto on franchise or ordinance may be exercised by a citizens' board.

(*r*) Compulsory, and requires three-fifths vote of electors to approve.

(*s*) Council may submit any franchise to voters.

(*t*) Petition of 25 per cent demanding the grant, renewal, or extension of a franchise requires special election to be called. — Art. VIII, Sec. 6.

(*u*) State constitution provides for referendum in cities, specifying 25 per cent, and compulsory referendum on franchises.

(*v*) Assent of two fifths of voters necessary for incurring of indebtedness beyond income. — Art. V, Sec. 8.

(*w*) Referendum only on vote to purchase public utilities. — Art. V, Sec. 5.

REFERENDUM AND INITIATIVE

TABLE 7 — *Continued*

A. Charters

City	Ordinances	Franchises	Bond Issues
Oklahoma —			
Tulsa	(x)	Compulsory (x)	—
McAlester	25 (a)	Compulsory (y)(z)	—
Muskogee	25 (b)	Compulsory (x)	—
Bartlesville	(x)	Compulsory (x)	—
Sapulpa	25	Compulsory (x)	—
Duncan	25	Compulsory (x)	—
Guthrie	(x)(c)	Compulsory (x)(c)	(c)
Colorado —			
Colorado Springs	(d) 15 (e)	Compulsory (f)	(d)
Grand Junction	(d) 10 (e)	Compulsory (f)	(d)
California —			
Berkeley	10 (e)	—	(g)
San Diego	7	(h)	(i)
Oakland	10 (e) (j)	Compulsory (k)	—

(x) State constitution provides for referendum in cities, specifying 25 per cent, and compulsory referendum on franchises.
(y) Sale or lease of any public utility requires vote of electors.
(z) Council may submit any franchise to voters.
(a) Charter may be amended on 25 per cent petition and majority vote at election.
(b) Council may also submit any ordinance to popular vote, without petition.
(c) Board of commissioners may authorize mayor to hold referendum election for bond issues, franchises, or other purpose.
(d) Referendum on purchase of public utility by city also provided, on petition. Referendum does not apply to emergency measures.
(e) Council may also submit any ordinance to popular vote, without petition.
(f) Referendum to taxpaying voters.
(g) See Art. IX, Sec. 47 (9) and (8).
(h) Referendum provisions as to all ordinances apply specifically to franchise ordinances. (i) See charter, Chapter II, Sec. 1 (53).
(j) But not less than 2000 signatures.
(k) For apparent conflict of provisions, see Secs. 177, 178.

TABLE 7 — Continued

A. Charters

City	Ordinances	Franchises	Bond Issues
California —			
Modesto	15	Compulsory	—
San Luis Obispo	10	(*l*) (*m*)	—
Santa Cruz	10 (*m*)(*n*)	10 (*n*)	—
Vallejo	10 (*m*)	5	—
Monterey	25	(*l*)	—
Washington —			
Tacoma	15 (*m*)	—	—
Spokane	10 (*m*)	—	—
Oregon —			
Baker	(*o*)	(*o*)	(*o*)
Minnesota —			
Mankato	20 (*m*)	—	—
Maryland —			
Cumberland	(*p*)	—	—
Michigan —			
Port Huron	25	—	—
Pontiac	20	Compulsory	—
Harbor Beach	25	Compulsory	—
Wyandotte	25	Compulsory	—

(*l*) Referendum provisions as to all ordinances apply specifically to franchise ordinances.

(*m*) Council may also submit any ordinance to popular vote, without petition.

(*n*) Applies to ordinances authorizing contracts, granting franchises, and "any penal ordinance adopted by the council." See charter, Sec. 234.

(*o*) State constitution applies, specifying 25 per cent.

(*p*) No provision in charter.

REFERENDUM AND INITIATIVE

TABLE 7 — *Continued*

B. *General Acts*

STATE	ORDINANCES	FRANCHISES	BOND ISSUES
Iowa	25	Compulsory	
Kansas — cities of first class	—	10	—
Kansas — cities of second class	25	Compulsory	—
South Dakota	5	Compulsory	Compulsory
North Dakota	25	—	Compulsory
Wisconsin	20	—	—
Minnesota	(*a*)	(*a*)	(*a*)
Illinois	10	Compulsory	—
New Mexico	—	Compulsory	—
Mississippi	—	Compulsory	—
Kentucky	25 (*b*)	—	—
Louisiana	33	Compulsory	—
South Carolina	20	Compulsory	—
Texas	—	—	(*c*)
Alabama — cities of 100,000 or over	—	1000 voters	—
Alabama — cities of 25,000–50,000	25	1000 voters	—
Alabama (general)	—	(*d*)	—
California (*f*)		25 (*e*)	—
Idaho	—	—	—
Montana	25	Compulsory	—

(*a*) City may provide for referendum in charter.

(*b*) Applies to ordinances ordering construction or reconstruction of any street, contracts involving more than $ 1000, and franchise ordinances. — Secs. 14 and 24. (*c*) State law applies.

(*d*) See also Act, Sec. 8, last sentence.

(*e*) Franchises are to be submitted to vote of electors upon petition: unusual provision: see Act.

(*f*) Separate act, relating to referendum, recall, and initiative in cities. Approved March 14, 1911.

227

TABLE 7 — *Continued*

B. *General Acts*

STATE	ORDINANCES	FRANCHISES	BOND ISSUE
New Jersey	15	—	Compulsory
Utah	—	—	—
Washington	25 (g)	Compulsory	—
Wyoming	35	10	—

(g) Special or general election.

From this table, it is clear that in each of the fifty-one special charters noted, some form of the referendum is provided, even though, as in Galveston, it is of the most limited sort, on bond issues. The same is true of all the general acts, except those of Utah and Idaho. A broad referendum on ordinances is provided in the charters, or according to state constitution or laws may be so provided, in 38 of the 51 cities, and in Huntington and Bluefield, where a citizens' board exercises the people's veto power. The general acts, except those for Kansas cities of the first class, New Mexico, Mississippi, Texas, two Alabama acts, Idaho and Utah, either make provision for such a referendum or permit cities to adopt it. The percentages for this broad referendum range from 35 in Wilmington, N.C., to 7 per cent in San Diego; and in the laws, from 35 per cent in Wyoming to 5 per cent in South Dakota. Fort Worth and High Point, N.C., provide a specific number of signatures — those of 500 voters. The average percentage required for the referendum on ordinances in the 38 charters in which a percentage is specified or fixed by state consti-

REFERENDUM AND INITIATIVE

tution or laws is slightly over 20 per cent; in the state laws, a little more than 22 per cent.

Initiative

Where the use of the initiative compels a special election, the percentage of signatures is usually higher than that for the submission of a measure at the next regular municipal election. The percentages in force in the two groups of cases are as follows:—

TABLE 8. INITIATIVE: PERCENTAGES REQUIRED FOR PETITION

A. Charters

CITY	SPECIAL ELECTION	GENERAL ELECTION
Texas—		
Galveston	——	——
Houston	——	——
Dallas	15	5
Fort Worth	(a)	500 voters (a)
El Paso	——	——
Denison	——	——
Greenville	——	——
Austin	25	
Waco	——	15 (b)
Palestine	——	——
Corpus Christi	——	——
Marshall	25	
Idaho—		
Lewiston	15	5

(a) At a general or special election.
(b) Is to be submitted at next general election, "unless otherwise provided for in said petition."

COMMISSION GOVERNMENT

TABLE 8 — *Continued*

A. *Charters*

City	Special Election	General Election
Massachusetts —		
Haverhill	25	10
Gloucester	25	
Lynn	25	10
Tennessee —		
Memphis	—	—
Chattanooga	—	—
North Carolina —		
High Point	—	—
Wilmington	35	10
West Virginia —		
Huntington	—	—
Bluefield	—	—
Parkersburg	20	10
Oklahoma —		
Ardmore	25	
Enid	(*c*)	
Tulsa	(*c*)	
McAlester	25	
Muskogee	25 (*d*)	
Bartlesville	(*c*)	
Sapulpa	25	
Duncan	(*c*)	
Guthrie	(*c*)	
Colorado —		
Colorado Springs	15	5
Grand Junction	10	5

(*c*) Provisions of state constitution apply, specifying 25 per cent.
(*d*) At a general or special election.

REFERENDUM AND INITIATIVE

TABLE 8 — *Continued*

A. *Charters*

City	Special Election	General Election
California —		
Berkeley	15	5
San Diego	15	5
Oakland	15	5
Modesto	25	15
San Luis Obispo	25	10
Santa Cruz	20 (*e*)	10
Vallejo	15	5
Monterey	20 (*f*)	10
Washington —		
Tacoma	20	5
Spokane	15	5
Oregon —		
Baker	(*g*)	(*g*)
Maryland —		
Cumberland		
Minnesota —		
Mankato	20	10
Michigan —		
Port Huron	25	10
Pontiac	20	5
Harbor Beach	25	10
Wyandotte	25	10

(*e*) See special provision in charter, Sec. 224.
(*f*) Charter may be amended on initiative petition of 20 per cent of voters.
(*g*) Provisions of state constitution apply, specifying 25 per cent.

COMMISSION GOVERNMENT

TABLE 8 — *Continued*

B. *General Acts*

STATE	SPECIAL ELECTION	GENERAL ELECTION
Iowa	25	10
Kansas — cities of first class	25	10
Kansas — cities of second class	40	10 to 25
South Dakota	5 (*a*)	(*a*)
North Dakota	25	25
Wisconsin	25	15
Minnesota	(*b*)	(*b*)
Illinois	25	10
New Mexico	——	——
Mississippi	——	——
Kentucky	——	25
Louisiana	33	——
South Carolina	20	——
Texas	——	——
Alabama — cities of 100,000 or over	——	——
Alabama — cities of 25–50,000	——	——
Alabama (general)	——	——
California (*c*)	30	15
Idaho	25	10
Montana	25	10
New Jersey	15	10
Utah	——	——
Washington	25 (*d*)	——
Wyoming	25	——

(*a*) Not specified whether general or special election.

(*b*) Each city adopting plan may provide for initiative in its charter. See under Mankato.

(*c*) Separate act, permitting initiative, recall, and referendum in cities.

(*d*) General or special election.

REFERENDUM AND INITIATIVE

The initiative is thus seen to be provided, either at a special or at a general election, in the city charter or permitted to the city under state law or constitution, in 38 out of the 51 cities, and in 17 of the 24 general acts tabulated. In the charters the percentage of signatures required to petitions requesting the submission of an ordinance range, for special elections, is from 25 to 10; for general elections, from 15 to 5. In the general acts, the range of signatures, for the initiative put into operation at special elections, is from 40 down; at general elections, from 25 to 10. The grand average of special election percentages is about 23; of general election percentages, a little more than 10 per cent.

CHAPTER XX

THE RECALL

The " recall " is the right of the voters to remove an official before his term of office has expired and to replace him by another. If the referendum and the initiative are means of effecting direct legislative action, the recall is a check upon administrative incapacity and dishonesty. The official whom it is sought to recall may be guilty of incompetence, of neglect of duty, or of official corruption. While the referendum and initiative make it possible to separate measures from men, and a bad ordinance may be negatived without ousting the honest though unwise commissioners who passed it, a series of weak and cowardly acts by a commissioner of public safety, or the repeated urging of corrupt measures by a venal mayor, may demand more drastic action.

The recall enables the voters to discharge an incompetent or faithless public servant promptly. Impeachment, in the nature of a court proceeding, being slow and accompanied often by great bitterness, has fallen into disuse. The recall — a political proceeding — is much more easy, prompt, and effective. There also attaches to the official who has been removed from office by impeachment a stigma of criminal guilt, which does not *necessarily* attach to an official removed by the re-

THE RECALL

call. The manager of a factory may discharge a foreman who is incapable or careless, but he does not prosecute him in the courts. So the voters, convinced of the necessity of a change in mayor or commissioner, may attempt to recall him, as in Huron, S.D., without his conviction of a violation of law, and without affecting his professional or business standing. The case may, of course, be so serious as to involve these also. The recall means that the people, who gave him his commission by election, withdraw that commission by election and give it to another.

The first requisite for the recall is that a petition, asking for the removal of the candidate in question, be signed by the required percentage of the voters at the last municipal election, and filed with the city clerk, who certifies to the commission or council the fact that it contains the requisite bona fide signatures. The council thereupon is required to call a special election, within a given number of days, at which the name of the former incumbent is placed on the ballot, together with that of the new candidate, or candidates, proposed. The person receiving a majority of the votes cast at this special election is declared elected: if the incumbent, he retains his office, the result amounting to a vote of confidence in him; if his opponent, the incumbent ceases to hold office, and his successor takes his place.

A petition signed by a considerable percentage of his fellows, asking an official, in the midst of his term, to stand for reëlection, shows such a lack of popular confidence that merely presenting the petition will frequently cause the official to resign, as did the mayor of Los Angeles not long ago.

COMMISSION GOVERNMENT

Even though it be not often actually exercised, the potential value of the recall is great. Few commissioners or councilmen will neglect their plain duty or abuse their powers when the people may so easily effect their removal from office. The recall puts into the hands of the electorate a powerful means of controlling representatives; and because so easily exercised, it is likely to be employed with caution by the voters.

The so-called "repeal" which has been recently advocated by some is the right of the people, upon proper petition, to revoke a law or ordinance already passed and in effect. It is more closely related to the referendum and initiative than to the recall, having to do with measures. It is probable that a broad construction of the initiative will be found to include the right to repeal a law already in existence, as well as to propose a new law.

In a very large number of charters, a statement of the grounds for demanding the recall must be included, usually as a part of the petition. In Oakland, Berkeley, Modesto, San Luis Obispo, Spokane, Mankato, and elsewhere, the official whose recall is sought has the right to present a justification of his acts, which is usually to consist of not more than 200 words, and is printed on the recall ballots.

Most provisions for the recall make it applicable to all elective officers; a few, to both elective and appointive officers, thus enabling the people to remove an official appointed by the commission. The petition must be verified usually by the city clerk or similar official. Under the Oakland charter, a statement of the intention to circulate a petition for recall must be filed with the city clerk in triplicate, one copy of which is to be sent

THE RECALL

to the office of the officer whose recall is to be demanded, and one to his residence.

The recall cannot be used in some charters until after an official has been in office for a reasonable period, — three or four or six months usually, — twelve months under the Illinois law. This prevents the use of this method of summary removal before the official has had time to get the work of his office well under way; it tends also to prevent recalls for purely partisan purposes.

The method of nominating a candidate to take the place of the person sought to be recalled, is, in many charters, not clearly provided. In many instances the usual provisions for election are made to apply. The Iowa law was amended in 1909 to cover this point, provision being made for nomination upon a petition of 10 percentum of the vote for mayor at the last general municipal election.[1]

To prevent a number of candidates from being nominated for a recall election, and the possibility that no one might have a majority, the law of Illinois prohibits more than one new candidate from being nominated for each office. In South Carolina, if no person receives a majority of votes at the recall election, a second election is held at which the ballot contains only the names of the incumbent and his opponent who received the highest vote at the first recall election.[2] So also in Oakland, and in the law of South Dakota as amended in 1911.

No officer who has been removed by recall can serve the city again in an official capacity for one year or more, according to provisions in many charters.

Failure to recall an official at an election operates, in

[1] Law as amended, 1909, sec. 1056–a 36.   [2] Sec. 2023 (14).

COMMISSION GOVERNMENT

Oakland, to require a higher percentage of signatures (30 per cent) for a subsequent recall petition for that officer.[1]

The commission (council) may make additional regulations on this subject, under many charters.

The following table summarizes the principal features of the recall provisions: —

TABLE 9. RECALL PROVISIONS
A. Charters

CITY (a)	PER CENT REQUIRED FOR PETITION (b)	PERIOD BEFORE BEING USED	STATEMENT REQUIRED OF GROUNDS OF RECALL (c)	METHOD OF NOMINATING OTHER CANDIDATE
Texas —				
Galveston	(No recall)	—	—	—
Houston	(No recall)	—	—	—
Dallas	35	—	x	—
Fort Worth	20	—	x	—
El Paso	—	—	—	—
Denison	20 (d)	—	—	—
Greenville	— (e)	—	—	—
Austin	25	—	x	—
Waco	30	—	x	(f)
Palestine	25	—	x	—
Corpus Christi	33⅓ (g)	—	x	—
Marshall	35 (g)	—	x	—
Idaho —				
Lewiston	25	90 days (h)	x	(i)

(a) Recall applies to all elective officers unless otherwise noted herein. A blank means no provision. (b) Percentage usually of last vote for mayor.
(c) x in this column means statement is required in petition for recall.
(d) Applies only to mayor. — Art. IV, Sec. 5.
(e) Mayor may be removed by majority of council, after hearing; this is not a recall provision.
(f) Any party may hold a primary election not less than five days before the recall election.
(g) Mayor or commissioner may be removed also after trial by majority of commissioners.
(h) No person shall be required to stand for reëlection more than once during his term of office. — Sec. 9. (i) Nominations may be made by petition.

[1] Charter, Sec. 7 (13).

THE RECALL

TABLE 9 — *Continued*

A. *Charters*

CITY	PER CENT REQUIRED FOR PETITION	PERIOD BEFORE BEING USED	STATEMENT REQUIRED OF GROUNDS OF RECALL	METHOD OF NOMINATING OTHER CANDIDATE
Massachusetts —				
Haverhill	25	—	x	(*j*)
Gloucester	—	—	—	—
Lynn	25	—	x	(*k*)
Tennessee —				
Memphis	—	—	—	—
Chattanooga	30	—	x	—
N. Carolina —				
High Point	(*l*)	—	—	—
Wilmington	35	—	x	—
W. Virginia —				
Huntington	(*m*)	—	—	—
Bluefield	(*m*)	—	—	—
Parkersburg	20	—	x	(*n*)
Oklahoma —				
Ardmore	30	—	x	(*j*)
Enid	30	6 months	x	(*j*)
Tulsa	35	—	x	(*j*)
McAlester	25	4 months (*o*)	—	(*p*)

(*j*) Election shall be conducted, returned, and the result thereof declared in all respects as are other city elections.

(*k*) Nomination to be " at a preliminary election."— Sec. 63.

(*l*) Mayor may be removed, after public hearing, by majority vote of all commissioners elected.— Sec. 26 (14).

(*m*) Any commissioner may be removed, after trial, by a citizens' board, elected by wards.

(*n*) Nomination of new candidate is upon petition of 10 per cent of voters.

(*o*) " Nor within 6 months after an election has been held upon a previous petition for recall of the same officer."— Art. IX, Sec. 5.

(*p*) Election conducted according to state laws.

COMMISSION GOVERNMENT

TABLE 9 — *Continued*

A. *Charters*

CITY	PER CENT REQUIRED FOR PETITION	PERIOD BEFORE BEING USED	STATEMENT REQUIRED OF GROUNDS OF RECALL	METHOD OF NOMINATING OTHER CANDIDATE
Oklahoma —				
Muskogee	30	6 months	x	(q)
Bartlesville	25 (r)	4 months (s)	—	(q)
Sapulpa	25	—	x	(t)
Duncan	25	—	x	(j)
Guthrie	35	6 months	x	primary
Colorado —				
Colorado Springs	30	6 months	x	usual (u)
Grand Junction	20 (v)	3 months	x	usual (u)
California —				
Berkeley	20	3 months	x	usual (u)
San Diego	25	—	x	(w)
Oakland	15 (x)(r)	6 months	x(y)	usual (u)
Modesto	15	—	x(y)	usual (z) (u)
San Luis Obispo	25	3 months	x(y)	usual (u)
Santa Cruz	15	3 months	x(y)	—
Vallejo	15 (a)	6 months	x(y)	usual (u)
Monterey	25	—	x	(w)

(q) Election conducted according to state laws.
(r) Applies to both elective officers and officers appointed to fill a vacancy.
(s) "Nor within 6 months after an election has been held upon a previous petition for recall of the same officer."— Art. IX, Sec. 5.
(t) Nomination of other candidate is at a special primary, and precedes recall election.
(u) Nominations made in same manner as for usual nominating elections — by petition.   (v) Of last vote for governor.
(w) Election shall be conducted, returned, and the result thereof declared in all respects as are other city elections.
(x) But not less than 3000 signatures, each a separate paper, acknowledged before a notary public.
(y) Statement of reasons for demanding recall of officer and a statement of officer justifying himself may both appear on the call for the election or on the ballot.   (z) Election for successor is separate from recall election.
(a) Subsequent petition to recall same officer requires signature of 30 per cent of voters.

THE RECALL

TABLE 9 — *Continued*

A. *Charters*

City	Per Cent required for Petition	Period before being Used	Statement required of Grounds of Recall	Method of Nominating Other Candidate
Washington —				
Tacoma	25 (*b*)	6 months	x	usual (*c*)
Spokane	20 (*d*)(*e*)	—	—	usual (*c*)
Oregon —				
Baker	(*f*)	—	—	—
Minnesota —				
Mankato	20	3 months	x (*g*)	(*h*)
Maryland —				
Cumberland	—	—	—	—
Michigan —				
Port Huron	—	—	—	—
Pontiac	20	3 months	x	usual (*c*)
Harbor Beach	—	—	—	—
Wyandotte	20	—	x	(*i*)

(*b*) But not less than 2500 signatures.

(*c*) Nominations made in same manner as for usual nominating elections — by petition.

(*d*) Applies to both elective officers and officers appointed to fill a vacancy.

(*e*) Petition of 20 per cent requires a special recall election; 15 per cent petition, recall is voted on at next regular municipal election.

(*f*) Election conducted according to state laws.

(*g*) Statement of reasons for demanding recall of officer and a statement of officer justifying himself may both appear on the call for the election or on the ballot.

(*h*) Election shall be conducted, returned, and the result thereof declared in all respects as are other city elections.

(*i*) Nomination of new candidate is upon petition of 10 per cent of voters.

COMMISSION GOVERNMENT

TABLE 9 — Continued

B. General Acts

City	Per Cent required for Petition	Period before being Used	Statement required of Grounds of Recall	Method of Nominating Other Candidate
Iowa	25	—	x	(a)
Kansas — cities of first class	25	—	x	—
Kansas — cities of second class	—	—	—	—
South Dakota	15	—	x	—
North Dakota	25	6 months	x	—
Wisconsin	25	—	x	(b)
Minnesota	(c)	—	—	—
Illinois	55 (d)	12 months	x	(e)
New Mexico	—	—	—	—
Mississippi	—	—	—	—
Kentucky	(f)	—	—	—
Louisiana	33	—	x	—
South Carolina	20	—	x	(g)
Texas	(h)	—	—	—
Alabama — cities of 100,000 or over	3000 voters	—	x	(g)
Alabama — cities of 25–50,000	1000 voters	—	x	—

(a) Nomination of new candidate is by petition of 10 per cent of voters.
(b) Primary election, if there are more than two candidates.
(c) Recall may be included by each city in its commission charter.
(d) Originally 75 per cent; amended in 1911 to 55 per cent.
(e) Only one candidate for each officer sought to be recalled may be nominated. — Sec. 42 (h).
(f) Any commissioner may be removed by unanimous vote of other four commissioners, after hearing, etc. — (Acts of Kentucky, 1910, p. 173, Sec. 22.)
(g) If no person receives a majority of votes, at the recall election, a second election is held at which the ballots contain only the names of the two candidates who received the highest vote at the preceding election.
(h) Texas general law applies only to cities of less than 10,000 population.

THE RECALL

TABLE 9 — *Continued*

B. *General Acts*

City	Per Cent required for Petition	Period before being Used	Statement required of Grounds of Recall	Method of Nominating Other Candidate
Alabama (general)	25	—	x	—
California (*i*)	25	4 months	x (*j*)	(*k*)
Idaho	35 (*l*)	3 months	x	(*m*)
Montana	25	—	x	(*n*)
New Jersey	25	12 months (*o*)	x	—
Utah	—	—	—	—
Washington	25	6 months	x	—
Wyoming	25	—	x	(*p*)

(*i*) Separate act, permitting recall, referendum, and initiative in cities.
(*j*) And also on ballot, officer may set forth statement justifying his course in office.
(*k*) Same as for general municipal election.
(*l*) A petition signed by 35 per cent of voters calls a special recall election unless a regular municipal election falls due within 90 days; 20 per cent, recall is voted on at next regular municipal election.
(*m*) Nomination procedure is same as in general municipal election.
(*n*) Nomination of new candidate is by petition of 10 per cent of voters.
(*o*) But one recall petition shall be filed against the same officer during his term of office.
(*p*) Special primary is held before recall election, at which only one candidate shall be chosen, if incumbent is a candidate.

The question as to what number of signers should be required, in order to make the recall operate most effectively, is difficult to answer in the absence of experience with this provision. The average percentage of signatures required for recall petitions is, in the charters here tabulated, approximately 25 per cent. In the general acts, exclusive of Illinois, where the extraordinary percentage of 75[1] seems to indicate an intention

[1] This percentage has since been reduced to 55 per cent.

COMMISSION GOVERNMENT

not to permit the recall to be used, the average of the general acts is also about 25 per cent.

A percentage as low as 5 is probably not sufficient to indicate a real demand for recall; while any such close approach to half the number of votes as 35 or 40 per cent is almost as certainly too high. While experience may modify present opinion, it is safe to say that 30 and 10 per cent are the upper and lower limits between which lies the percentage of signatures which may reasonably be required. Different percentages may be desirable for different cities; or it may prove best to adopt generally a reasonably low limit such as that in Oakland, 15 per cent, while at the same time requiring that each signature shall be a separate paper, sworn to before a notary public. This will have the effect of discouraging the ready and thoughtless signing of petitions, so common among Americans, while not preventing the recall from being used. At the same time it adds to the expense of securing the recall of an official. Not less than three thousand individual petitions in a city the size of Oakland[1] means a real demand for the removal of an official. Tacoma requires at least 2500 signatures, but not individual petitions.

Spokane provides that a petition signed by 25 per cent of the voters shall operate to require a special recall election; a petition of 15 per cent compels a vote only at the next regular municipal election, which occurs every two years, though the term of the council is four years.

[1] Population, 1910, 150,174.

THE RECALL

Use of Recall

The actual use of the recall has not been extensive enough yet to ascertain fully its value in practice. In Los Angeles, which is not a commission city, though it possesses several commission features, the mayor resigned after the required petition was signed and before the election was held, and at the election in the spring of 1909 another mayor was chosen. In Seattle, the mayor was recently recalled (Feb. 8, 1911). In Dallas, members of the school board were recalled in 1910. In Tacoma, in 1911, the mayor and two commissioners were recalled, but the two other commissioners were reëlected. In Huron, S.D., the petition for the recall of mayor and council was signed by a sufficient number to require action at the spring election of 1911, but the voters refused to recall the officials.[1] A petition is now pending [2] for the recall of the mayor of McAlester, Okla. In Des Moines, though threatened twice, the recall has never been used. In the one instance, the appointment, for local political reasons, of an unsuitable chief of police, aroused much public indignation; but his resignation shortly afterward allayed the agitation. In the other case, those who opposed a commissioner, on account of his vigorous enforcement of police regulations, particularly in the removal of slot machines and the extinction of the "red light district," joined forces with certain disgruntled automobile owners who had been arrested for violating the speed laws in the city

[1] See also for additional data "The Practice of the Recall," by H. S. Gilbertson, in Beard's "Digest of Short Ballot Charters."

[2] July, 1911.

and opened headquarters to recall the commissioner. They failed, however, to secure the necessary number of signers. In Cedar Rapids, the suggestion that the recall be used, because of the failure of the commissioners to remove certain accused policemen, was never acted upon. The fear expressed by some earnest students of the subject that honest officials will be intimidated by the dread of the recall from the proper performance of their duties does not seem to have been realized. The opposite danger seems more likely, that bad officials will not fear the recall where the percentage of signatures is placed too high.

It may be that the recall will prove to be a transitory method of control, and be superseded by some other; on the other hand, it may become an integral part, not only of our municipal, but of our state and national election machinery as well. Why might not a state legislator whose vote betrays his lack of care for the interests of his constituents be recalled; or a congressman whose vote on a tariff measure or conservation bill shows him to be not representing his district? The recall bids fair to receive wide attention during the next few years, and whether of permanent or transient nature, is of interest as affording at present an important extension of the right of suffrage — the right to change officials before the usual term of office has expired. "There appears no reason," said the Court of Appeals of California, "why a representative should not be made to retire at any time at the request of the people as well as at the end of a fixed period."

CHAPTER XXI

NONPARTISAN PRIMARIES AND ELECTIONS

THE system of nonpartisan primaries and elections, inaugurated by Des Moines and the other Iowa cities, has been adopted as a part of many recent commission laws. By it, candidates are nominated by petition, and the names are arranged alphabetically on the ballot, both for the primary and for the regular election, no party designation being permitted. Galveston, it will be remembered, has neither broad referendum, initiative, recall, nor nonpartisan primaries. The charter of Austin, adopted in 1909, incorporated all of these features. Haverhill, also, provides for the nomination of candidates on petition of twenty-five voters and allows no party designation. "No ballot," runs Section 11, " . . . shall have printed thereon any party or political designation or mark, and there cannot be appended to the name of any candidate any such party or political designation or mark, or anything showing how he was nominated, or indicating his views or opinions."

Twice the number of candidates to be elected may be nominated. The mayor is usually voted for separately, but the commissioners in a group. At the first primary in Des Moines, there were fifty candidates for the five commissionerships; at Cedar Rapids there were fifty-seven. The primary reduced this number to ten. At

COMMISSION GOVERNMENT

the election each voter faced, in the booth, a ballot which contained the names of two candidates for mayor and eight for commissioners (councilmen), none of which were marked with a party name. Of these, he voted for one candidate for mayor and for four commissioners. The candidates for commissionerships who received the four highest votes were elected.

The Kansas law for cities of the first class, and for those cities of the second class having over 10,000 population, is similar to the Iowa law. The Wisconsin law provides for nomination by twenty-five voters, for the alphabetical arrangement of names on the ballot, and prohibits party designation. Cities in Minnesota may provide for nominations without "any party designation or mark indicating that any candidate is a member of any party whatsoever, whether on said primary election ballot or upon said municipal election ballot." The South Dakota act and the Kentucky law contain provisions substantially similar to those of the Iowa law.

Colorado Springs and Berkeley have a similar method, except that if any candidate at the primary — called the first election — has a clear majority of the ballots cast at such first election, he is declared elected, and it is not necessary to vote for him at the second, or "regular" election. This is probably an advantage, as it eliminates from the second contest those candidates who are clearly the choice of more than half of the voters. In a contest where the candidates number thirty or forty, as in the Iowa cities, a majority for any one candidate would indicate a decided preference on the part of the voters.

NONPARTISAN PRIMARIES, ELECTIONS

In Berkeley twenty-five names are required on the nominating petition; in San Diego, fifty. The new Tacoma charter contains a provision for a "first election," similar to that of Berkeley and Colorado Springs. The nomination requires twenty-five *individual* petitions or certificates, each signed by one person, acknowledged before a notary public, and filed with the city clerk; and the candidate, in filing his acceptance, must state that he is the nominee of no political party. Oakland provides for not less than fifty nor more than two hundred and fifty "individual certificates."

Huntington and Bluefield, W. Va., treat the matter quite differently. Frankly recognizing the national partisanship fomerly existing in those cities, and assuming it to be inevitable, as it was under the old system, they provide that no party shall have more than three commissioners on the board of four, nor more than half the membership of the citizens' referendum board (the body which acts as a check on the board of commissioners). At the same time, by dividing the present city government evenly between the two largest parties, Republican and Democratic, even down to the policemen, each party is satisfied and a good start made toward equitable relations in the future.

It may be that the ordinary commission features will remove partisanship without supplementary provisions by giving the commissioners power enough to be independent of the party bosses and by providing a referendum and recall; but the charters of many commission cities indicate a belief that nonpartisan nominating and election provisions are of substantial value. These are summarized in the following table:—

COMMISSION GOVERNMENT

TABLE 10. NOMINATING AND ELECTION PROVISIONS

A. Charters

City	Elected at Large	Nominated at Large	Number of Signers Required to Candidate's Petition	Twice as Many Candidates Nominated as Elected	Names Arranged Alphabetically on Ballot — Primary	Names Arranged Alphabetically on Ballot — Election	No Party Designation on Ballot — Primary	No Party Designation on Ballot — Election
Texas —								
Galveston	x (a)	(b)	(b)	—	—	—	—	—
Houston	x	x (c)	(d)	(d)	—	—	—	—
Dallas	x	x (c)	100(e)	x	—	—	(e)	—
Fort Worth	x	(f)		—	—	—	—	—
El Paso	x	(g)		—	—	—	—	—
Denison	x			—	—	—	—	—
Greenville	x			—	—	—	—	—
Austin	x	x	25	x	x	x	x	x
Waco	x	(h)		—	—	—	—	—
Palestine	x	—		—	—	x	—	(i)
Corpus Christi	x	x		—	—	—	—	—
Marshall	x	—		—	—	—	—	—
Idaho —								
Lewiston	x	x (j)	100	—	—	—	—	—

(a) In practice, but not specified in charter.
(b) Commissioners are usually nominated by a club of citizens, or they may run independently, in which case each Commissioner has to secure a petition signed by five per cent of the qualified voters. This petition, presented to the Board, has the effect of placing the name of the candidate on the ballot.
(c) In case a primary is held, nominations are to be at large; and independent candidates may have names placed on ballot by petition of one hundred qualified voters.
(d) Council may prescribe manner of holding primary elections. — Art. IX, Sec. 2.
(e) May be party primaries; or independent nominations by petition.
(f) Primary not a prerequisite for a general election. See Chap. II, Sec. 7.
(g) Elections and nominations to be in accordance with state laws.
(h) In practice, a committee of fifteen is selected by a mass meeting of citizens, to recommend candidates.
(i) Party designation shall be made where candidates have been nominated by a party. — Art. V, Sec. 2.
(j) City council may prescribe manner of holding primary election.

NONPARTISAN PRIMARIES, ELECTIONS

TABLE 10 — *Continued*
A. *Charters*

CITY	ELECTED AT LARGE	NOMINATED AT LARGE	NUMBER OF SIGNERS REQUIRED TO CANDIDATE'S PETITION	TWICE AS MANY CANDIDATES NOMINATED AS ELECTED	NAMES ARRANGED ALPHABETICALLY ON BALLOT — Primary	NAMES ARRANGED ALPHABETICALLY ON BALLOT — Election	NO PARTY DESIGNATION ON BALLOT — Primary	NO PARTY DESIGNATION ON BALLOT — Election
Massachusetts —								
Haverhill	x	x	25	x	—	—	x	x
Gloucester	x	—	—	—	—	—	—	—
Lynn	x	x	25	x	—	—	x	x
Tennessee —								
Memphis	x (*k*)	—	—	—	—	—	—	—
Chattanooga	x	x	25	x	—	—	—	—
N. Carolina —								
High Point	x	(*l*)	(*m*)	—	—	—	—	—
Wilmington	x (*o*)	x	25	(*p*)	x	(*n*)	x	(*n*)
W. Virginia —								
Huntington	x (*q*)	(*r*)	(*s*)	(*t*)	—	—	—	(*u*)
Bluefield	x	(*s*)	(*s*)	(*t*)	—	—	—	(*u*)
Parkersburg	x	x	25	x	x	(*n*)	x	(*n*)

(*k*) In practice, but not specified in charter.

(*l*) City council may prescribe manner of holding primary election.

(*m*) Candidate must file notice of candidacy.

(*n*) The ballot at the general municipal election shall be in the same general form as for the primary election, so far as applicable.

(*o*) "The councilmen shall be nominated and elected by the qualified voters of the city, but no two or more of said councilmen shall be elected from one ward." — Charter, Sec. 14.

(*p*) "The two candidates living in each *ward* who receive the greatest number of votes for councilmen shall be the only candidates whose names shall be placed on the ballots for councilmen at the general municipal election." — Charter, Sec. 15 (*c*). (*q*) Citizens' board, however, is elected by wards.

(*r*) Independent candidates must file written notice of candidacy as is required of candidates for a political party nomination.

(*s*) Candidates may be nominated by convention, primary, or petition. — Sec. 27.

(*t*) No political party shall nominate more than three (of four) candidates for commissioners, no two of whom shall be from the same ward.

(*u*) Every person nominated for commissioner shall file statement of political party to which he belongs; Bluefield adds, "or if he belongs to no party, he shall so state."

COMMISSION GOVERNMENT

TABLE 10 — *Continued*
A. *Charters*

City	Elected at Large	Nominated at Large	Number of Signers Required to Candidate's Petition	Twice as Many Candidates Nominated as Elected	Names Arranged Alphabetically on Ballot — Primary	Names Arranged Alphabetically on Ballot — Election	No Party Designation on Ballot — Primary	No Party Designation on Ballot — Election
Oklahoma —								
Ardmore	x	—	—	—	—	—	—	—
Enid	x	x	—	—	—	—	—	(v)
Tulsa	x	x(w)	100	x(x)	—	—	—	—
McAlester	x(y)	x	—	—	—	—	—	(v)
Muskogee	x	x(z)	—	—	—	—	—	—
Bartlesville	x	x	—	—	—	—	—	(v)
Sapulpa	x	x	—	x	x	—	(a)	—
Duncan	x(b)	x	—	—	—	—	—	(v)
Guthrie	x	x	25	x	x	(c)	x	(c)
Colorado —								
Col. Springs	x	x(d)	25 (e)	x(x)	x	x(d)	x(f)	x(d)
Grand Junction	x	(g)	25 (e)	(g)	(g)	x	(g)	x

(*v*) Independent candidates must file written notice of candidacy as is required of candidates for a political party nomination.

(*w*) In case a primary is held, nominations are to be at large; and independent candidates may have names placed on ballot by petition of one hundred qualified voters.

(*x*) If candidate has majority at first election (primary), his name is not voted on at second election. For candidates not receiving such majority, first election serves as a primary election.

(*y*) In practice, but not specified in charter.

(*z*) But two of the four commissioners shall be residents of the district east of Main Street, and two west of Main Street.

(*a*) Candidate must file written notice of candidacy, stating he is not the representative of any political party.

(*b*) Wording ambiguous. — Art. II, Sec. 4.

(*c*) General municipal election is to be conducted in same manner as primary.

(*d*) The provisions as to the conduct of first election (primary) as far as applicable, govern the second election.

(*e*) Individual certificates, and each certificate a separate paper.

(*f*) "Nothing on the ballot shall be indicative of the source of the candidacy or of the support of any candidate."

(*g*) Preferential ballot combines primary and election.

NONPARTISAN PRIMARIES, ELECTIONS

TABLE 10 — *Continued*

A. Charters

CITY	ELECTED AT LARGE	NOMINATED AT LARGE	NUMBER OF SIGNERS REQUIRED TO CANDIDATE'S PETITION	TWICE AS MANY CANDIDATES NOMINATED AS ELECTED	NAMES ARRANGED ALPHABETICALLY ON BALLOT — Primary	NAMES ARRANGED ALPHABETICALLY ON BALLOT — Election	NO PARTY DESIGNATION ON BALLOT — Primary	NO PARTY DESIGNATION ON BALLOT — Election
California —								
Berkeley	x	x(*h*)	25(*i*)	x(*j*)	x	x	x(*k*)	x
San Diego	x	x	50	x	x	x	x	x
Oakland	x	x(*h*)	50(*l*)	x	x	x	x	x
Modesto	x	x(*h*)	25	x(*j*)	x	x	x(*k*)	x
San Luis Obispo	x	x(*h*)	25(*m*)	(*n*)	(*n*)	x	(*n*)	x(*k*)
Santa Cruz	x	x	25(*i*)	x	x	x	x(*k*)	x
Vallejo	x	x	25(*o*)	x	x	x(*p*)	x	x(*p*)
Monterey	x	x(*h*)	25(*m*)	(*n*)	(*n*)	x	(*n*)	x(*k*)
Washington —								
Tacoma	x	x	25(*i*)	x(*j*)	x	x(*j*)	x(*r*)	x(*j*)
Spokane	x	(*q*)	25(*i*)	(*q*)	(*q*)	x	(*q*)	x(*r*)
Oregon —								
Baker	x(*h*)	(*n*)	25(*i*)	(*n*)	(*n*)	x	(*n*)	x

(*h*) In practice, but not specified in charter.
(*i*) Individual certificates, and each certificate a separate paper.
(*j*) If candidate has majority at first election (primary), his name is not voted on at second election. For candidates not receiving such majority, first election serves as a primary election.
(*k*) "Nothing on the ballot shall be indicative of the source of the candidacy or of the support of any candidate."
(*l*) Not less than fifty nor more than two hundred fifty individual certificates.
(*m*) Not less than twenty-five nor more than one hundred individual certificates.
(*n*) There appears to be no primary election; a petition puts name of candidate on final election ballot.
(*o*) Not less than twenty-five nor more than fifty *individual* certificates.
(*p*) The provisions as to the conduct of first election (primary), as far as applicable, govern the second election.
(*q*) Preferential ballot combines primary and election.
(*r*) Candidate also, in accepting nomination, makes affidavit that he is not a candidate of any political party.

COMMISSION GOVERNMENT

TABLE 10 — *Continued*

A. Charters

City	Elected at Large	Nominated at Large	Number of Signers required to Candidate's Petition	Twice as many Candidates Nominated as Elected	Names arranged Alphabetically on Ballots — Primary	Names arranged Alphabetically on Ballots — Election	No Party Designation on Ballot — Primary	No Party Designation on Ballot — Election
Minnesota —								
Mankato	x	x(*s*)	25	x	x	(*t*)	x	(*t*)
Maryland —								
Cumberland	x	x	100	x	x	x	x	x
Michigan —								
Port Huron	x	x	100(*u*)	x	x	x	x	x
Pontiac	x	x	25 (*v*)	x	(*w*)	(*w*)	x	x
Harbor Beach	x	x	10	x	x	x	x	x
Wyandotte	x	x	25 (*v*)	x	x	x	x	x

(*s*) In practice, but not specified in charter.

(*t*) The ballot at the general municipal election shall be in the same general form as for the primary election, so far as applicable.

(*u*) Not less than one hundred nor more than one hundred and twenty-five signatures to petition.

(*v*) Not less than twenty-five nor more than fifty signatures to petition.

(*w*) Rotation of names on ballots.

The purpose of the petition, signed by twenty-five or fifty voters, is to effectually avoid the party convention or caucus, and to make it easy to be a candidate for office, but not so easy as to encumber the ballot with candidates. The arrangement of names alphabetically permits an order clearly not partisan, and, by the omission of party column or designation, compels the voter to select his mayor and four commissioners, both at the

NONPARTISAN PRIMARIES, ELECTIONS

TABLE 10 — *Continued*
B. *General Acts*

STATE	ELECTED AT LARGE	NOMINATED AT LARGE	NUMBER OF SIGNERS REQUIRED TO CANDIDATE'S PETITION	TWICE AS MANY CANDIDATES NOMINATED AS ELECTED	NAMES ARRANGED ALPHABETICALLY ON BALLOT — Primary	NAMES ARRANGED ALPHABETICALLY ON BALLOT — Election	NO PARTY DESIGNATION ON BALLOT — Primary	NO PARTY DESIGNATION ON BALLOT — Election
Iowa	x	x	25	x	x	(*a*)	x	(*a*)
Kansas — cities of 1st class	x	x(*b*)	25	x	x	—	x	—
Kansas — cities of 2d class	x(*b*)	x(*b*)	25	x	x	—	x	—
South Dakota	x(*c*)	—	(*d*)	x	—	x	—	x(*e*)
North Dakota	x	—		—	—	—	—	—
Wisconsin	x	x	25	x	x	—	x	—
Minnesota	x(*f*)	x(*b*)		(*b*)	—	—	x(*f*)	x(*f*)
Illinois	x	x	25	x	x	x	x	x
New Mexico	x	—		—	—	—	—	—
Mississippi	x	—		—	—	—	—	—
Kentucky	x	x(*b*)	100	x	x	x	x	(*g*)
Louisiana	x(*b*)	—		—	—	—	—	—
South Carolina	x	—		x	x	—	(*h*)	—
Texas	x (*i*)	—		—	—	—	—	—
Alabama — cities of 100,000 or over	x	x	500	x	x	x	—	—

(*a*) "The ballot at such general municipal election shall be in the same general form as for such primary election so far as applicable."
(*b*) In practice, though not specified in the law.
(*c*) Inferred, but not specifically stated; only one commissioner is elected each year.
(*d*) Fifteen electors for each one thousand population or major fraction thereof, but not less than twenty-five nor over one hundred and fifty signatures. — Sec. 107.
(*e*) "Without other designation than that of the office for which they are candidates." — Sec. 100.
(*f*) State law specifically permits each city adopting commission plan to incorporate this provision in its charter.
(*g*) Election ballot similar to nominating ballot. See Sec. 37.
(*h*) "Party primary."
(*i*) Provision in title of act.

COMMISSION GOVERNMENT

TABLE 10 — *Continued*

B. General Acts

STATE	ELECTED AT LARGE	NOMINATED AT LARGE	NUMBER OF SIGNERS REQUIRED TO CANDIDATE'S PETITION	TWICE AS MANY CANDIDATES NOMINATED AS ELECTED	NAMES ARRANGED ALPHABETICALLY ON BALLOT — Primary	NAMES ARRANGED ALPHABETICALLY ON BALLOT — Election	NO PARTY DESIGNATION ON BALLOT — Primary	NO PARTY DESIGNATION ON BALLOT — Election
Alabama — cities of 25–50,000	x	x	100	x	x	x	—	—
Alabama (general)	x	x	(*j*)	(*k*)	x	(*k*)	—	—
California	x (*l*)	—	—	—	—	—	—	—
Idaho	x	x	25	x	(*m*)	(*m*)	x	x
Montana	x	x	25	x	x	x (*n*)	x	x (*n*)
New Jersey	x	x	25 (*o*)	x	x	(*n*)	x	x (*n*)
Utah	x	x	100	x	x	x	x	x
Washington	x	x	100	x	x	x	x	x
Wyoming	x	x (*p*)	25	x (*p*)	x (*p*)	x	x (*p*)	x

(*j*) Three per cent of voters.
(*k*) Preferential ballot combines primary and election.
(*l*) In practice, though not specified in the law.
(*m*) Rotation of names on ballots.
(*n*) "The ballot at such general municipal election shall be in the same general form as for such primary election so far as applicable."
(*o*) "At least one half of one per centum of the entire vote at the last preceding general election, but in no event less than 25 individual certificates." — Laws of 1911, Chap. 221, 13.
(*p*) No primary held if there are but two candidates for mayor and four candidates for commissioners.

primary and at the election, without regard to their national politics.

The limitation of names on the final ballot to twice the number to be elected, is designed to prevent three-cornered contests, in which frequently two good candidates divide the votes of the better citizens, and a less

NONPARTISAN PRIMARIES, ELECTIONS

desirable candidate wins. It is not difficult at the primary to select two candidates for mayor and eight for commissioners, out of forty or fifty names; and it is still easier at the election to select for mayor, one of two, and for commissioners, four out of eight. Even where the ballot does not designate the candidate to a particular department, the voters know practically what place in the city hall each man will fill, and the choice really amounts to that of one of two candidates for each position.

It has been urged that alphabetical arrangement of names gives, especially in the primaries, an advantage to the candidate whose name begins with one of the earlier letters of the alphabet. In practical operation in Des Moines and Cedar Rapids, this has not proved to be true. If necessary, however, the tickets can be printed with the names revolved alphabetically; that is, if there are ten candidates, one-tenth of the ballots begin with the name of each candidate. This is done in Pontiac, Mich., and elsewhere, and is a simple method of solving the problem.

In a sense, these municipal nominations and elections are nonpartisan only in the sense of "free from national or state politics." So defined, the term is correct. There will always be local politics and parties and partisanship, and it is impossible to eliminate them. People must divide on local issues and candidates, as on other questions; but much is gained by separating local from state or national matters. It submits to the voters, unconfused with such national issues as tariff changes or regulation of railroad rates, such questions as the building of new wharves, subways, water-supply aqueducts, or, for the smaller city, the establishment of a system of parks, a municipal lighting plant, or a sewerage system. "The motto of every sensible man," says the mayor of New York City, "should be national politics and issues for national elections, state politics and issues for state elections, and local politics and issues, and none other, for local elections."[1]

Preferential Ballot

The method of electing members of the commission, adopted in Grand Junction, Col., as already described,[2] permits voters to express not only their first choice for commissioners, but also second and third choices. In Des Moines, Dallas, and many other commission cities, there are three processes involved in electing commissioners. First, names are put on the nominating ballot, by petition — as many candidates as can secure the necessary number of signatures (twenty-five in Des Moines). Second, from these, the voters select, at the primary, two candidates for mayor, and eight candidates for the four commissionerships. Each voter, therefore, expresses two choices for mayor and eight choices for four commissioners, which, in practice, is nearly equivalent to two choices for each commissioner. Third, at the final election, substantially the same group of voters pick, as their first choice, one of the two candidates for mayor whom they have previously chosen as first and second choices; and four first-choice commissioners out of the eight. Under the method at Grand Junction, the first step — that of placing names on the ballot by petition

[1] Mayor William J. Gaynor, in the *Century Magazine* for September, 1910.   [2] See pp. 100 ff.

NONPARTISAN PRIMARIES, ELECTIONS

— is similar to that in Des Moines; but primary and election are consolidated, by permitting the voters to express, on the only ballot taken, their first, second, and third choices for each office. A minor difference is that the Grand Junction plan provides for the election of candidates to specific places; instead of electing the four commissioners as a group and permitting the board to assign later each of its members to a department.

The main advantage over the Des Moines system, which is urged for the preferential ballot, is that it simplifies the process of choosing commissioners, at the same time permitting the election of candidates who are really the choice of a majority of the voters.

Spokane adopted a preferential ballot, similar in many of its provisions to that of Grand Junction. The legislature of Alabama passed, in 1911, a general act providing for two choices on the election ballot.

The method of counting the preferential ballots under the Grand Junction plan, is, that when there is no majority of first-choice votes, the name of the candidate having the fewest first-choice votes is thrown out, and the second-choice votes of each remaining candidate are added to the first-choice votes of that candidate, in order to arrive at a majority. The third-choice votes are added, if the first and second-choice votes do not supply a majority for any one candidate.

Under the "Hare" plan,[1] the ballots of the candidates having the fewest number of first-choice votes are

[1] See for further discussion, Beard's "Digest of Short Ballot Charters," pp. 21501, 21502 ("Preferential Voting," by Robert Tyson); also 21301–21304 ("Preferential Representation through the Single Transferable Vote").

distributed to the other candidates who are indicated as second-choices on those ballots, if necessary to arrive at a majority. Which of these plans is preferable remains to be seen.

How valuable the preference ballot is, must be determined later, from its actual use in elections. While it is no necessary part of the commission form, it is of interest as affording a possibly simpler method of choosing officials. The argument in favor of the primary-and-election system of Des Moines is that it gives the voters an opportunity to reconsider, if necessary, their judgment of candidates, during the period of time elapsing between the primary and the election.

The commission form of government aims to abolish national and state party lines in local elections, by several most fundamental features. First, it gives the municipal governing body power enough so that there is none left for the state or national party boss to run his local machine with. Second, the commissioners are independent, since responsible alone to the city electorate who chose them, and not to the party machine. Third, by the referendum and recall, readily exercised on municipal matters, the separate consideration of local affairs is made still easier. Fourth, by means of specific ballot provisions, such as prohibiting the use of national party names on the ticket, and by other restrictions, it is made still harder to inject national or state issues into local campaigns. Finally, as described in the following chapter, a municipal civil service commission is also provided in many charters. The elimination of national and state party politics is thus almost completely assured; and reports from commission cities confirm, by actual results, what might naturally be expected. If the commission plan results in nothing else than the entire separation of municipal questions from state or national politics, it will on this account alone merit the hearty support of American citizens and lovers of good government, and be worthy of general adoption by our cities.

CHAPTER XXII

MUNICIPAL CIVIL SERVICE, AND OTHER CHECKS

MANY of the laws and charters, as those of Iowa and Kansas, add, as an additional safeguard, a civil service commission. The number, qualifications, and duties of this commission differ in the various acts, the main provisions being for a small number, appointed by the board of commissioners for a long term, and usually paid.

Most of the Texas cities make no provision for a civil service commission. The charter of Austin merely prohibits soliciting for political contributions, and that of Marshall provides against party assessments of city employees. Palestine and other cities have a corrupt practices act, besides stipulating that "all policemen and firemen shall hold office during good behavior." Beyond these general provisions they do not go.

Under the Iowa law, a civil service commission of three is appointed by the board of commissioners to serve for six years, the term of one member expiring every two years. Any of these civil service commissioners may be removed by the council (board of commissioners), by a four-fifths vote, and the vacancy filled similarly. The council supplies a clerk and such equipment as may be needed. Twice a year the civil service commission holds examinations to select persons qualified to fill various positions under the city government, and, from the list secured, all appointments to places under the civil service must be made. The provisions of the law apply to all appointive offices and employees, except the city clerk, fire chief, assessor, street commissioner, and those who may be designated as chiefs of subdepartments and "commissioners of any kind, laborers whose occupation requires no special skill or fitness, election officials, and mayor's secretary and assistant solicitor, where such officers are appointed." Existing employees were to be retained without examination, unless removed for cause.

The promise of a position or any benefit in return for political support is prohibited. Every election officer must file, within thirty days after taking office, a sworn statement of his election expenses, with the city clerk, specifying by whom such funds were contributed; and the statement must be published "at least once in a daily newspaper of general circulation." Violation of these provisions is made a misdemeanor and a ground for removal from office.

The Iowa law provides that "all persons subject to such civil service examinations shall be subject to removal from office or employment by the council for misconduct or failure to perform their duties"; and the chiefs of subdepartments (fire, police, and the like) and foremen may peremptorily discharge any subordinate, subject to later revocation or approval by the superintendent of the department. The employee discharged has the right of appeal to the council. These provisions are necessary, in the eyes of the framers of the law, in order to give the city board authority to control its employees.

COMMISSION GOVERNMENT

It is a question whether the civil service commission is needed, as an additional means of removing partisan politics from the administration of city affairs since several other features of the commission plan look toward the same end. If the possession of enough power frees the council-commissioners from subservience to the party boss, and removes national issues from the arena of local questions; if the checks already mentioned make it possible to hold strictly accountable the men chosen as city directors; and if primaries and elections, freed from national party names and connections, supplement the results otherwise likely,— it may be that no municipal civil service commission will be necessary, or that the board of commissioners (council) may itself best act as the civil service commission, as in Huntington and Bluefield. Until this shall clearly appear, however, it is undoubtedly safer to demand a separate, nonpartisan civil service board, rather than to lose any ground already gained. If the board prove unnecessary, it can be discarded.

The Kansas law for cities of the first class and the South Carolina act follow Iowa in their most important features. No civil service board is provided for Kansas cities of the second class. In Lewiston, Ida., the mayor and council have "power to provide for the selection of agents, officers, and employees of the city under civil service rules." Comprehensive provisions are contained in the charter of Memphis. In Colorado Springs and Grand Junction, Col., and Tacoma, a civil service board of three is to serve without pay, for six-year terms in the first two, and three years in Tacoma. Muskogee, Okla., in its new charter, also provides for

MUNICIPAL CIVIL SERVICE

such a board. The tendency of recent charters seems to be toward a separate civil service board, though the inclination in this direction is not so marked as that toward "nonpartisan primaries." Most of the municipal civil service boards report annually to the council.

The following table summarizes the provisions for a municipal civil service: —

TABLE 11. CIVIL SERVICE COMMISSION (*a*)

A. *Charters*

City	Number of Commissioners	By Whom Appointed	Term (Years)	Salary	Jurisdiction (Depts.)
Texas —					
Galveston	—	—	—	—	
Houston	—	—	—	—	(*b*)
Idaho —					
Lewiston	(*c*)	—	—	—	
Tennessee —					
Memphis	3	Bd. of Com'rs (*d*)	3	$300	All appointive officers and employees (*e*)

(*a*) General provisions against appointment or removal for political reasons are not included in table.

(*b*) Charters of Texas cities usually have no provision for a civil service commission.

(*c*) Mayor and council have power to provide for selection of agents, officers, and employees of city under civil service rules.

(*d*) Removal by vote of four commissioners.

(*e*) See Sec. 34 of charter for exceptions. Employees, though appointed under civil service rules, are subject to removal by board of commissioners (or council) for cause. — See Sec. 29 of charter.

COMMISSION GOVERNMENT

TABLE II — *Continued*

A. *Charters*

CITY	NUMBER OF COMMISSIONERS	BY WHOM APPOINTED	TERM (YEARS)	SALARY	JURISDICTION (DEPTS.)
Tennessee — Chattanooga	3	Bd. of Com'rs	3	$300	(*f*)
North Carolina — Wilmington	3	Council	6	—	Fire and Police (*g*)
West Virginia — Huntington	(*h*)	—	—	—	—
Bluefield	(*h*)	—	—	—	—
Parkersburg	3	Council	—	—	Police, Fire, and Water W'ks
Oklahoma — Muskogee	3	Council	3	(*i*)	All appointees (*j*)
Colorado — Colorado Springs	3	Council	6	No	Depts. of Pub. Safety and Pub. Works and Pr'p'ty (*k*)
Grand Junction	3	City Council (*m*)	(*l*)	No	City Depts. (*n*) (*o*)

(*f*) See Charter of Chattanooga, Sec. 24, subsec. 8.
(*g*) And other employees as council may determine. — Sec. 19 (*f*).
(*h*) Board of commissioners acts as civil service board.
(*i*) "All necessary expenses of civil service commissioners" to be paid by city, and a reasonable compensation for time actually spent in official duties, may be allowed by the council, if deemed expedient. — Sec. 130.
(*j*) Except day laborers; see Secs. 134–136.
(*k*) See Sec. 149 for wording; does not seem to be limited to these two departments.
(*l*) Prescribed by ordinance.
(*m*) Removal only for cause, unless by unanimous vote of council.
(*n*) See Sec. 132. (*o*) No political test can be imposed for holding office

MUNICIPAL CIVIL SERVICE

TABLE 11 — *Continued*

A. *Charters*

City	Number of Commissioners	By Whom Appointed	Term (Years)	Salary	Jurisdiction (Depts.)
California—					
Berkeley	(*p*)	(*p*)	—	(*p*)	
Oakland	3	Mayor (*q*)	6	$10 per meeting (*r*)	City Depts. (*s*) (*p*)
Modesto	(*t*)	—	—	—	—
Vallejo	(*u*)	Council	—	(*u*)	—
Monterey	(*u*)	Council	—	(*u*)	—
Washington—					
Tacoma	3	Council (*v*)	3	No	City Depts. (*w*) (*x*)
Spokane	3	Council	6	No	All employees (*y*)
Michigan—					
Wyandotte	3	City Commission	6	No	—

(*p*) City has power to establish a civil service commission to serve without compensation.

(*q*) Confirmed by council. Removal by vote of four members of council, after public hearing. — Sec. 71.   (*r*) But not over $40 in any one month.

(*s*) See Sec. 80 of charter for employees to which provisions do not apply.

(*t*) No political test shall be imposed for holding office.

(*u*) City is authorized to establish a civil service commission, to serve without compensation. Charter, Sec. 47 (61).

(*v*) Removable for cause, by council, upon vote of four members.

(*w*) Secs. 181, 183.

(*x*) Civil service appointees may be removed by commissioner in charge of department for cause.

(*y*) Except day laborers and certain others. — See Sec. 53.

COMMISSION GOVERNMENT

TABLE 11 — *Continued*

B. *General Acts*

STATES	NUMBER OF COMMISSIONERS	BY WHOM APPOINTED	TERM (YEARS)	SALARY	JURISDICTION (DEPTS.)
Iowa	3	Council (*a*) (*b*)	6	——	Officers and employees (*c*) (*d*)
Kansas — cities of first class	3	Board of Commissioners (*b*)	4	——	Officers and employees (*e*) (*d*)
Minnesota	——	——	——	——	——
Illinois	(*f*)	——	——	——	——
South Carolina	3	City Council (*b*)	6 (*g*)	$200	Police and Fire Depts. (*h*)
Montana	3	Council	6 (*g*)	——	(*i*)

(*a*) Council shall appoint a civil service commission, in cities of 25,000 and over, and *may* appoint such a commission, in cities of less population; if no civil service commission is appointed, council shall act as such.

(*b*) Council may remove for cause, on vote of four members, any civil service commissioner.

(*c*) For detailed exceptions, see Sec. 1056–*a* 23 (*f*) of act as revised, 1909.

(*d*) Employees under civil service rules are subject to removal by council, for cause. (*e*) For exceptions, see Sec. 4.

(*f*) Cities may adopt state civil service act.

(*g*) Term of one expires every two years.

(*h*) Or any other line of service placed by city council under civil service regulations. (*i*) See Act, Sec. 25 (*f*).

Other Provisions

In many commission charters, there are sundry specific provisions which add to the effectiveness of the public control of municipal servants, but, as these are also found

MUNICIPAL CIVIL SERVICE

in the charters of other cities, they can hardly be said to be more than incidental features of the commission plan.

One of these provisions, already briefly mentioned, is that against officers or employees being interested financially in contracts for furnishing city supplies, or constructing municipal public works, or supplying municipal utilities. This applies usually not only to the commissioners, but to all subordinates and employees also. The wording of the Iowa law on the subject is specific. Wisconsin, South Dakota, and South Carolina have inserted sections to cover this point. Dallas, Fort Worth, El Paso, Denison, and many other cities prohibit such interest in contracts in the most comprehensive terms.

Other provisions, such as those relating to franchises, limit the term, insure adequate compensation to the city, reserve the right to regulate rates and to have access to accounts and records, specify the method of taxation, and provide for a referendum on franchises. The subject of franchises and the relation of the city to public utility corporations is so broad as to have already received attention in a volume devoted entirely to those topics.[1] It is sufficient to note here that the commission charters contain many of the provisions which recent progressive thought has come to regard as essential for the proper control of public utilities. Whether all these specific prohibitions and regulations are needed, in view of the broad power of control exercised by the voters over their representatives by means of the recall, referendum, and initiative, is seriously questioned by some students. Experience only will enable us to wisely de-

[1] See "Municipal Franchises" by Delos F. Wilcox, in two volumes, — a comprehensive work.

termine this. A reasonable degree of caution, however, favors retaining these provisions until they prove to be unnecessary.

Many minor points of interest occur in the charters examined, but they are not of sufficient importance to be treated here. It is sufficient to say that the public interests are safeguarded, not only in the method of adoption, specified in many charters, but by a provision for a return to the old system after a trial of three, four, or six years, upon proper preliminary petition and a majority vote in favor of abandoning the commission plan. So far, no city has shown any intention of availing itself of this opportunity.

CHAPTER XXIII

SUMMARY OF "CHECKS"; CLASSIFICATION OF COMMISSION CITIES

THE various types of commission government in cities are so numerous that their classification can be made according to any one of several different principles, the presence of one or more of the elements already noted being taken as the basis. For example, commission cities may be grouped according to the number of commissioners, though this is of minor importance; whether other officials are elective besides the commissioners (not including school or library boards), and how many; and whether the commission is wholly or only partially renewed at each election. Under the head of election at large may be considered those cities which have also nominations at large; charters requiring the entire time of commissioners may be separated from those requiring only part time; and well-paid commissioners may be contrasted with commissioners who are poorly paid. The concentration of power in the hands of the commission may be made the basis of differentiating those charters and general acts in which administrative and legislative powers are specifically granted to the board as a whole from those under which there is merely a personal union, the commissioners acting collectively in a legislative capacity, but only individually in an ad-

COMMISSION GOVERNMENT

ministrative capacity. Cities may be classified not only according to the relation of each commissioner to the commission as a whole, but also according to the relation of the mayor to the other commissioners, noting particularly the "strong-mayor type," of Houston, and considering in connection therewith whether the mayor or the board assigns the heads of departments.

Perhaps the most important classification, however, may be made on the basis of the "checks" provided. A city like Galveston has few checks — publicity, and the narrowest of referendums, that on bond issues, which is required by state law; Des Moines, under the Iowa statute, has many checks. The following table presents a résumé of the methods of popular control discussed in the previous chapters, including under the head of "Election and Nominating Provisions" the small number of the governing body ("short ballot"), election at large, and nonpartisan nominations; and confining the term "checks" to those means of control applicable *after* election. The degree of publicity, the extent to which the referendum is applicable, the percentage of signatures required for the recall, — indeed, nearly every item — differs in some respect from the corresponding provision in other charters, as has been seen; but the definite presence of the principle involved is sufficient to place it here in the columns "publicity," "referendum," etc.[1]

This table is subject to those previously presented, and is intended as a broad summary of their principal points: —

[1] See note at end of table.

SUMMARY OF "CHECKS"

TABLE 12. SUMMARY OF POPULAR CONTROL UNDER COMMISSION CHARTERS AND LAWS

A. Charters

City	Short Ballot (a)	Election at Large	Nonpartisan Primary and Election Methods	Publicity	Referendum	Initiative	Recall	Civil Service Commission
Texas —								—
Galveston	x	x	—	x	(b)	—	—	—
Houston	x	x	—	x	x	—	—	—
Dallas	x	x	(c)	x	x	x	x	—
Fort Worth	x	x	—	x	x	x	x	—
El Paso	x	x	—	x	x	—	—	—
Denison	x	x	—	x	x	—	x	—
Greenville	x	x	—	x	x	—	—	—
Austin	x	x	x	x	x	x	x	—
Waco	x	x	—	x	x	x	x	—
Palestine	x	x	—	x	x	—	x	—
Corpus Christi	x	x	—	x	x	—	x	—
Marshall	x	x	—	x	x	x	x	—
Idaho —								
Lewiston	x	x	(c)	x	x	x	x	(d)
Massachusetts —								
Haverhill	x	x	x	x	x	x	x	—
Gloucester	x	x	—	x	x	x	—	—
Lynn	x	x	x	x	x	x	x	—
Tennessee —								
Memphis	x	x	—	x	x (e)	—	—	x
Chattanooga	x	x	(c)	x	x (e)	—	x	x

(a) Election of less than 10 commissioners or councilmen.
(b) Referendum only on bond issues, under state law.
(c) Partial. See table, pp. 250–251.
(d) Mayor and council have power to provide for selection of agents, officers, and employees, under civil service rules. (e) See referendum table, p. 224.

COMMISSION GOVERNMENT

TABLE 12 — *Continued*

A. Charters

City	Short Ballot	Election at Large	Nonpartisan Primary and Election Methods	Publicity	Referendum	Initiative	Recall	Civil Service Commission
N. Carolina —								
High Point	x	x	—	x	x	—	—	—
Wilmington	x	x	x	x	x	x	x	x
W. Virginia —								
Huntington	x	x	(*f*)	x	(*g*)	—	(*g*)	(*h*)
Bluefield	x	x	(*f*)	x	(*g*)	—	(*g*)	(*h*)
Parkersburg	x	x	x	x	x	x	x	x
Oklahoma —								
Ardmore	x	x	(*j*)	x	x(*i*)	x(*i*)	x	—
Enid	x	x	(*j*)	x	x	x	x	—
Tulsa	x	x	(*k*)	x	x	x	x	—
McAlester	x	x	(*j*)	x	x	x	x	—
Muskogee	x	x	(*j*)	x	x	x	x	x
Bartlesville	x	x	(*j*)	x	x	x	x	—
Sapulpa	x	x	x	x	x	x	x	—
Duncan	x	x	(*j*)	x	x	x	x	—
Guthrie	x	x	x	x	x	x	x	—
Colorado —								
Col. Springs	x	x	x	x	x	x	x	x
Grand Jct.	x	x	(*l*)	x	x	x	x	x

(*f*) Unusual provisions, as previously noted. See p. 249.
(*g*) Exercised by citizens' board. See p. 239.
(*h*) Board of commissioners acts as civil service board.
(*i*) Provisions for referendum and initiative are contained in Oklahoma constitution. (*k*) Partial. See table, p. 252.
(*j*) No provision in charter. May have either partisan or nonpartisan primaries, in accordance with state constitution. (*l*) Preferential ballot.

SUMMARY OF "CHECKS"

TABLE 12 — *Continued*

A. *Charters*

CITY	ELECTION AND NOMINATING PROVISIONS			"CHECKS" AFTER TAKING OFFICE				
	Short Ballot	Election at Large	Nonpartisan Primary and Election Methods	Publicity	Referendum	Initiative	Recall	Civil Service Commission
California —								
Berkeley	x	x	x	x	x	x	x	x
San Diego	x	x	x	x	x	x	x	—
Oakland	x	x	x	x	x	x	x	x
Modesto	x	x	x	x	x	x	x	—
San Luis Obispo	x	x	x	x	x	x	x	—
Santa Cruz	x	x	x	x	x	x	x	—
Vallejo	x	x	x	x	x	x	x	(*m*)
Monterey	x	x	x	x	x	x	x	(*m*)
Washington —								
Tacoma	x	x	x	x	x	x	x	x
Spokane	x	x	(*n*)	x	x	x	x	x
Oregon —								
Baker	x	x	x (*o*)	x	x (*p*)	x (*p*)	x (*p*)	—
Minnesota —								
Mankato	x	x	x	x	x	x	x	—
Maryland —								
Cumberland	x	x	x	x	—	—	—	—
Michigan —								
Port Huron	x	x	x	x	x	x	—	—
Pontiac	x	x	x	x	x	x	x	—
Harbor Beach	x	x	x	x	x	x	—	—
Wyandotte	x	x	x	x	x	x	x	x

(*m*) Council may establish civil service commission.
(*n*) Preferential ballot.
(*o*) No primary proper. See table and note, p. 253.
(*p*) State laws apply, permitting referendum, initiative, and recall.

COMMISSION GOVERNMENT

TABLE 12 — *Continued*
B. *General Acts*

STATE	Short Ballot (a)	Election at Large	Nonpartisan Primary and Election Methods	Publicity	Referendum	Initiative	Recall	Civil Service Commission
Iowa	x	x	x	x	x	x	x	x
Kansas — cities of first class	x	x	x	x	x	x	x	x
Kansas — cities of second class	x	x (b)	x (c)	x	x	x	—	—
South Dakota	x	x	x	x	x	x	x	—
North Dakota	x	x	—	x	x	x	x	—
Wisconsin	x	x	x	x	x	—	—	—
Minnesota	x	x	x	x	x (d)	x (d)	x (d)	—
Illinois	x	x	x	x	x	x	x	x (e)
New Mexico	x	x		(b)	x	—	—	—
Mississippi	x	x		x	x	—	—	—
Kentucky	x	x	x	x	x	x	—	—
Louisiana	x	x (b)	—	x	x	x	x	—
South Carolina	x	x (b)	(f)	x	x	x	x	x
Texas	x	x	—	x	(g)	—	—	—
Alabama — cities of 100,000 or over	x	x	x	x	x	—	x	—
Alabama — cities of 25–50,000	x	x	x			—	x	—
Alabama (general)	x	x	—	x	x	—	x	—
California (i)	x	x	(h)	x	x (j)	x (j)	x (j)	—

(a) Less than 10 commissioners or councilmen elected.
(b) In practice, but not specified in commission law.
(c) Does not apply to cities of less than 10,000 population.
(d) City may provide for this feature in charter.
(e) City may adopt state civil service laws.
(f) Partial; unusual provision. See table and note, p. 255.
(g) Referendum only on bond issues, under state laws.
(h) Preferential ballot.   (i) Applies to cities of fifth and sixth classes.
(j) Separate act permits referendum, initiative, and recall.

SUMMARY OF "CHECKS"

TABLE 12 — *Continued*

B. *General Acts*

STATE	Short Ballot	Election at Large	Nonpartisan Primary and Election Methods	Publicity	Referendum	Initiative	Recall	Civil Service Commission
	\multicolumn{3}{} Election and Nominating Provisions		"Checks" after taking Office				
Idaho	x	x	x	x	—	x	x	—
Montana	x	x	x	x	x	x	x	x
New Jersey	x	x	x	x	x	x	x	—
Utah	x	x	—	x	—	—	—	—
Washington	x	x	x	x	x	x	x	—
Wyoming	x	x	x	x	x	x	x	—

NOTE. In this summary table, in the column headed "Referendum," an x has been placed opposite each city or state making provision for either a referendum on all ordinances, or a referendum on franchises. Houston, for example, since it provides for a referendum on franchises — a most important sort of referendum — is here credited in the referendum column.

It will be observed that all of the charters and laws contain provisions for the election of a small board, at large, and for publicity features; nearly all of them, for some sort of referendum, and most of them for the recall and initiative. A great number employ nonpartisan primary and election features, while a dozen special charters and at least five state laws add a separate civil service board.

Cities with "few checks" — that is, which have neither initiative, recall, civil service commission, nor nonpartisan primary — are Galveston, Houston, Greenville, El Paso,

High Point, and those operating under the acts of New Mexico, Utah, Mississippi, and Texas. Memphis just escapes inclusion in this list by virtue of her civil service commission, while in the state of Wisconsin, usually so advanced in matters political, a nonpartisan primary and election provision was the one feature which raised its statute to the middle class of commission forms, until the inclusion of the recall and other checks by the legislature, in 1911. Cities with all the checks are Colorado Springs and Grand Junction, Berkeley, Oakland, Tacoma, Spokane, and others, and the cities operating under the general laws of Iowa, Kansas (cities of the first class), Montana, and Illinois, the last named permitting cities to adopt the provisions of the state civil service law. Between these two classes — some twenty cities with "few checks," and over forty with "all checks" — lies a numerous class, which include those with *many* controlling devices, but not all. It is sufficient at this time to roughly group the commission forms, upon this basis.

Which of these "checks" is most important and therefore most necessary of inclusion in a city charter is a question difficult to answer, because there is no means of determining the value of each safeguard separately with any degree of exactness. Publicity features are certainly indispensable, for the public must know what ordinances are passed and what is the condition of the city in its many departments, in order to intelligently use any of the other safety devices. The referendum and initiative naturally go together; and while the former is likely to be more frequently employed, the experience of Oregon shows that in state

SUMMARY OF "CHECKS"

affairs, at least, the latter will not be unused. The two together constitute a unit, permitting a constant control of legislation. The recall is of no less value for its continuing control of legislators, — the city commissioners, in a municipality. Nonpartisan primary and election features seem to be clearly helpful, and there is at present demand for a municipal civil service in connection with the other provisions. It will be impossible to determine the relative importance of these controlling levers, most of which are clearly in the nature of improvements, until after a longer period of trial has supplied more data.

The broader question as to what element of the five noted as fundamental parts of the commission form is most essential and the cause of the great improvement in governmental efficiency, is of much greater import. It is even more difficult to answer. Is it more important to give the governing body adequate power, or to hold it strictly accountable to the will of the people? How can these elements be separated? Are they not the two sides of the shield? Must not power and responsibility go together? The great fault of the aldermanic system is not only that adequate means for holding councilmen responsible to their constituents are not provided, but that not enough power is given to the council to enable it to direct the city's activities effectively. These two principles, inseparably connected, and each to be given its proper weight, lie at the bottom of all well-conducted collective enterprises, corporate or governmental. The commission form recognizes, first, the need of authority reasonably centralized, and hence gives the council administrative and appointing, as well as legislative, power; and second, provides means of popular control which are numerous and direct, compelling publicity of council proceedings; means of referring all ordinances, including franchises, to the people; of bringing a public servant up sharply for a vote of confidence or lack of confidence; of eliminating national politics from municipal elections; of insuring a system of appointment for merit among employees and assistants. Both the "short ballot" and election-at-large are safeguards in the system applied prior to election, and hence rather fundamental in determining the conditions under which officials are chosen; yet they are not sufficient. Control must be adequate *after* election, and the more numerous and direct the means of control, the less likelihood that there will be need to use them. One other important element of control must not be lost sight of, — closely connected, indeed, with the exercise of administrative power by the commission, — and that is the division of duties among the commissioners. The simple and effective method of putting one commissioner in charge of each department at once conveniently subdivides the work and localizes responsibility. In each department, employees and assistants and chiefs are accountable to the commissioner; the commissioner is, in turn, chargeable to the entire board for his department; and both single commissioners and the board as a whole are answerable to the people for the proper conduct of all the city's affairs. There is no break in the chain of responsibility. There is enough power; it is definitely located; it is simply organized; it is linked with means of enforcing accountability. The similarity to the business corporation is marked.

SUMMARY OF "CHECKS"

The same chain of responsibility was there successfully worked out long ago. American business is contributing perhaps its best element, its effective form of organization, its excellent machinery for collective action, to aid in solving the problems of city government. In place of careful attention to cutting down operating expenses and increasing receipts, in order to yield resulting profits, there is substituted careful attention to cutting down operating expenses and increasing public revenue (aside from taxes), for the general benefit. The same means are used in both instances, but for different ends. The city will probably never push the rate of wages down to the limit sometimes forced by private business; but the same care may be exercised and similar energy to secure a reasonable return for service rendered; and similar correct principles of organization may be followed. Of no less value because first inaugurated to meet a crisis, not necessarily less substantial because adopted rapidly, the commission form seems to be the first earnest attempt to apply to governmental conditions the successful experience of the corporation. The American citizen appears to believe so thoroughly in commission government for cities, not because the governing body is called a commission, nor because the plan is new; but because he is thoroughly familiar with its main principles as employed in business. In those cities where it has been tried, its introduction has been followed by sufficient financial, engineering, moral, and general civic improvement to convince him that the application of these principles to the management of municipal affairs is likely to yield better results than heretofore secured under the aldermanic form.

CHAPTER XXIV

UNUSUAL AND PARTIAL FORMS OF COMMISSION GOVERNMENT

Among the cities included in some of the earlier lists of those which have the commission form are several of peculiar and unusual types, and others in which one or more fundamental elements are lacking. Both should be briefly described, in order to more fully realize what commission government means, and to afford information concerning the cities in question.

Washington, D.C., and Chelsea, Mass., have uncommon types of government, the former being the national capital, and to some extent different from other cities; the latter having an emergency control instituted immediately after its disastrous fire in 1908. Washington is governed by three commissioners, who are appointed by the President, with the consent of the Senate, — one commissioner a Republican, one a Democrat, and one an army engineer. In many matters the national Congress acts as a municipal council, and certain days are set aside for the consideration of bills relating to the District of Columbia. The inhabitants of Washington have no vote; they do not elect their commissioners; they have no direct voice in the management of municipal affairs. For this reason the city government of Washington is not comparable with that of other municipalities.

UNUSUAL AND PARTIAL FORMS

The features already observed to be characteristic of commission governments, in Texas, Iowa, Kansas, California, and elsewhere, do not apply; there is no election of a small governing body, no election at large, no initiative nor referendum nor recall. These all depend upon the possession of the right to vote, locally. Ordinance power remains largely in the hands of the national Senate and House of Representatives. Only limited legislative authority and narrow administrative and appointing power is exercised by the commissioners. The inclusion of the national capital in the list of commission cities is therefore not of much significance to the average American city, since the sort of commission form in use here is not at all similar to that likely to be adopted elsewhere.

Chelsea has a Board of Control, consisting of five members, appointed by the governor, with the consent of the council, and their compensation fixed by the governor. They were given the powers of mayor and aldermen, — broad and comprehensive authority, including the right to establish departments and appoint the officers thereof. In 1911, however, the people are to elect a mayor and aldermen once more, who will act, subject to the veto of the Board of Control, until 1913, when the people may vote on the continuation of the Board of Control. If they vote favorably, the governor is to appoint a new board of three members, which will exercise a veto power, as in 1911 and 1912, evidently leaving the mayor and aldermen as the governing body, their acts subject to the approval of the Board of Control.

It is at once seen that this is no ordinary commission form. It is an appointed emergency board, and may or may not be included in the list of commission cities, as the reader prefers. The reason why it is not here placed in the list is because it is, like the city of Washington, outside the usual type and not serviceable as a model for the average municipality.

Commission Government Defined

Of partial commission forms there are many. The definition of commission government here accepted, based on the common features *actually present* in the great majority of so-called commission cities, is that form of city government in which (1) substantially the entire municipal authority — executive and legislative — is exercised (2) by a commission or small council, elected (3) at large, (4) simply organized by placing each member in charge of a definite field of municipal activity; and the acts of the commissioners being subject to (5) ample control by the voters through publicity provisions, referendum, initiative, recall, or other "checks." The phrase, "substantially the entire municipal authority," is here interpreted broadly to admit those cities in which the main civic power is unquestionably lodged in a small board, but in which, also, one or more relatively unimportant city officers are elected as in El Paso or Tacoma. The commission has never more than ten members, and usually not over five. Cities are included where the first commissioners were appointed by the governor, provided they are thereafter to be elected and the form is otherwise of the usual commission type. Election-at-large may include, as it does in most cases, nomination at large — that is, by *all* the voters, from any section of the city, or it may be associated with nomina-

UNUSUAL AND PARTIAL FORMS

tion by all the voters *from* certain wards. The method of organization may be that in which every commissioner is designated as head of a specific department, or the mayor may have only general oversight without a separate department assigned to him; and the mayor may possess more power than the other commissioners, less power, or have about equal authority. The presence in a charter or general act of *one or more* of the "checks" referred to, is regarded as sufficient to fulfill the fifth requirement, though, as already seen, there are usually several such "checks." This definition, broad and yet specific, is seen to include Galveston, Houston, Des Moines, and nearly all of the cities to which the term "commission governed" has been applied.

It was inevitable that in time the term should be used loosely in the case of charters known to contain only a few commission features — provision for election at large, for example, or a small council, or the referendum, or recall. It has been recognized, however, by these very cities that such a charter should not be so classed, and their officials have pointed out the features lacking. Those charters have been excluded, therefore, which distribute authority widely among several boards or between two chambers of a council or which do not clearly center both administrative and executive powers in one small body. Cities have been excluded in which the commission or council has more than ten members; in which the members are elected by wards; in which a rather definite division of labor does not exist among the members of the board; and in which there are not provided at least one of the methods of direct control referred to.

COMMISSION GOVERNMENT

For example, Riverside, Cal., has the referendum and recall, but ward councilmen, many elected officers, including mayor, city clerk, and assessor, auditor and city treasurer and tax collector, and many administrative boards, including a department of public utilities consisting of five commissioners appointed by the mayor, a board of health of five members, a board of park commissioners, and others. Santa Cruz, Santa Monica, and Long Beach, Cal., have somewhat similar charters, the latter adding a civil service commission as well as the other checks. Alameda, Cal., has a mayor and a council of nine members, all elected at large, but seven nominated by wards (and two nominated at large); a board in charge of each department, instead of single heads; and recall, initiative, and referendum. The California constitution permits cities of over 3500 population to frame their own charters, and the charters so adopted offer opportunity for many interesting studies not here possible. Among the cities which have the initiative, referendum, and recall are Santa Barbara, Palo Alto, Richmond, and others. Oakland, however, Santa Cruz, Vallejo, and other cities have recently framed new charters providing for the full commission plan.

Temple, Tex., has ward aldermen, and the council does not possess administrative oversight; but in many other respects its charter resembles that of Houston. Beaumont, Tex., has an aldermanic form of government, but provides for the referendum and initiative. St. Joseph, Mo., which appears at first sight to have the commission form, proves, upon examination, only to be operating under a new state law, which, applying to cities of between 75,000 and 150,000, provides for a small council (five), elected at large, includes the initiative, referendum, and recall, and permits some officials to be appointed by the mayor, some to be elected, and administrative power to be widely distributed among several boards, members of the council not being heads of departments. The mayor retains the veto power.

At least five cities in Tennessee have been included, at various times, in the list of commission cities, — Bristol, Clarksville, Richmond City, Ashland City, and Etowah. While these have certain commission features, they retain the council committees and, so far as ascertained, do not concentrate administrative power in the council.

San Antonio, Tex., has been included in some lists by mistake; the effort to secure a commission plan there has not yet been successful. Many cities, however, which voted at first in the negative, later adopted a commission by a good majority. Among such cities are the following : —

City	Date Rejected Plan	Date Adopted Plan
Kansas City, Kan.	June, 1908	July, 1909
Sapulpa, Okla.	——, 1909	——, 1910
Oklahoma City, Okla.	Defeated three times	March 9, 1911
Guthrie, Okla.	1908; April 5, 1910	Jan. 30, 1911
Mankato, Minn.	September 27, 1909	May, 1910.
Sioux City, Ia.	January 21, 1908	February 15, 1910
Sioux Falls, S. D.	November 5, 1907 (a)	Sept'ber 29, 1908 (b)

(a) Vote, 549—579.   (b) Vote, 857—353.

Boise, Ida., has a board of five, known as mayor and common council, elected "on a general ticket," but the councilmen are not heads of departments and do not seem to exercise administrative authority or appointing power, to any considerable extent. The mayor appoints and may remove all the heads of departments and all officers and employees, except city clerk and city magistrate, but he is required to give due consideration to the recommendations of the heads of departments in regard to positions requiring special qualifications. The heads of departments, however, may employ and remove laborers in their respective departments, subject to the approval of the mayor. There are no checks provided, except a referendum on bond issues, certain publicity provisions, and no party designation allowed on the election ballot. Nominations are to be by a convention attended or called by at least fifty qualified electors. Each candidate must be voted for at election by a cross placed opposite his name, the voting of a whole ticket by the use of one cross mark being specifically prohibited.

The new charter of Boston provides for a mayor and a city council of nine, elected at large, for a term of three years, three members being elected annually. The mayor holds office for four years, and may be recalled after two years. The mayor and council are recognized as distinct and separate authorities, as under the old aldermanic charters, and the members of the council are not heads of departments. This charter, therefore, cannot be properly included in the list of commission cities.

Taunton, Mass., under a special charter adopted Nov. 2, 1909, has a mayor and municipal council of nine. While approaching the commission type, this charter fails to constitute the councilmen as heads of depart-

UNUSUAL AND PARTIAL FORMS

ments; and they do not appear to exercise both administrative and legislative functions.

Several other cities have quasi-commission charters.

Cities Rejecting the Plan

A list of the cities which have voted against the commission plan, and have not yet reconsidered their votes, so far as ascertained, are as follows: —

CITIES WHICH HAVE VOTED AGAINST THE COMMISSION FORM

City	Date of Vote
Portland, Ore.	May, 1909
Auburn, Me.	September, 1909
Arkansas City, Kan.	1909
Orange, Tex.	December, 1909
El Dorado, Kan.	March, 1910
Fort Scott, Kan.	February, 1910
Hiawatha, Kan.	February, 1910
Winfield, Kan.	1910
Janesville, Wis.	January, 1910
Pueblo, Col.	February, 1910
Watertown, S. Dak.	February, 1910
Mitchell, S. Dak.	March, 1910
Spearfish, S. Dak.	March, 1910
Grand Forks, N. Dak.	March, 1910
Fargo, N. Dak.	July 22, 1910
Gulfport, Miss.	March 15, 1910
Biloxi, Miss.	Twice; last time in June, 1910
Cuero, Tex.	April, 1910
Durant, Okla.	October 25, 1910
Boulder, Col.	November 8, 1910
Lexington, Ky.	November, 1910
Bellingham, Wash.	December, 1910
Chickasha, Okla.	December 15, 1910
San Antonio, Tex.	February, 1911
Rockford, Ill.	January, 1911

COMMISSION GOVERNMENT

CITIES WHICH HAVE VOTED AGAINST THE COMMISSION FORM — *Continued*

CITY	DATE OF VOTE
Monmouth, Ill.	January, 1911
Champaign, Ill.	January 18, 1911
Joliet, Ill.	January 15, 1911
Galesburg, Ill.	February 7, 1911
Virginia, Ill.	February 20, 1911
Danville, Ill.	February, 1911
Quincy, Ill.	January 24, 1911
Sullivan, Ill.	February 14, 1911
Taylorville, Ill.	February 17, 1911
Peoria, Ill.	February 28, 1911
Greenville, Ill.	February 28, 1911
Havana, Ill.	March 1, 1911
Woodward, Okla.	March 2, 1911
Highland Park, Mich.	March 13, 1911
Paolo, Kan.	March 21, 1911
Ottawa, Kan.	March 22, 1911
Raleigh, N.C.	March, 1911
Asheville, N.C.	March 21, 1911
Winston-Salem, N.C.	April, 1911
Cameron, Tex.	April, 1911
Taylor, Tex.	April 2, 1911
Temple, Tex.	April 10, 1911
Salina, Kan.	April 4, 1911
Altus, Okla.	April 20, 1911
Norwich, Conn.	June 5, 1911
Kingsville, Tex.	June, 1911
Bayonne, N. J.	June 13, 1911
Hoboken, N. J.	June, 1911
Lansing, Mich.	June 19, 1911
Jersey City, N. J.	July 18, 1911 (*a*)
Fort Madison, Ia.	July 21, 1911

(*a*) Vote, 11,505 "for," 13,068 "against." About 30 per cent of total vote is said to have been cast.

CHAPTER XXV

LIMITATIONS OF THE COMMISSION FORM

THAT the operation of the commission form of municipal government has been accompanied by distinctly favorable results where adopted has led to many extravagant claims for it. It is asserted that once the Galveston or Des Moines plan is adopted by a municipality, the battle for efficient government is won; that no further attention is necessary from the mass of voters; and that the danger of extravagance or carelessness, of laxity in law enforcement, and of corruption, is practically removed. Such an attitude comes from a failure to estimate accurately the value of the commission system and leads to over-confidence. This attitude, if generally assumed, must evidently result in the return of the same evil conditions many of which it has abolished. A review of the elements of the new form reveals wherein lies its strength and what are its limitations.

The central principle of the commission plan — that of placing in the hands of a single small body legislative authority and administrative control — concentrates both power and responsibility, and when reasonably capable men are elected, greatly increases the efficiency of municipal government. If bad men be chosen, such concentrated power enables them to do possibly more damage than under the present council system, unless subject to easily exercised and effective "checks." Herein lies the value of the referendum, recall, and other methods of public control.

The assignment of each commissioner or councilman to a given department fixes his responsibility for that department. In most cities it is known before election who is to head each department of the city's work, even where not so provided under the charter. The commission plan changes *ward* representation to departmental representation, if such a phrase be permissible — a definite field of municipal work for each commissioner. For street repairs, go to Commissioner A; for water works extensions or more electric lights, see Commissioner B, etc. The primary interest of each alderman at present is to look after the *many* interests of his ward — its water, lights, sewers, police protection, and sidewalks. Under the commission plan, the commissioner is elected by all the city to look after one division or class of its work. The commission plan substitutes for ward representation and an unsatisfactory general oversight of all municipal affairs, because based on a loose supervision of particular departments by council committees, representation of the entire city and close oversight of all the city's business, partly by virtue of the control of a *particular section of the business*, by each commissioner.

Under the commission plan, the governing body is small. This results in centering attention upon a few officials, and the selection of better and abler men. An increase in the degree of public scrutiny of councilmen promotes, but it does not necessarily *assure*, the election

LIMITATIONS OF COMMISSION FORM

of competent officials. Should the electors put dishonest men into office, the board could and probably would wield its large power to the detriment of the public interest.

Election at large does not preclude the choice of incompetent or venal men. It only decreases the chance of their being nominated or elected.

The "checks" provided supply only opportunities to control. *Methods of publicity* inform the voters; the *referendum* permits them to decide questions of municipal policy, but it does not insure a right decision. The *initiative* permits the people to originate needed measures, and afterward vote upon them. Whether or not wise measures are adopted depends upon the character of the electorate. The whole principle of democracy, however, is, that the people should rule; and this is what they have an opportunity to do under the commission plan. The *recall* permits the retirement of a bad official before his term of office has expired, and the substitution of another. Whether or not the recall will be used against good men can only be determined after longer experience. So far it has not thus been employed.

The commission plan enables the citizens to select better men, clothes the council with more power than under the aldermanic system, organizes the government more simply and definitely, and provides more effective popular control. To claim more than this would seem to be going too far. The commission form does not insure good government; it merely makes it easier to obtain. It does not supply character to the voters, nor capacity and honesty to officials. The same need exists as formerly for an intelligent consideration of public questions by a citizenship forceful and courageous in using the means of control provided. It supplies one of the elements requisite for good government — the *form* of government, the machinery. The other element must be supplied by the voters and by the men whom they choose. No governmental method or system can reasonably be expected to do more.

The excellent financial results which have been secured seem clearly to be due to the definite location of responsibility in one board and usually in one commissioner, and adequate provisions for publicity. If dishonest or careless men are elected, extravagance and corruption are almost sure to result.

In the field of public health, provisions for adequate sewerage disposal and the enforcement of rules as to contagious diseases have produced excellent results in many of the cities noted; but here again, we have the equation — " system plus men equals results " — and, while the system is vastly improved, no one should forget the other half. A vigorous doctor or business man in charge of the city's health, backed by a strong sentiment for clean alleys, garbage disposal, enforcement of quarantine regulations, pure water, and no slums, will improve conditions wonderfully.

Finances, streets, health, morals, education, civic beauty, — in all these fields the commission form means opportunity to accomplish, but does not insure results. These must depend upon the men who compose the governmental and civic units called municipalities.

Does the commission plan abolish partisanship? It seems to have largely eliminated national party politics from local elections, but not municipal politics. The experience of Des Moines, Cedar Rapids, and Galveston, and almost every commission city is to this effect. Des Moines turned down at the first election under the commission plan a ticket presumably excellent, since it was selected by a committee of business men, but stigmatized as a "slate," and chose as commissioners a well-known ex-mayor, a popular local judge, two union labor men, and a former assessor. Local politics served to defeat for reelection the first police and fire commissioner of that city, who had given an excellent administration of the affairs of his department, but who, in the vigorous enforcement of law, had incurred the enmity of the "liberal" element, in addition to certain personal opposition. Men previously officeholders have been elected as commissioners in Cedar Rapids, Houston, Huntington, and elsewhere. Personal popularity is still an asset; local men and issues remain. "Parties will be formed and partisanship aroused," says Mr. Horace E. Deming, "to give expression and effect to . . . prevailing opinion."[1] While the elimination of national politics from city elections is an achievement of great value, there will continue to be differences as to officials and as to questions of municipal policy.

Will the commission form abolish saloons, gambling, and the social evil? To this question, of interest to a constantly increasing element of our people, the answer must be "not necessarily." But the reasonably rigid enforcement of law is easier under the commission plan because officials can be effectively controlled by public opinion; and the great improvement in this field in nearly

[1] "Government of American cities," p. 116.

all of the commission cities indicates that the better citizens have more influence under the new plan than under the old. But if public opinion actively desires those institutions, or does not want them suppressed, or is indifferent, they will remain. The question comes back again to the character of citizenship and of the officials elected. "Ours is a government of laws, but ... no law is worth anything unless there is the right kind of a man behind it."[1] A vigorous police commissioner may secure marked reforms, as in Des Moines; or an active chamber of commerce or city club may so effectively represent a large element of the community as to compel action by weak commissioners and strengthen the hands of strong ones. This is a most hopeful feature of the situation; but the plan will not run itself. It takes active public opinion to secure results. "One of the primary tests of efficient municipal organization," says Professor Rowe, "is the extent to which such organization not only develops, but demands the alertness and watchfulness of the people."[2]

A great increase of interest in municipal affairs on the part of citizens is reported from every commission city. Part of this is due undoubtedly to the novelty of the plan; but much is accounted for by the general belief that the voters have now a *chance* to secure democratic government. A few men to elect possessing substantially equal power and all the power — how easy to understand! Each commissioner head of a department — how definite the division of responsibility! Compre-

[1] Theodore Roosevelt, in the *Outlook*, Jan. 21, 1911.
[2] L. S. Rowe, "Problems of City Government," p. 51.

LIMITATIONS OF COMMISSION FORM

hension of the simple form of organization and the effective means of control provided in the referendum, recall, and initiative, is followed by renewed confidence that good municipal government can be attained. Public spirit is aroused and civic effort is stimulated by a returning faith in democracy.

In Large Cities

Is the commission form applicable to large cities? Will the same principles which have been successful in managing municipal affairs for cities of less than 100,000 prove adequate for those of half a million or a million population, or more — for New York or Chicago or Philadelphia or Boston?

The commission cities which have more than 100,000 population are Memphis (131,000), Oakland (125,000), Spokane (104,000), and Birmingham, Ala. (132,000). Pittsburg, Pa. (553,000), and Boston, as already noted, have certain features of the commission plan,[1] particularly a council of nine members. Of these, only Memphis has had the plan in operation for a year or more. Dallas with 92,000, Houston with 78,000, and Des Moines with 86,000 are typical cities of slightly less population. While it will not be possible to determine definitely how far the commission plan can be applied to the larger cities until it has actually been in operation for a time in several, the marked improvement in governmental efficiency in all the cities, large and small, in which the plan has yet been tried raises a strong presumption in favor of a similar improvement in the larger centers. While different problems confront cities of different size,

[1] See p. 288.

COMMISSION GOVERNMENT

are not the *principles of administration* essentially similar for all? Is the large private corporation not managed on lines approximately the same as the smaller ones? May not differences in civic needs be met by certain modifications necessary to suit size or local conditions, as already seen in a number of new municipal charters? These are questions which suggest themselves to those who wonder whether the commission form will succeed in large cities.

CHAPTER XXVI

OBJECTIONS TO COMMISSION GOVERNMENT

THE objections which have been urged to the commission form are numerous, coming from both interested and disinterested conservatives. Rarely has there been any question raised as to the facts in individual cities; but the interpretation of the facts as well as the correctness of the principles involved have been vigorously contested.

Commission Cities not Typical

That the cities in which the plan has been tried and proved successful are not typical American municipalities, was one of the first objections raised; but it has not been urged since the new form has spread to cities of all sections and varying sizes. Texas, Massachusetts, Wisconsin, California, Tennessee, Washington, are represented. Seaports like Galveston and Tacoma, containing a large floating population; centers of mixed farming and manufacturing interests, such as Cedar Rapids, Des Moines, Dallas, Eau Claire (Wis.), and Huntington (W. Va.); river ports, as Memphis, Burlington, Keokuk; more purely agricultural communities, as are many of the cities of Oklahoma, Kansas, and the Dakotas; manufacturing centers like Haverhill and Lynn, — all are represented among the number of commission cities. Memphis, Oakland, and Spokane have a population of over 100,000 each; there are some thirty cities of between 25,000 and 100,000 population; while Texas, Kansas, and Oklahoma contain more than 20 commission cities of less than 5000 population each. With the adoption of the system by cities of the size of Pittsburg (Pa.), and Buffalo,[1] N.Y., we shall have an opportunity to test the argument, already noted, that this form of organization is not applicable to the government of large cities.

Too Brief a Trial

That the form has had too short a trial to justify any general statement as to its success or permanent value is an objection of weight and requires examination. Of the cities which are now governed by commissions (or small councils), one (Galveston) has had the plan in effect for about ten years — since September, 1901; another (Houston) six years — since July 5, 1905; Dallas, Fort Worth, Denison, Greenville, and Lewiston, Ida., since 1907; Des Moines, Cedar Rapids, and Leavenworth, since 1908; and a considerable group of cities — six in Texas, five in Kansas, three in Oklahoma, one in South Dakota, two in North Dakota, two in Massachusetts, two in Colorado, two in California, two in West Virginia, and one in North Carolina, beginning in 1909. Twenty-six cities have therefore had approximately two years' use of the plan; three have had three years' experience; five, four years; one, six years; and one, ten years' experience — thirty-six in all.

In the city which has had the commission plan the longest, which is confronted on account of its location

[1] Bill pending before legislature, June, 1911.

OBJECTIONS

and large shipping interests with many of the problems common to places of much greater population, there is no indication that the new broom sweeps any the less clean now than at first. "It is a different kind of broom," said a citizen — "an improved vacuum cleaner." The continued reëlection of the same commission would indicate satisfaction with the plan in actual operation. Houston seems to be solving its municipal problems no less successfully than at the beginning. While it is to be expected that some decrease in active public attention will occur after the novelty and first interest wear off, such interest seems to have remained to an unusual degree. While it is always difficult to determine the answer to such a problem with certainty except by time and the sifting of a great mass of facts thoroughly, no marked decrease in municipal efficiency — but rather an increase, as added experience gives confidence to the commissioners — is manifest in Cedar Rapids, Dallas, Fort Worth, Lewiston, and elsewhere. While it is too soon to say how the commission plan will work in all cities, the results so far attained and the presumption they raise as to its efficiency elsewhere should be frankly recognized.

Too much Power in a Few Hands

The strongest arguments advanced against the commission plan have been aimed at some one of the fundamental features noted. Election at large rather than by wards has been generally commended; but the large powers granted to the small board, and the "checks" provided, particularly the referendum and the recall, have been vigorously attacked by opponents of the new

COMMISSION GOVERNMENT

form. It is argued that it is dangerous to popular government to put into the hands of a small group of men the large powers granted to them under most commission charters; that it creates an oligarchy which cannot be controlled by the citizens; and that it tends to upbuild an irresistible political machine. The referendum and the recall have also been attacked as untried experiments, and incompatible with stable government, since "the violence of political sentiment and preference for municipal offices" would lead to anarchy. On the other hand, the mayor of Riverside argues that without these checks, particularly the recall, such concentration of power is dangerous.

It cannot be denied that the small elective commission is given large authority, which must be subject to adequate control; and the question seems to turn upon the opinion held of the sufficiency of the referendum, the recall, and other "checks." Accountability must be coupled with authority, and the two considered together. Galveston, for example, with no checks except publicity and its influential though unofficial City Club, might well hesitate to grant municipal authority to five commissioners unless it had great confidence in the competence and character of those commissioners. The argument against the bestowal of extensive power without corresponding means of holding responsible the wielders of such power, seems entirely reasonable; but there is a conflict between the objection that the commission system grants too great power, and the other objection sometimes urged that too many checks are provided. A close analysis of these objections reveals the belief, either that a *larger* body is more representative as a

OBJECTIONS

municipal governing board, or that the people are not safely to be trusted with control such as is provided by the recall and the referendum. Both of these positions have already been considered in the chapters on "Election at Large" and the "Checks" provided.

Constitutionality

Another argument, forcefully urged against one of the central ideas of the commission plan, was presented in the case of Eckerson *vs.* the city of Des Moines, and was carried to the supreme court of Iowa. In brief, it is that the commission form violates the constitution, in that it is not a republican, that is, a representative, form of government, — since it combines the legislative and administrative functions in the same body. But the supreme court held that the new form *is* representative, since the commissioners are elective; and that in any event the legislature of the state has the power to grant cities the right to have both legislative and executive functions exercised by the same body.[1]

[1] Additional decisions affirming the constitutionality of various charters and acts, and one (that of Texas) denying the constitutionality of certain features, such as referendum and recall, have appeared since the above was written, but demand consideration at greater length than is here possible.

CHAPTER XXVII

CONCLUSION

THE beginning of the commission idea has been described, its spread traced from Texas north and later east and west, and the results of its operations considered in the several sections. We have seen that Galveston supplied the main idea, that of a small board of directors with large powers, each member head of an administrative department; that the *election* of all the members of the board was forced by a court decision, election at large being the method adopted; that Houston modified the form by adding a referendum on franchises, and greatly enlarging the power of the mayor-commissioner; that Des Moines increased the number and efficiency of the methods of popular control by broadening the referendum to include all ordinances, adding the initiative, recall, a nonpartisan ballot, and a civil service commission, besides minor provisions. Des Moines followed Galveston rather than Houston in the main outline of its commission plan, and the "strong mayor" type is found principally in Texas. Kansas and other states and cities adopted the salient features of the small board plan, adding most of the important "checks." Grand Junction, Spokane, and a general act in Alabama have included a preferential ballot as a desirable improvement. A wide variety of

CONCLUSION

charters and statutes thus exist, but possessing the same essential elements, as disclosed by analysis.

Which of these elements is most important is a matter of opinion; but their joint presence in the commission types has been attended with most favorable results. There has been a long enough period of trial to indicate the success of the plan in cities of less than 100,000, and to raise a strong presumption that the application of the same principles in larger cities will greatly improve present conditions. The essential similarity of structure of municipal and private corporations argues toward the same conclusion.

The wide adoption of the commission form indicates that important changes are taking place in the political beliefs of the American people. In the first place, it reveals an altered conception of representation; a small governing body is accepted, so far as the city is concerned, as being as truly representative as one of large membership — more representative, in fact, because more easily held accountable to public opinion. It is recognized that the city is a unit, and that election by wards has led in the past to an overemphasis of the parts, to the neglect of the interests of the whole. Very important is the clear acknowledgment that at least, in the municipality, legislative power and close administrative oversight may well be exercised by the same governing body, — that the "separation of powers" is not so necessary as the location of responsibility. In this respect, the commission plan marks the emphasis of principles of business organization in the field of political theory. Lastly, for a system of supposedly self-acting and independent "checks" — one part of the

COMMISSION GOVERNMENT

governmental machinery working to offset another — is substituted a system of direct popular control, which many believe should accompany concentration of power.

These fundamental changes are in the nature of a return to time-honored political principles — an attempt to apply to modern conditions the essentials of the New England town meeting, where a public assembly chose annually a few " selectmen " and vested them with sufficient power to act for the community during the ensuing year. It is rather remarkable that these principles of simple organization, and direct general control have not been applied more widely to municipal government previously — principles applicable to the administration of all corporate bodies. At the present rate of adoption, however, it is not improbable that the commission type will be soon in use in a majority of our American cities, modified as may be needed to meet the requirements of the larger centers.

The widespread civic awakening coincident with the adoption of this improved form of municipal organization augurs well for the future. If this shall prove to be permanent, it will constitute the element which no mere form of government, however perfect, can be expected to supply — that active interest of citizens in public affairs so necessary for the successful continuance of democratic institutions.

PREFERENTIAL BALLOT PROVISIONS OF CHARTER OF GRAND JUNCTION, COL.

18. Preferential Ballot—Form.—The city clerk shall cause ballots for each general and special election to be printed, bound, numbered, endorsed, and authenticated, as provided by the constitution and laws of the State, except as otherwise required in this Charter. The ballots shall contain the full list and correct name of all the respective offices to be filled, and the names of the candidates nominated therefor. It shall be in substantially the following form with the cross (**X**) omitted when there are four or more candidates for any office. (When there are three and not more candidates for any office, then the ballot shall give first and second choice only; when there are less than three candidates for any office, all distinguishing columns as to choice, and all reference to choice, may be omitted):

GENERAL (OR SPECIAL) MUNICIPAL ELECTION, CITY OF GRAND JUNCTION. . . . (Inserting date thereof.)

Instructions.—To vote for any person, make a cross (**X**) in ink in the square in the appropriate column according to your choice, at the right of the name voted for. Vote your first choice in the first column; vote your second choice in the second column; vote any other choice in the third column; vote only one first and only one second choice. Do not vote more than one choice for one person, as only one choice will count for any candidate by this ballot.

COMMISSION GOVERNMENT

Omit voting for one name for each office, if more than one candidate therefor. All distinguishing marks make the ballot void. If you wrongly mark, tear, or deface this ballot, return it, and obtain another.

Commissioner of Public Affairs	First Choice	Second Choice	Third Choice
John Doe			X
James Foe	X		
Louis Hoe		X	
Dick Joe			X
Richard Roe			
Commissioner of Highways			
Mary Brown	X		
Harry Jones		X	
Fred Smith			
Commissioner of Water and Sewers			
Joe Black	X		
Robert White			

Charter Amendments, Ordinances, or Other Referendum Propositions

19. **Blank Spaces for Additional Candidates.** — One space shall be left below the printed names of the

candidates for each office to be voted for, wherein the voter may write the name of any person for whom he may wish to vote.

20. Requirements of Ballots. — All ballots printed shall be identical, so that without the numerical number thereon it would be impossible to distinguish one ballot from another. Space shall be provided on the ballot for Charter Amendments or other questions to be voted on at the municipal elections, as provided by this charter. The names of candidates for each office shall be arranged in alphabetical order of the sur-names. Nothing on the ballot shall be indicative of the source of the candidacy, or of the support of any candidate. No ballot shall have printed thereon any party or political designation or mark, and there shall not be appended to the name of any candidate any such party or political designation or mark, or anything indicating his views or opinions.

21. Sample Ballots. — The city clerk shall, at least five days before the election, cause to be printed not less than five hundred sample ballots, upon paper of different color, but otherwise identical with the ballot, to be used at the election, and shall distribute the same, upon application of the candidates, to the registered voters at his office.

22. Canvass and Election. — As soon as the polls are closed, the election judges shall immediately open the ballot boxes, take therefrom and count the ballots, and enter the total number thereof on the tally sheet provided therefor. They shall also carefully enter the number of the first, second, and third choice votes for each candidate on said tally sheet and make return thereof to the city clerk as provided by law. No vote shall be counted for any candidate more than once on any ballot, all subsequent votes on that ballot for that candidate being void.

The person receiving more than one half of the total number of ballots cast at such election as the first choice of the electors for any office shall be elected to that office; provided, that if no candidate shall receive such a majority of the first choice votes for such office, then and in that event, the name of the candidate printed on the ballot having the smallest number of first choice votes, and all names written on the ballot having a less number of votes, than such last-named candidate, shall be excluded from the count, and votes for such candidate or persons so excluded shall not thereafter be counted. A canvass shall then be made of the second choice votes received by the remaining candidates for said office; said second choice votes shall then be added to the first choice votes received by each remaining candidate for such office, and the candidate receiving the largest number of said first and second choice votes, if such votes constitute a majority of all ballots cast at such election, shall be elected thereto; and provided, further, that if no such candidate shall receive such a majority after adding the first and second choice votes, then and in that event, the name of the candidate then having the smallest number of first and second choice votes shall be excluded from the count, and no votes for such candidate so excluded shall thereafter be counted. A canvass shall then be made of the third choice votes received by the remaining candidates for such office;

PREFERENTIAL BALLOT

said third choice votes shall then be added to the first and second choice votes received by each remaining candidate for such office, and such remaining candidate receiving the highest number of first, second, and third choice votes shall be elected thereto. When the name of but one person remains as a candidate for any office, such person shall be elected thereto regardless of the number of votes received.

A tie between two or more candidates is to be decided in favor of the one having the greatest number of first choice votes. If all are equal in that respect, then the greatest number of second choice votes determine the result. If this will not decide, then the tie shall be determined by lot, under the direction of the canvassing board.

Whenever the word "majority" is used in this section, it shall mean more than one half of the total number of ballots cast at such election.

23. Informalities in Election. — No informalities in conducting municipal elections shall invalidate the same, if they have been conducted fairly and in substantial conformity with the requirements of this charter.

TEXT OF IOWA LAW

("DES MOINES PLAN" OF COMMISSION GOVERNMENT)[1]

INDEX TO PLAN

Bribery, Sec. 5-b.
Civil Service, Sec. 14.
Contracts with city, interest in, prohibited, Sec. 13.
Contracts with public service companies prohibited, Sec. 13.
Commissions, Civil Service, Sec. 14-a-b-c-d-e-f.
Candidates, how to become, Sec. 5.
Candidates assisting for pay prohibited, Sec. 5-A.
Departments, city of, Sec. 7.
Examination of books and accounts, Sec. 15.
Election of officers, Sec. 4.
Initiative, ordinances by the people, Sec. 19.
Merit system established, Sec. 14.
Officials to be elected, Sec. 4.
Officers elected by Council, Sec. 8.
Ordinances, Secs. 12-19.
Primary, nomination for office, Sec. 5.
Powers of City Council, Secs. 6-7-8-9.
Political or machine politics a crime, Sec. 13.
Petition by voters, Sec. 22.
Recall, right of, Sec. 18.
Referendum, franchise voted upon, Sec. 12.
Return to present system, Sec. 21.
Rights of people, Secs. 11-12-18-19.
Removal of officials by the people, Sec. 18.
Statement of receipts and expenditures, Sec. 15.
State statutes remaining unchanged, Sec. 3.
Salaries, Mayor and Councilmen, Sec. 10.
Words and terms defined, Sec. 17.

[1] Passed by the Thirty-second General Assembly of Iowa, and adopted at a special election held June 20, 1907. The election of the first Council (Commissioners) provided for in the act, took place in March, 1908. The "plan" became operative April 1, 1908.

TEXT OF IOWA LAW

AN ACT TO PROVIDE FOR THE GOVERNMENT OF CERTAIN CITIES, AND THE ADOPTION THEREOF BY SPECIAL ELECTION "ADDITIONAL TO TITLE V (FIVE) OF THE CODE."

Be It Enacted by the General Assembly of the State of Iowa:

SECTION 1.—That any city of the first class, or with special charter, now or hereafter having a population of twenty-five thousand[1] or over, as shown by the last preceding state census, may become organized as a city under the provisions of this act by proceeding as hereinafter provided.

SEC. 2.—Upon petition of electors equal in number to twenty-five per centum of the votes cast for all candidates for mayor at the last preceding city election of any such city, the mayor shall, by proclamation, submit the question of organizing as a city under this act at a special election to be held at a time specified therein, and within two months after said petition is filed. If said plan is not adopted at the special election called, the question of adopting said plan shall not be resubmitted to the voters of said city for adoption within two years thereafter, and then the question to adopt shall be resubmitted upon the presentation of a petition signed by electors equal in number to twenty-five per centum of the votes cast for all candidates for mayor at the last preceding general city election.

---

[1] Amended in 1909 to apply to cities of over 7000 population: cities of 7000–25,000 population have three commissioners instead of five. See Chap. 64, Acts of 1909; also Chaps. 65, 66, 67.

At such election the proposition to be submitted shall be, "Shall the proposition to organize the city or (name of a city) under chapter (naming the chapter containing this act) of the acts of the Thirty-second General Assembly be adopted?" and the election thereupon shall be conducted, the vote canvassed, and the result declared in the same manner as provided by law in respect to other city elections. If the majority of the votes cast shall be in favor thereof, the city shall thereupon proceed to the election of a mayor and four (4) councilmen, as hereinafter provided. Immediately after such proposition is adopted, the mayor shall transmit to the governor, to the secretary of state, and to the county auditor, each a certificate stating that such proposition was adopted.

At the regular city election after the adoption of such proposition, there shall be elected a mayor and four (4) councilmen. In the event, however, that the next regular city election does not occur within one year after such special election, the mayor shall, within ten days after such special election, by proclamation, call a special election for the election of a mayor and four councilmen, sixty days' notice thereof being given in such call; such election in either case to be conducted as hereinafter provided.

SEC. 3. — All laws governing cities of the first class and not inconsistent with the provisions of this act, and Sections 955, 956, 959, 964, 989, 1000, 1023 and 1053 of the Code, now applicable to special charter cities and not inconsistent with the provisions of this act shall apply to and govern cities organized under this act.

TEXT OF IOWA LAW

All by-laws, ordinances and resolutions lawfully passed and in force in any such city under its former organization shall remain in force until altered or repealed by the council elected under the provisions of this act. The territorial limits of such city shall remain the same as under its former organization, and all rights and property of every description which were vested in any city under its former organization shall vest in the same under the organization herein contemplated, and no right or liability either in favor of or against it, existing at the time, and no suit or prosecution of any kind shall be affected by such change, unless otherwise provided for in this act.

SEC. 4. — In every such city there shall be elected at the regular biennial municipal election, a mayor and four councilmen.

If any vacancy occurs in any such office, the remaining members of said council shall appoint a person to fill such vacancy during the balance of the unexpired term.

Said officers shall be nominated and elected at large. Said officers shall qualify and their terms of office shall begin on the first Monday after their election. The terms of office of the mayor and councilmen or aldermen in such city in office at the beginning of the terms of office of the mayor and councilmen first elected under the provisions of this act shall then cease and determine, and the terms of office of all other appointive officers in force in such city, except as hereinafter provided, shall cease and determine as soon as the council shall by resolution declare.

COMMISSION GOVERNMENT

SEC. 5. — Candidates to be voted for at all general municipal elections at which a mayor and four councilmen are to be elected under the provisions of this act shall be nominated by a primary election, and no other names shall be placed upon the general ballot except those selected in the manner hereinafter prescribed. The primary election for such nomination shall be held on the second Monday preceding the general municipal election. The judges of election appointed for the general municipal election shall be the judges of the primary election, and it shall be held at the same place, so far as possible, and the polls shall be opened and closed at the same hours, with the same clerks as are required for said general municipal election.

Any person desiring to become a candidate for mayor or councilman shall, at least ten days prior to said primary election, file with the said clerk a statement of such candidacy, in substantially the following form:

State of Iowa_____County—ss:

   I (_____), being first duly sworn, say that I reside at_____street, city of_____ county of_____state of Iowa; that I am a qualified voter therein; that I am a candidate for nomination to the office of (mayor or councilman), to be voted upon at the primary election to be held on the _____Monday of_____19_____, and I hereby request that my name be printed upon the official primary ballot for nomination by such primary election for such office.

          Signed_____

   Subscribed and sworn to (or affirmed) before me by _____
_____on this_____day of_____19_____.

          Signed_____,

and shall at the same time file therewith the petition of at least twenty-five qualified voters requesting such candidacy. Each petition shall be verified by one or more persons as to the qualifications and residence, with street number, of each of the persons so signing the said petition, and the said petition shall be in substantially the following form:

Petition Accompanying Nominating Statement

The undersigned, duly qualified electors of the city of _____, and residing at the places set opposite our respective names hereto, do hereby request that the name of (name of candidate) be placed on the ballot as a candidate for nomination for (name of office) at the primary election to be held in such city on the _____ Monday of _____ 19_____. We further state that we know him to be a qualified elector of said city and a man of good moral character, and qualified, in our judgment, for the duties of such office.

Names of Qualified Electors	Number	Streets

Immediately upon the expiration of the time of filing the statements and petitions for candidacies, the said city clerk shall cause to be published for three successive days in all the daily newspapers published in the city, in proper form, the names of the persons as they are to appear upon the primary ballots, and if there be no daily newspaper, then in two issues of any other newspapers that may be published in said city; and the said clerk shall thereupon cause the primary ballots to be printed, authenticated with a facsimile of his signature. Upon the said ballot the names of the candidates for mayor, arranged alphabetically, shall first be placed, with a square at the left of each name, and immediately below the words "Vote for one." Following these names, likewise arranged in alphabetical order, shall appear the names of the candidates for councilmen, with a square at the left of each name, and below the names of such candidates shall appear the words "Vote for four." The ballots shall be printed upon plain, substantial, white paper, and shall be headed:

CANDIDATES FOR NOMINATION FOR MAYOR AND COUNCILMEN OF_____CITY AT THE PRIMARY ELECTION,

but shall have no party designation or mark whatever. The ballots shall be in substantially the following form:

(Place a cross in the square preceding the names of the parties you favor as candidates for the respective positions.)

OFFICIAL PRIMARY BALLOT

CANDIDATES FOR NOMINATION FOR MAYOR AND COUNCILMEN OF_____CITY AT THE PRIMARY ELECTION

For Mayor

☐ (Name of candidate.)
(Vote for one.)
For Councilman.

☐ (Name of candidate.)
(Vote for four.)

Official ballot attest:
(Signature)
_____
City Clerk.

TEXT OF IOWA LAW

Having caused said ballots to be printed, the said city clerk shall cause to be delivered at each polling place a number of said ballots equal to twice the number of votes cast in such polling precinct at the last general municipal election for mayor. The persons who are qualified to vote at the general municipal election shall be qualified to vote at such primary election, and challenges can be made by not more than two persons, to be appointed at the time of opening the polls by the judges of election; and the law applicable to challenges at a general municipal election shall be applicable to challenges made at such primary election. Judges of election shall, immediately upon the closing of the polls, count the ballots and ascertain the number of votes cast in such precinct for each of the candidates, and make return thereof to the city clerk, upon proper blanks, to be furnished by the said clerk, within six hours of the closing of the polls. On the day following the said primary election the said city clerk shall canvass said returns so received from all the polling precincts, and shall make and publish in all the newspapers of said city at least once, the result thereof. Said canvass by the city clerk shall be publicly made. The two candidates receiving the highest number of votes for mayor shall be the candidates and the only candidates whose names shall be placed upon the ballot for mayor at the next succeeding general municipal election, and the eight candidates receiving the highest number of votes for councilman, or all such candidates if less than eight, shall be the candidates and the only candidates whose names shall be placed upon the ballot for councilman at such municipal election.

COMMISSION GOVERNMENT

All electors of cities under this act who, by the laws governing cities of the first class and cities acting under special charter, would be entitled to vote for the election of officers at any general municipal election in such cities, shall be qualified to vote at all elections under this act; and the ballot at such general municipal election shall be in the same general form as for such primary election, so far as applicable, and in all elections in such city the election precincts, voting places, method of conducting election, canvassing the votes and announcing the results, shall be the same as by law provided for election of officers in such cities, so far as the same are applicable and not inconsistent with the provisions of this act.

SEC. 5-A. — Any person who shall agree to perform any services in the interest of any candidate for any office provided in this act, in consideration of any money or other valuable thing for such services performed in the interest of any candidate shall be punished by a fine not exceeding three hundred dollars ($300), or be imprisoned in the county jail not exceeding thirty (30) days.

SEC. 5-B. — Any person offering to give a bribe, either in money or other consideration, to any elector, for the purpose of influencing his vote at any election provided in this act, or any elector entitled to vote at any such election receiving and accepting such bribe or other consideration; any person making false answer to any of the provisions of this act relative to his qualifications to vote at said election; any person wilfully voting or offering to vote at such election who has not been a resident of this state for six months next preceding said election, or who is not twenty-one years of age, or is not a citizen of the United States, or knowing himself not to be a qualified elector of such precinct where he offers to vote; any person knowingly procuring, aiding or abetting any violation hereof shall be deemed guilty of a misdemeanor, and, upon conviction, shall be fined a sum not less than one hundred dollars ($100) nor more than five hundred dollars ($500), and be imprisoned in the county jail not less than ten (10) nor more than ninety (90) days.

SEC. 6.— Every such city shall be governed by a council, consisting of the mayor and four councilmen, chosen as provided in this act, each of whom shall have the right to vote on all questions coming before the council. Three members of the council shall constitute a quorum, and the affirmative vote of three members shall be necessary to adopt any motion, resolution or ordinance, or pass any measure, unless a greater number is provided for in this act. Upon every vote the yeas and nays shall be called and recorded, and every motion, resolution or ordinance shall be reduced to writing and read before the vote is taken thereon. The mayor shall preside at all meetings of the council; he shall have no power to veto any measure, but every resolution or ordinance passed by the council must be signed by the mayor, or by two councilmen, and be recorded before the same shall be in force.

SEC. 7.— The council shall have and possess and the council and its members shall exercise all executive, legislative and judicial powers and duties now had, possessed and exercised by the mayor, city council, board of public works, park commissioners, board of police and fire commissioners, board of water works trustees, board of library trustees, solicitor, assessor, treasurer, auditor, city engineer, and other executive and administrative officers in cities of the first class and cities acting under special charter. The executive and administrative powers, authority and duties in such cities shall be distributed into and among five departments, as follows:

1. Department of Public Affairs.
2. Department of Accounts and Finance.
3. Department of Public Safety.
4. Department of Streets and Public Improvements.
5. Department of Parks and Public Property.

The council shall determine the powers and duties to be performed by, and assign them to the appropriate department; shall prescribe the powers and duties of officers and employes; may assign particular officers and employes to one or more of the departments; may require an officer or employe to perform duties in two or more departments; and may make such other rules and regulations as may be necessary or proper for the efficient and economical conduct of the business of the city.

SEC. 8.— The mayor shall be superintendent of the department of Public Affairs, and the council shall, at the first regular meeting after election of its members, designate by majority vote one councilman to be superintendent of the department of Accounts and Finance, one to be superintendent of the department of Public Safety, one to be superintendent of the department of Streets and Public Improvements, and one to be superintendent of the department of Parks and Public Property; but such designation shall be changed whenever it appears that the public service would be benefited thereby.

The council shall, at said first meeting, or as soon as practicable thereafter, elect by majority vote the following officers: A city clerk, solicitor, assessor, treasurer, auditor, civil engineer, city physician, marshal, chief of fire department, market master, street commissioner, three library trustees, and such other officers and assistants as shall be provided for by ordinance and necessary to the proper and efficient conduct of the affairs of the city; and shall appoint a police judge in those cities not having a superior court. Any officer or assistant elected or appointed by the council may be removed from office at any time by vote of a majority of the members of the council, except as otherwise provided for in this act.

Sec. 9.—The council shall have power from time to time to create, fill and discontinue offices and employments other than herein prescribed, according to their judgment of the needs of the city, and may, by majority vote of all the members, remove any such officer or employe, except as otherwise provided for in this act; and may, by resolution or otherwise, prescribe, limit or change the compensation of such officers or employes.

Sec. 10.—The mayor and council shall have an office at the city hall, and their total compensation shall be as follows: In cities having by the last preceding state or national census from 25,000 to 40,000 people, the annual salary of the mayor shall be $2,500, and of each councilman $1,800. In cities having by such census from 40,000 to 60,000 people, the mayor's annual salary shall be $3,000, and that of each councilman $2,500; and in cities having by such census over 60,000 population, the mayor's annual salary shall be $3,500, and that of each councilman $3,000. Such salaries shall be payable in equal monthly installments.

Any increase in salary occasioned under the provisions of this scale by increase in population in any city shall commence with the month next after the official publication of the census showing such increase therein.

Every other officer or assistant shall receive such salary or compensation as the council shall by ordinance provide, payable in equal monthly installments.

The salary or compensation of all other employes of such city shall be fixed by the council, and shall be payable monthly or at such shorter periods as the council shall determine.

SEC. 11. — Regular meetings of the council shall be held on the first Monday after the election of councilmen, and thereafter at least once each month. The council shall provide by ordinance for the time of holding regular meetings, and special meetings may be called from time to time by the mayor or two councilmen. All meetings of the council, whether regular or special, at which any person not a city officer is admitted, shall be open to the public.

The mayor shall be president of the council and pre-

TEXT OF IOWA LAW

side at its meetings, and shall supervise all departments and report to the council for its action all matters requiring attention in either. The superintendent of the department of Accounts and Finance shall be vice-president of the council and in case of vacancy in the office of mayor, or the absence or inability of the mayor, shall perform the duties of the mayor.

Sec. 12. — Every ordinance or resolution appropriating money or ordering any street improvement or sewer, or making or authorizing the making of any contract or granting any franchise or right to occupy or use the streets, highways, bridges or public places in the city for any purpose, shall be complete in the form in which it is finally passed, and remain on file with the city clerk for public inspection at least one week before the final passage or adoption thereof. No franchise or right to occupy or use the streets, highways, bridges or public places in any city shall be granted, renewed or extended, except by ordinance, and every franchise or grant for interurban or street railways, gas or water works, electric light or power plants, heating plants, telegraph or telephone systems, or other public service utilities within said city, must be authorized or approved by a majority of the electors voting thereon at a general or special election, as provided in Section 776 of the Code.

Sec. 13. — No officer or employe elected or appointed in any such city shall be interested, directly or indirectly, in any contract or job for work or materials, or the profits thereof, or services to be furnished or performed for the city; and no such officer or employe shall be interested, directly or indirectly, in any contract or job for work or materials, or the profits thereof, or services to be furnished or performed for any person, firm or corporation operating interurban railway, street railway, gas works, water works, electric light or power plant, heating plant, telegraph line, telephone exchange, or other public utility within the territorial limits of said city. No such officer or employe shall accept or receive, directly or indirectly, from any person, firm or corporation operating within the territorial limits of said city, any interurban railway, street railway, gas works, water works, electric light or power plant, heating plant, telegraph line or telephone exchange, or other business using or operating under a public franchise, any frank, free ticket or free service, or accept or receive, directly or indirectly, from any such person, firm or corporation, any other service upon terms more favorable than is granted to the public generally. Any violation of the provisions of this section shall be a misdemeanor, and every such contract or agreement shall be void.

Such prohibition of free transportation shall not apply to policemen or firemen in uniform; nor shall any free service to city officials heretofore provided by any franchise or ordinance be affected by this section. Any officer or employe of such city who, by solicitation or otherwise, shall exert his influence, directly or indirectly, to influence other officers or employes of such city to adopt his political views or to favor any particular person or candidate for office, or who shall in any manner contribute money, labor, or other valuable thing to any person for election purposes, shall be guilty of a misdemeanor, and upon conviction shall be punished by a fine not exceeding three hundred dollars ($300) or by im-

TEXT OF IOWA LAW

prisonment in the county jail not exceeding thirty (30) days.

SEC. 14.— Immediately after organizing, the council shall, by ordinance, appoint three civil service commissioners, who shall hold office, one until the first Monday in April in the second year after his appointment, one until the first Monday in April of the fourth year after his appointment, and one until the first Monday in April of the sixth year after his appointment. Each succeeding council shall, as soon as practicable after organizing, appoint one commissioner for six years, who shall take the place of the commissioner whose term of office expires. The chairman of the commission for each biennial period shall be the member whose term first expires. No person while on the said commission shall hold or be a candidate for any office of public trust. Two of said members shall constitute a quorum to transact business. The commissioners must be citizens of Iowa, and residents of the city for more than three years next preceding their appointment.

The council may remove any of said commissioners during their term of office for cause, four councilmen voting in favor of such removal, and shall fill any vacancy that may occur in said commission for the unexpired term. The city council shall provide suitable rooms in which the said civil service commission may hold its meetings. They shall have a clerk, who shall keep a record of all its meetings, such city to supply the said commission with all necessary equipment to properly attend to such business.

(a) Before entering upon the duties of their office,

each of said commissioners shall take and subscribe an oath, which shall be filed and kept in the office of the city clerk, to support the constitution of the United States and the state of Iowa, and to obey the laws, and to aim to secure and maintain an honest and efficient force, free from partisan distinction or control, and to perform the duties of his office to the best of his ability.

(b) Said commission shall, on the first Monday of April and October of each year, or oftener if it shall be deemed necessary, under such rules and regulations as may be prescribed by the council, hold examinations for the purpose of determining the qualifications of applicants for positions, which examination shall be practical and shall fairly test the fitness of the persons examined to discharge the duties of the position to which they seek to be appointed. Said commission shall, as soon as possible after such examination, certify to the council double the number of persons necessary to fill vacancies, who, according to its records, have the highest standing for the position they seek to fill as a result of such examination, and all vacancies which occur, that come under the civil service, prior to the date of the next regular examination, shall be filled from said list so certified; provided, however, that should the list for any cause be reduced to less than three for any division, then the council or the head of the proper department may temporarily fill a vacancy, but not to exceed thirty days.

(c) All persons subject to such civil service examinations shall be subject to removal from office or employment by the council for misconduct or failure to perform their duties under such rules and regulations as it may adopt, and the chief of police, chief of the fire depart-

TEXT OF IOWA LAW

ment, or any superintendent or foreman in charge of municipal work, may peremptorily suspend or discharge any subordinate then under his direction for neglect of duty or disobedience of his orders, but shall, within twenty-four hours thereafter, report such suspension or discharge, and the reason therefor, to the superintendent of his department, who shall thereupon affirm or revoke such discharge or suspension, according to the facts.

Such employe (or the officer discharging or suspending him) may, within five days of such ruling, appeal therefrom to the council, which shall fully hear and determine the matter.

(d) The council shall have the power to enforce the attendance of witnesses, the production of books and papers, and power to administer oaths in the same manner and with like effect, and under the same penalties, as in the case of magistrates exercising criminal or civil jurisdiction under the statutes of Iowa.

Said commissioners shall make annual report to the council, and it may require a special report from said commission at any time; and said council may prescribe such rules and regulations for the proper conduct of the business of the said commission as shall be found expedient and advisable, including restrictions on appointment, promotions, removals for cause, roster of employes, certification of records to the auditor, and restrictions on payment to persons improperly employed.

(e) The council of such city shall have power to pass ordinances imposing suitable penalties for the punishment of persons violating any of the provisions of this act relating to the civil service commission.

(f) The provisions of this section shall apply to all appointive officers and employes of such city, except those especially named in Section 8 of this act, commissioners of any kind, laborers whose occupation requires no special skill or fitness, election officials, and mayor's secretary and assistant solicitor, where such officers are appointed; provided, however, that existing employes heretofore appointed or employed after competitive examination or for long service under the provisions of Chapter 31, acts of the Twenty-ninth General Assembly, and subsequent amendments thereto, shall retain their positions without further examinations unless removed for cause.

All officers and employes in any such city shall be elected or appointed with reference to their qualifications and fitness, and for the good of the public service, and without reference to their political faith or party affiliations.

It shall be unlawful for any candidate for office, or any officer in any such city, directly or indirectly, to give or promise any person or persons any office, position, employment, benefit, or anything of value, for the purpose of influencing or obtaining the political support, aid or vote of any person or persons.

Every elective officer in any such city shall, within thirty days after qualifying, file with the city clerk, and publish at least once in a daily newspaper of general circulation, his sworn statement of all his election and campaign expenses, and by whom such funds were contributed.

Any violation of the provisions of this section shall be a misdemeanor and be a ground for removal from office.

TEXT OF IOWA LAW

Sec. 15.—The council shall each month print in pamphlet form a detailed itemized statement of all receipts and expenses of the city and a summary of its proceedings during the preceding month, and furnish printed copies thereof to the state library, the city library, the daily newspapers of the city, and to persons who shall apply therefor at the office of the city clerk. At the end of each year the council shall cause a full and complete examination of all the books and accounts of the city to be made by competent accountants, and shall publish the result of such examination in the manner above provided for publication of statements of monthly expenditures.

Sec. 16.—If, at the beginning of the term of office of the first council elected in such city under the provisions of this act, the appropriations for the expenditures of the city government for the current fiscal year have been made, said council shall have power, by ordinance, to revise, to repeal or change said appropriations and to make additional appropriations.

Sec. 17.—In the construction of this act the following rules shall be observed, unless such construction would be inconsistent with the manifest intent, or repugnant to the context of the statute:

1. The words "councilman" or "alderman" shall be construed to mean "councilman" when applied to cities under this act.

2. When an office or officer is named in any law referred to in this act, it shall, when applied to cities under this act, be construed to mean the office or officer having the same functions or duties under the provisions

of this act, or under ordinances passed under authority thereof.

3. The word "franchise" shall include every special privilege in the streets, highways and public places of the city, whether granted by the state or the city, which does not belong to the citizens generally by common right.

4. The word "electors" shall be construed to mean persons qualified to vote for elective offices at regular municipal elections.

SEC. 18. — The holder of any elective office may be removed at any time by the electors qualified to vote for a successor of such incumbent. The procedure to effect the removal of an incumbent of an elective office shall be as follows: A petition signed by electors entitled to vote for a successor to the incumbent sought to be removed, equal in number to at least twenty-five per centum of the entire vote for all candidates for the office of mayor at the last preceding general municipal election, demanding an election of a successor of the person sought to be removed shall be filed with the city clerk, which petition shall contain a general statement of the grounds for which the removal is sought. The signatures to the petition need not all be appended to one paper, but each signer shall add to his signature his place of residence, giving the street and number. One of the signers of each such paper shall make oath before an officer competent to administer oaths that the statements therein made are true as he believes, and that each signature to the paper appended is the genuine signature of the person whose name it purports to be.

TEXT OF IOWA LAW

Within ten days from the date of filing such petition the city clerk shall examine, and from the voters' register ascertain whether or not said petition is signed by the requisite number of qualified electors, and, if necessary, the council shall allow him extra help for that purpose; and he shall attach to said petition his certificate, showing the result of said examination. If, by the clerk's certificate, the petition is shown to be insufficient, it may be amended within ten days from the date of said certificate. The clerk shall, within ten days after such amendment, make like examination of the amended petition, and if his certificate shall show the same to be insufficient, it shall be returned to the person filing the same; without prejudice, however, to the filing of a new petition to the same effect. If the petition shall be deemed to be sufficient, the clerk shall submit the same to the council without delay. If the petition shall be found to be sufficient, the council shall order and fix a date for holding the said election, not less than thirty days or more than forty days from the date of the clerk's certificate to the council that a sufficient petition is filed.

The council shall make, or cause to be made, publication of notice and all arrangements for holding such election, and the same shall be conducted, returned, and the result thereof declared, in all respects as are other city elections. The successor of any officer so removed shall hold office during the unexpired term of his predecessor. Any person sought to be removed may be a candidate to succeed himself, and unless he requests otherwise in writing, the clerk shall place his name on the official ballot without nomination. In any such removal election, the candidate receiving the highest number of votes shall be declared elected. At such election, if some other person than the incumbent receives the highest number of votes, the incumbent shall thereupon be deemed removed from the office upon qualification of his successor. In case the party who receives the highest number of votes should fail to qualify within ten days after receiving notification of election, the office shall be deemed vacant. If the incumbent receives the highest number of votes, he shall continue in office. The same method of removal shall be cumulative and additional to the methods heretofore provided by law.

SEC. 19. — Any proposed ordinance may be submitted to the council by petition signed by electors of the city equal in number to the percentage hereinafter required. The signatures, verification, authentication, inspection, certification, amendment and submission of such petition shall be the same as provided for petitions under Section 18 hereof.

If the petition accompanying the proposed ordinance be signed by electors equal in number to twenty-five per centum of the votes cast for all candidates for mayor at the last preceding general election, and contains a request that the said ordinance be submitted to a vote of the people if not passed by the council, such council shall either

(a) Pass said ordinance without alteration within twenty days after attachment of the clerk's certificate to the accompanying petition, or,

(b) Forthwith, after the clerk shall attach to the petition accompanying such ordinance his certificate of

TEXT OF IOWA LAW

sufficiency, the council shall call a special election, unless a general municipal election is fixed within ninety days thereafter, and at such special or general municipal election, if one is so fixed, such ordinance shall be submitted without alteration to the vote of the electors of said city.

But if the petition is signed by not less than ten nor more than twenty-five per centum of the electors, as above defined, then the council shall, within twenty days, pass said ordinance without change, or submit the same at the next general city election occurring not more than thirty days after the clerk's certificate of sufficiency is attached to said petition.

The ballots used when voting upon said ordinance shall contain these words: "For the ordinance" (stating the nature of the proposed ordinance), and "Against the ordinance" (stating the nature of the proposed ordinance). If a majority of the qualified electors voting on the proposed ordinance shall vote in favor thereof, such ordinance shall thereupon become a valid and binding ordinance of the city; and any ordinance proposed by petition, or which shall be adopted by a vote of the people, cannot be repealed or amended except by a vote of the people.

Any number of proposed ordinances may be voted upon at the same election, in accordance with the provisions of this section; but there shall not be more than one special election in any period of six months for such purpose.

The council may submit a proposition for the repeal of any such ordinance or for amendments thereto, to be voted upon at any succeeding general city election;

and should such proposition so submitted receive a majority of the votes cast thereon at such election, such ordinance shall thereby be repealed or amended accordingly. Whenever any ordinance or proposition is required by this act to be submitted to the voters of the city at any election, the city clerk shall cause such ordinance or proposition to be published once in each of the daily newspapers published in said city; such publication to be not more than twenty or less than five days before the submission of such proposition or ordinance to be voted on.

SEC. 20. — No ordinance passed by the council, except when otherwise required by the general laws of the state or by the provisions of this act, except an ordinance for the immediate preservation of the public peace, health or safety, which contains a statement of its urgency and is passed by a two-thirds vote of the council, shall go into effect before ten days from the time of its final passage; and if during said ten days a petition signed by electors of the city equal in number to at least twenty-five per centum of the entire vote cast for all candidates for mayor at the last preceding general municipal election at which a mayor was elected, protesting against the passage of such ordinance, be presented to the council, the same shall thereupon be suspended from going into operation, and it shall be the duty of the council to reconsider such ordinance; and if the same is not entirely repealed, the council shall submit the ordinance, as is provided by Subsection b of Section 19 of this act, to the vote of the electors of the city, either at the general election or at a special municipal election to be called for that purpose; and such ordinance shall not go into effect or become operative unless a majority of the qualified electors voting on the same shall vote in favor thereof. Said petition shall be in all respects in accordance with the provisions of said Section 19, except as to the percentage of signers, and be examined and certified to by the clerk in all respects as therein provided.

SEC. 21. — Any city which shall have operated for more than six years under the provisions of this act may abandon such organization hereunder, and accept the provisions of the general law of the state then applicable to cities of its population, or if now organized under special charter, may resume said special charter by proceeding as follows:

Upon the petition of not less than twenty-five per centum of the electors of such city a special election shall be called, at which the following proposition only shall be submitted: "Shall the city of (name the city) abandon its organization under Chapter — of the acts of the Thirty-second General Assembly and become a city under the general law governing cities of like population, or if now organized under special charter shall resume said special charter?"

If a majority of the votes cast at such special election be in favor of such proposition, the officers elected at the next succeeding biennial election shall be those then prescribed by the general law of the state for cities of like population, and upon the qualification of such officers such city shall become a city under such general law of the state; but such change shall not in any manner or degree affect the property, right or liabilities of any nature of such city, but shall merely extend to such change in its form of government.

The sufficiency of such petition shall be determined, the election ordered and conducted, and the results declared, generally as provided by Section 18 of this act, insofar as the provisions thereof are applicable.

SEC. 22. — Petitions provided for in this act shall be signed by none but legal voters of the city. Each petition shall contain, in addition to the names of the petitioners, the street and house number in which the petitioner resides, his age and length of residence in the city. It shall also be accompanied by the affidavit of one or more legal voters of the city, stating that the signers thereof were, at the time of signing, legal voters of said city, and the number of signers at the time the affidavit was made.

SEC. 23. — This act, being deemed of immediate importance, shall take effect and be in force from and after its publication in The Register and Leader and Des Moines Capital, newspapers published in Des Moines, Iowa.

Approved March 29, A.D., 1907.

LIST OF REFERENCES

LIST OF REFERENCES (1)

I. Commission Charters and Laws (2)

State	General Act or Special City Charter	Session Laws (Year and Chapter)	
Alabama — Cities of 100,000 pop. or over	(3)	1911	No. 163
Cities of 25–50,000 pop.	General	1911	No. 254
Other cities	General	1911	
California —	Special — Berkeley	1909	
	Modesto	1911	
	Monterey	1911	
	Pomona	1911	
	Oakland	1911	
	San Diego	1909	
	Santa Cruz	1911	
	San Luis Obispo	1911	
	Vallejo	1911	
	General (4) (5)	1911	

(1) In the preparation of this list, free use has been made of the bibliographies of the Library of Congress (H. H. B. Meyer, Chief Bibliographer), of the Municipal Reference Bureau of the University of Wisconsin (Ford H. MacGregor in charge), and of the Legislative Reference Library of the State of New York (C. B. Lester, Librarian), on this subject. In view of the complete bibliography now in preparation by the Library of Congress, no attempt has been made to present here a full list of references.

(2) Charters are available, not only in the session laws of the respective states, but can also usually be secured from the city clerk of the municipality: general acts are found in the session laws, or may be had from the secretary of state.

(3) Applies only to Birmingham, and is equivalent to a special charter.

(4) Applies to cities of fifth and sixth classes.

(5) Separate act permits recall, initiative, and referendum in cities; **laws of 1911**, Chap. 185.

LIST OF REFERENCES

State	General Act or Special City Charter	Session Laws (Year and Chapter)	
Colorado —	Special — Colorado Springs	1909 (1)	
	Grand Junction	1909 (1)	
Idaho —	Special — Lewiston	1907	
	General	1911	Chap. 82
Illinois —	General	1910	Special sessions, 1909–10, p. 12
Iowa —	General	1907 (2)	Chap. 48
Kansas — Cities of 1st class	General	1907 (3)	Chap. 114
Cities of 2d class	General	1907 (3)	Chap. 123
Kentucky —	General	1910	Chap. 50
Louisiana —	General	1910	Act 302
Maryland —	Special — Cumberland	1910	
Massachusetts —	Special — Haverhill	1908	Chap. 574
	Gloucester	1908	Chap. 611
	Lynn	1910	Chap. 602 (Part I)
Michigan —	(4) Port Huron		(5)
	Pontiac		(5)
	Harbor Beach		(5)
	Wyandotte		(5)
	Owosso		(5)
Mississippi —	General (6)	1908	Chap. 108
Minnesota —	General (6)	1909	Chap. 170

(1) Framed by charter convention: approval by legislature not necessary.
(2) Amended 1909; Chaps. 64, 65, 66, 67, laws of 1909.
(3) Acts amended 1909; see Laws of Kansas, 1909, Chap. 74.
(4) Under "home rule," any city may frame its own charter.
(5) Ratification of legislature not necessary; approval of governor only required. Charter can be secured usually by writing to the city clerk, enclosing stamp.
(6) General act specifically permits cities to frame commission charter.

LIST OF REFERENCES

State	General Act or Special City Charter	Session Laws (Year and Chapter)	
Montana —	General	1911	Chap. 57
New Jersey —	General	1911	Chap. 221
New Mexico —	General	1909	Chap. 87
North Carolina —	Special — High Point (1)	1909	Chap. 395
	Greensboro (1)	1911	Chap. 2
	Wilmington (1)	1911	Chap. 75
North Dakota —	General	1907 (2)	Chap. 45
Oklahoma —	Special (3) (4)		
Oregon —	Special (4)		
South Carolina —	General	1910	No. 277
South Dakota —	General	1907 (5)	Chap. 86
Tennessee —	Special — Memphis	1909	Chap. 298
	Chattanooga	1911	
Texas —	Special — Austin	1909	Chap. 2 (6)
	Corpus Christi	1909	Chap. 33
	Dallas	1907	Chap. 71 (7)
	Denison	1907	Chap. 33 (8)
	El Paso	1907	Chap. 5
	Fort Worth	1907	Chap. 7
		1909	Chap. 31
	Galveston	1901	Chap. 12 (9)

(Texas entries are under Local and Special Laws.)

(1) Public Laws of North Carolina.

(2) Amended by laws of 1911, Chap. 67.

(3) Ratification of legislature not necessary; approval of governor only required. Charter can be secured usually by writing to the city clerk, enclosing stamp.

(4) Under "home rule," any city may frame its own charter.

(5) Amended in 1909, Chaps. 57 and 158; and in 1911, Chap. 97.

(6) Minor amendments in Local and Special Laws, 1909, Chap. 90.

(7) Minor amendments to Dallas Charter in Local and Special Laws, 1909, Chaps. 93 and 14, p. 870.

(8) Minor amendments to Denison Charter in Local and Special Laws, 1909, Chap. 9 (second called session) and 1910, Chap. 2 (third called session).

(9) Amended in 1903.

LIST OF REFERENCES

State	General Act or Special City Charter	Session Laws (Year and Chapter)	
Texas —	Greenville	1907	Chap. 24
		1909	Chap. 89 (1)
	Houston	1905	Chap. 17
	Marshall	1909	Chap. 6
	Palestine	1909	Chap. 85
	Waco	1909	Chaps. 3 and 91
	General	1909	Chap. 106
Utah —	General	1911	Chap. 125
Washington —	Special—Tacoma(2) Spokane (2)		
	General	1911	Chap. 116
West Virginia —	Special — Huntington	1909	Chap. 3
	Bluefield	1909	Chap. 1
	Parkersburg	1911	Chap. 83
Wisconsin —	General	1909 (3)	Chap. 448
Wyoming —	General	1911	Chap. 84

(Texas special city charters noted as "Local and Special Laws.")

(1) Minor amendments in Local and Special Laws (second called session), 1909, Chaps. 6 and 17.

(2) Under "home rule," any city may frame its own charter.

(3) Amended by laws of 1911, Chap. 287.

LIST OF REFERENCES

II. GENERAL REFERENCES

ALLEN, S. B.: The Des Moines plan. (In National municipal league. Proceedings, 1907. [n. p.], 1907, pp. 156-165.)

BEARD, C. A.: American government and politics. New York: The Macmillan Co., 1910, pp. 483-484, 598-602.

—— Loose leaf digest of short ballot charters. New York: The Short Ballot Organization, 383 Fourth Ave. 1911. Contains digest of many commission charters and an account of the operation of the plan in a large number of cities.

BERRYHILL, JAS. G.: The Des Moines plan of municipal government. (In Iowa state bar association. Proceedings of the fourteenth annual meeting, 1908. Iowa City, Ia., pp. 35-50.)

—— Commission government. A general statement prepared for the Commercial club of Des Moines.

BRADFORD, ERNEST S.: Commission government in American cities. [Philadelphia? 1910], pp. 217-228. Reprinted from Proceedings of the Cincinnati conference for good city government and the fifteenth annual meeting of the National municipal league, 1909.

—— A comparison of the forms of commission government in cities. (In National municipal league. Proceedings, 1910. [n. p.], 1910, pp. 246-280.)

—— Commission government in American cities. New York: The Macmillan Co., 1911, 350 pp.

BRYCE, JAMES: American commonwealth, vol. I., pp. 662-666.

CAMPBELL, ROBERT A.: Commission system of municipal government — Des Moines plan. American political science review, Aug., 1907, v. 1: 621-626.

—— Commission form of government. American political science review, Nov., 1908, v. 2: 571-574.

—— Municipal government. Commission system. American political science review, Feb., 1910, v. 4: 80-87.

CHADWICK, F. E.: The Newport charter. (In American political science association. Proceedings of the third annual meeting, 1906. Lancaster, Pa., 1907, pp. 58-66.) Includes a brief comparison of the Newport charter with that of Galveston.

—— The Newport plan. (In National municipal league. Proceedings, 1907. [n. p.], 1907, pp. 166-177.)

LIST OF REFERENCES

CHEESBOROUGH, E. R.: The success of the Galveston experiment. (In National municipal league. Proceedings, 1906, pp. 181–193.)

—— Galveston plan of city government by commission. Galveston, Tex., 1910. Reprinted from Galveston Tribune, Dec. 31, 1909.

CHILDS, RICHARD S.: The story of the short ballot cities. New York: The Short Ballot Organization [1910], 20 pp.

CLARK, C. A.: Municipal government. (In Iowa state bar association. Proceedings, 1904, pp. 129–134.)

Commission government luncheon (Buffalo). (In National municipal league. Proceedings, 1910. [n. p.], 1910, pp. 555–567.) Remarks by E. S. Bradford, K. Mixer, A. Wilcox, L. Stockton, W. B. Wright, Jr., W. B. Howland, A. D. Mason, J. W. S. Peters, S. Sumner, S. P. Jones, R. Bowman, S. Fleischmann, and A. R. Hatton.

COMMONS, JOHN R.: In Political science quarterly, Dec., 1902, v. 17: 609–630. Referendum and initiative in city government.

DEMING, H. E.: The government of American cities. New York: G. P. Putnam's sons, 1909, 323 pp. "City government by a board of directors," pp. 97–101.

DES MOINES. Auditor's office. Annual report of the city of Des Moines. [Des Moines, 1909–date.] Text of Iowa law, pp. 11–34.

DURAND, E. D.: Council government *vs.* mayor government. Political science quarterly, Sept., Dec., 1900, v. 15: 426–451, 675–709. Reprinted in part in Percy L. Kaye's "Readings in civil government," New York, 1910, pp. 349–356.

Economic club of Boston. Municipal government: shall it be carried on by a small board of administrators elected at large by the people? Two discussions before the club, Jan. 11, 1907, and Jan. 21, 1908, [Boston? 1908?], 74 pp. Includes papers and addresses by George K. Turner, James M. Head, Charles W. Eliot, Harvey S. Chase, Arthur Warren, Sidney J. Dillon, J. H. Beale, Jr., and William M. Ivins.

ELIOT, CHAS. W.: Municipal government. New England magazine, June, 1909, v. 40: 393–397. "Originally delivered as an address before the Economic club of Boston, Jan., 1907." Discusses the commission form of city government.

LIST OF REFERENCES

ELIOT, CHAS. W.: Municipal government by commission. South Atlantic quarterly, April, 1909, v. 8: 174–183.

FAIRLIE, J. A.: American municipal councils. Political science quarterly, June, 1904, v. 19: 234–251.

——Essays in municipal administration. New York: The Macmillan Co., 1908, 374 pp. Commission form of city government, pp. 13, 127.

FORD, HENRY JONES: Principal of municipal organization. Annals of American academy, March, 1904, v. 195–222.

FULLER, A. M.: Municipal government by commission. Address before Chamber of commerce of Erie, Pa., April 15, 1909. Erie, Pa.: Chamber of commerce, 1909, 20 pp.

Galveston Charter. Charter of the city of Galveston as passed by the 28th Legislature of the state of Texas and approved by the Governor, March 30, 1903. Galveston: F. J. Finck stationery and printing Co. [1907?], 90, xxxix pp.

The Galveston idea. (In Bliss, William D. P., ed. New encyclopedia of social reform. New York, 1908, pp. 529–530.)

GOODNOW, F. J. Municipal government. New York: The Century Co., 1909, 401 pp. The "commission system," pp. 175–178.

HAMILTON, J. J.: The dethronement of the city boss. New York: Funk & Wagnalls Co., 1910, 285 pp.

Iowa University. Forensic league. Speeches of the representatives of the State university of Iowa in the inter-collegiate debate, 1908–1909. 2d ed. Subject, Commission form of city government. Iowa City, Ia.: Forensic league, 1910, 32 pp.

Kansas University. Extension division; Debating and public discussion. The Commission plan of city government. Lawrence: University of Kansas, 1910, 45 pp. (Bulletin of the University of Kansas, July, 1910, v. 11, no. 10; Debating series, no. 2.)

KAYE, P. L.: Readings in civil government. New York: The Century Co., 1910, 535 pp. "Additional readings" at end of chapters. "The Des Moines plan of city government [partial text of the Iowa law of 1907]," pp. 356–360.

KING, J. A.: Legislative *vs.* business management of municipalities. (In League of Michigan municipalities. Report of the ninth annual convention, 1907. [Detroit? 1907], pp. 70–74.)

LIST OF REFERENCES

LYTTON, E. C., compiler. The Des Moines plan of commission government, digest and references. Des Moines, Ia.: [Arcade ptg. Co.], 1910, 11 pp. "Digest of the Des Moines plan, by Mayor James R. Hanna," pp. 4–5. References, pp. 6–9.

MACGREGOR, FORD H.: City government by commission; address delivered before the League of Wisconsin municipalities at Marinette, Wis., July 23, 1909. [Madison? Wis., 1909], 12 pp.

—— City government by commission. Bulletin of the University of Wisconsin, no. 428. Madison, Wis., April, 1911, 151 pp. Contains bibliography.

MUNRO, WILLIAM BENNETT: The Galveston plan of city government. (In National municipal league. Proceedings, 1907. [n. p.], 1907, pp. 142–155.)

NIDAY, J. E.: Business idea in municipal government. Houston, Tex., 19–

North Dakota University: Brief and bibliography on commission plan of city government. University of North Dakota, 1910, 8 pp. (Circular, new ser., no. 3.)

OSTROGORSKIĬ, M. ĪA.: Democracy and the party system in the United States. New York: The Macmillan Co., 1910, 469 pp. "Municipal government by commission," pp. 356–358.

PEARSON, P. M., ed.: Intercollegiate debates ; being briefs and reports of many intercollegiate debates. New York city: Hinds, Noble & Eldredge [1909], 507 pp. "The commission system of municipal government [with bibliographical references]," pp. 461–477. Affirmative argument also printed in Speaker (Philadelphia), Sept., 1908, v. 3: 404–408.

RICE, H. B.: Address of mayor of Houston, Texas, on the commission form of government, Charlotte, N.C., Nov. 18, 1908. [Houston ? Tex., 1908 ?], 15 pp.

ROBBINS, E. C., compiler: Selected articles on the commission plan of municipal government. 2d and enl. ed. Minneapolis: The H. W. Wilson Co., 1910, 178 pp. Debater's handbook series. Bibliography, pp. xv–xxvi.

ROWE, L. S.: Problems of city government. New York: D. Appleton and Co., 1908, 358 pp. Commission form of city government, pp. 183–190.

LIST OF REFERENCES

SHAMBAUGH, B. F.: The commission plan of [city] government. (In Minnesota academy of social sciences. Papers and proceedings of the third annual meeting. [Minneapolis] 1910, pp. 150-165.)

—— The Des Moines plan of city government. (In American political science association. Proceedings at its fourth annual meeting, 1907. Baltimore, 1908, pp. 189-192.)

TURNER, G. K.: Galveston: a business corporation. McClure's magazine, Oct., 1906, v. 27 : 610-620.

—— The new American city government; the Des Moines plan. McClure's magazine, May, 1910, v. 35 : 97-108.

WEBSTER, W. A.: The problem of city government, the charter of Boston, government by commission, council *vs.* mayor, future of down town Boston, city debts, limited suffrage, business and politics, home rule. Boston, 1908, 45 pp.

WILLIS, U. G.: The commission form of municipal government, 98 pp. Thesis — (A. M.) — Bates college. Bibliography, pp. 91-98. Typewritten manuscript.

Wisconsin University. University extension division. Dept. of debating and public discussion. Commission plan of city government (Bulletin, 2d revision). Madison, The University, 1910, 18 pp.

Wisconsin University. University extension division. (Bulletin No. 423.) City government by commission, by Ford H. MacGregor. Madison, The University, April, 1911, 151 pp.

WOODRUFF, CLINTON ROGERS: American municipal tendencies. (In National municipal league. Proceedings of the Pittsburg conference for good city government and fourteenth annual meeting, Nov., 16-19, 1908. [Pittsburg] 1908. pp. 145-203. "The Boston finance commission," pp. 154-157; "Concentration of power and responsibility [the Des Moines plan]," pp. 164-166.

—— New forms of city charters: The commission system. (In American year book, 1910. New York, 1911. pp. 218-220.) Bibliography, p. 224.

—— City government by commission. Papers and addresses before the National municipal league. Edited by Clinton Rogers Woodruff. D. Appleton and Co., N.Y., 1911.

LIST OF REFERENCES

III. REFERENCES IN PERIODICALS

ARNDT, W. T.: Municipal government by commission. Nation, Oct. 18, 1906, v. 83 : 322.

—— The American city the storm center in the battle for good government. Arena, Oct., 1907, v. 38 : 428–436. Commission government, pp. 431–436.

BATES, F. G.: Municipal government — commission form. American political science review, Feb., 1910, v. 4 : 75–76.

—— City government by commission: a symposium on the Galveston, Newport, and Des Moines plans. Chautauquan, June, 1908, v. 51 : 108–141. Contents. — Munro, W. B., The Galveston plan. — Chadwick, F. E., The Newport plan. — Allen, S. B., The Des Moines plan.

City government: Three great experiments. [Galveston, Tex.; Des Moines, Ia.; Newport, R. I.] Independent, June 18, 1908, v. 64 : 1409–1410.

BENET, CHRISTIE: A campaign for a commission form of government [in Columbia, S.C.] American city, Dec., 1910, v. 3 : 276–278.

CARLSON, S. A.: Simplified city government. American city, Jan., 1911, v. 4 : 34–36.

CHILDS, R. S.: Will commission government succeed in large cities? American city, Feb., 1911, v. 4 : 79–82.

COCHRANE, C. H.: Should New York be governed by a commission? Broadway magazine, Feb., 1907, v. 17 : 547–552.

Commission government: Cities which have adopted it to date. What is meant by the term, etc. Municipal journal and engineer, Feb. 22, 1911, v. 30 : 253–256.

DEHONEY, CARL: Breaking down ward lines in American cities. World to-day, May, 1910, v. 18 : 487–490.

—— Commission government and democracy. American city, Feb., 1910, v. 2 : 76–78.

ELIOT, C. W.: City government by fewer men. World's work, Oct., 1907, v. 14 : 9419–9426.

GAETZ, H. H.: Government a question of business. Public service (Chicago), June, 1909, v. 6 : 177–179.

GRESHAM, WALTER: Galveston's charter government. City hall, Dec., 1905, v. 4 : 183–184.

LIST OF REFERENCES

HART, A. B.: Commission Government in Texas. Boston evening transcript, April 11, 1908: 2.

HASKELL, H. J.: The Texas idea: city government by a board of directors. Outlook, April 13, 1907, v. 85: 839–843.

HUSTON, CHAS. D.: Commission plan in Cedar Rapids. Address at Burlington, Ia., Mar. 30, 1909. Cedar Rapids Evening gazette, March 31, 1909.

HUTSON, ETHEL: Galveston; an achievement story. Reader, Oct., 1906, v. 8: 545–556.

JAMES, G. W.: Two successful experiments in civic government: Galveston and Houston, Texas. Arena, July–Aug., 1907, v. 38: 8–13, 144–149.

JONES, NEAL: A city upon a hill. Solving municipal problems in Des Moines. Circle, July, 1909, v. 6: 8–9, 55.

KENDALL, CLARENCE: The city government of Galveston. University of Texas record, March 15, 1907, v. 7: 186–191.

LANDES, H. A.: Galveston's civic management. League of American municipalities. Bulletin, Feb., 1907, v. 7: 50–52.

—— The Galveston plan of city government. Municipal engineering, April, 1907, v. 32: 255–258. From a paper read before the League of American municipalities.

—— The government of Galveston. (Letter from the mayor-president of Galveston.) Pacific municipalities, May, 1907, v. 16: 99–103.

MOORHEAD, F. G.: Bringing dead cities to life. Technical world magazine, Feb., 1910, v. 12: 621–628.

MOWRY, D. E.: Governing cities by commissions. La Follette's magazine, v. 1, March 27, 1909: 7–8. Reprinted in Central law journal, May 14, 1909, v. 68: 372–373; and in Chicago legal news, June 12, 1909, v. 41: 370.

—— The various forms of commission government. Central law journal, May 27, 1910, v. 70: 384–388.

—— New forms of city government. Municipal engineering, Aug., 1907, v. 33: 100–101 and Oct., 1907, v. 33: 244–245.

Papers and discussion on municipal government by board (or commission) *vs.* mayor and council. League of American municipalities. Bulletin, Oct., 1907, v. 8: 100–121. Papers read before the eleventh annual convention of the League of Ameri-

LIST OF REFERENCES

can municipalities by F. E. Chadwick, J. M. Head, E. Coatsworth, R. G. Rhett, and J. B. Mahool. Discussion by H. A. Landes and others. Reprinted in Bulletin of the League of American municipalities, Jan., 1908, v. 9: 42–60.

RICH, B. A.: Business government for cities. Case and comment, June, 1910, v. 17: 4–7.

RUSSELL, C. E.: Sanity and democracy for American cities. Everybody's magazine, April, 1910, v. 22: 435–447.

RYAN, OSWALD: The commission plan of city government. American political science review, Feb., 1911, v. 5: 38–56.

SAMPSON, H. E.: Discussion of the Des Moines plan. (In favor of the plan.) Midwestern (Des Moines, Ia.), June, 1909, v. 3: 25–28.

SHERMAN, ERNEST R.: Commission plan in Cedar Rapids. Address before Commercial club, Sioux Falls, S.D., March 24, 1909. Cedar Rapids Evening gazette, March 25, 1909.

SLOSSON, W. B.: Government by commission in Texas. Independent, July 25, 1907, v. 63: 195–200.

—— The new Galveston. Independent, June 16, 1904, v. 56: 1382–1387.

Spread of the Texas idea. Outlook, August 3, 1907, v. 86: 707–708.

Spread of the Galveston plan. American monthly review of reviews, Nov., 1907, v. 36: 623–624.

THURNAU, AGNES: Criticizes Des Moines plan. City hall, Feb., 1910, v. 11: 251–252. Summary of an article by Miss Agnes Thurnau, in Los Angeles Sunday times.

WHITE, WILLIAM ALLEN: Progress in American cities. American magazine, April, 1909, v. 67: 603–610.

WILLIAMS, C. A.: Government of municipalities by boards of commissioners. Gunton's magazine, Dec., 1904, v. 27: 559–570.

—— Governing cities by commissions. World to-day, Sept., 1906, v. 11: 943–946.

WISE, W. W.: Discussion of the Des Moines plan. (Opposed to the plan.) Midwestern (Des Moines, Ia.), June, 1909, v. 3: 29–37.

—— The Des Moines plan. Midwestern (Des Moines, Ia.), Jan.,

LIST OF REFERENCES

1910, v. 4: 25–38. Two papers opposing the commission form of city government.

WOODRUFF, C. R.: Government by commission. Municipal journal, Jan. 28, 1911, v. 20: 85–86.

III (a). PARTICULAR PERIODICALS CONTAINING MANY REFERENCES ON THE SUBJECT

Arena:

Jan., 1902, 27: 39–46. Responsibility in municipal government.

32: 377–391. Democracy and municipal government. B. O. Flower.

July, 1907, 38: 8–13. Galveston. G. W. James.

Aug., 1907, 38: 144–149. Houston and its city commission. G. W. James.

Oct., 1907, 38: 429–436. American city the storm center in the battle for good government.

Oct., 1907, 38: 431–432. Unguarded commission government.

Oct., 1907, 38: 432–436. Des Moines plan: a model of guarded city government.

Jan., 1909, 41: 38–41. Better city government. L. F. C. Garvin.

Jan., 1909, 41: 109–110. Direct legislation in municipal government. R. T. Paine, Jr.

Bulletin of the League of American municipalities [at present, the City hall], Des Moines, Ia.:

Nov., 1905. Galveston's charter government. Walter Gresham.

Feb., 1907. Galveston's civic management.

Feb., 1908. Galveston's commission government. H. A. Landes, mayor of Galveston.

Feb., 1908. The Des Moines plan. Sidney J. Dillon.

City hall, Des Moines, Ia.:

July, 1908, 10: 15–18. Neal Jones — Des Moines plan.

Jan., 1909, 10: 265–270, 272. Des Moines plan charter.

Feb., 1909, 10: 284–287. Commission plan of city government.

March, 1909, 10: 316–319.

April, 1909, 10: 357–359.

May, 1909, 10: 376–378.

June, 1909, 10: 408–413. Debate between John MacVicar and W. W. Wise. Des Moines plan.

LIST OF REFERENCES

City hall, Des Moines, Ia. (*Continued*)
>July, 1909, 11 : 15-17.
>Sept., 1909, 11 : 85-91 ; 91-93. Commission government in San Diego.
>Jan., 1910, 11 : 235-236.
>Feb., 1901, 11 : 253-254.
>March, 1910, 11 : 286-290.
>April, 1910, 11 : 316-317.
>May, 1910, 11 : 328-335. Mayor Guthrie of Pittsburg opposes plan.
>June, 1910, 11 : 368-370.
>July, 1910, 12 : 26-27.
>Sept., 1910, 12 : 99-100.
>Nov., 1910, 12 : 193-194 ; 195-198.

Independent :
>June 16, 1904, 56 : 1382. The New Galveston. W. B. Slosson.
>March 30, 1905, 58 : 706-709. City government. Goldwin Smith.
>April 4, 1907, 62 : 806-807. Way to decent city government.
>June 6, 1907, 62 : 1367. One man city government.
>July 25, 1907, 63 : 195-200. Government by commission in Texas. W. B. Slosson.
>Jan. 18, 1908, 64 : 1409-1410. Three great experiments.
>Jan. 28, 1909, 66 : 194-195. Example of Haverhill. Demont Goodyear.
>Feb. 24, 1910, 68 : 415-416. Experience of Haverhill. D. Goodyear.

Municipal engineering :
>April, 1907, 32 : 255-258. The Galveston plan of city government.
>March, 1908, 34 : 160-162. Government of cities by commission.
>Jan., 1909, Cedar Rapids under the commission plan. Chas. D. Huston.
>May, 1909, 36 : 279-281. A business manager for Staunton, Va. Ernest S. Bradford.
>Feb., 1910, 38 : 105-107. Nominations for office under the commission plan. (Editorial.)

LIST OF REFERENCES

March, 1910, 38:180–181. Illinois bill for commission government.

May, 1910, 38:345–346. The commission form of government and the Indianapolis charter.

Municipal journal and engineer:

March 25, 1908. Newport plan vs. Galveston plan. Rear Admiral F. E. Chadwick.

Dec. 23, 1908. Commission government in Iowa.

June 3, 1908. Galveston plan successful. Ernest S. Bradford.

Aug. 5, 1908. Commission government in Houston. E. S. Bradford.

Oct. 28, 1908. Finances under commission government. Chas. Mulford Robinson.

May 19, 1909. Commission government at Cedar Rapids.

June 23, 1909. Spread of the commission idea. Ernest S. Bradford.

July 28, 1909. Commission government for Kansas City.

Feb. 22, 1911. List of cities having commission plan, to date.

Outlook:

Jan. 6, 1906, 82:5. Concentration of power in the hands of the mayor at Houston.

May 12, 1906, 83:54. Experiments.

April 13, 1907, 85:834–835. Texas idea.

April 13, 1907, 85:839–843. Texas idea. City government by a board of directors. H. J. Haskell.

May 25, 1907, 86:127–128. Municipal efficiency.

Aug. 3, 1907, 86:707–708. Spread of the Texas idea: Peculiarities of the Des Moines plan.

Jan. 4, 1908, 88:9. Breakdown of ward government in St. Louis.

July 4, 1908, 89:495–497. Spread of the commission plan.

Nov. 7, 1908, 90:510–511. Are our cities free?

Aug. 14, 1909, 92:865–866. City government.

Sept. 4, 1909, 93:13, 14. Should a city govern itself?

Sept. 18, 1909, 93:90–92. Form of city government.

April 16, 1910, 94:422. Rapid growth of commission government.

INDEX

Administrative control by the commission, 188-190.

Alabama, three commission acts, 98, 99; Birmingham, 98; tables 1-12.

Alameda, Cal., partial commission form, 286.

Alphabetical arrangement of names of candidates on ballot, table (10), 250-256.

Appointing power of commission, 186-188.

Aransas Pass, Tex., adoption, 76; tables 1-12.

Ardmore, Okla., tables 1-12.

Assignment of commissioners as heads of departments, by the commission, 200; table, 201-203.

Austin, Tex., provisions of charter, 76; results, 78; tables 1-12.

Baker, Ore., 107; tables 1-12.

Barry, Tex., adoption, 76; tables 1-12.

Bartlesville, Okla., tables 1-12.

Beaumont, Tex., aldermanic form of government, 286.

Berkeley, Cal., 103, 106; tables 1-12.

Biloxi, Miss., rejects plan, 95, 96.

Bluefield, W. Va., commission form, 93; tables 1-12.

Board of directors of corporation similar to city commission, 192-196.

Boise, Ida., partial commission form, 72, 288.

Boss eliminated under commission form, 210, 212.

Boston, Mass., not commission government, 288.

Bristol, Tenn., partial commission form, 287.

Buffalo, N.Y., chart of city government, 1910, 208; chart for same city under commission form, 211.

Business corporation and municipal government similar, 192-196; 278, 279.

Business manager for city, Staunton, Va., 119-124.

California cities, 103-106; Berkeley, 103, 106; San Diego, 104, 105; Oakland, 104; tables 1-12.

California, general act, 108; tables 1-12.

Cedar Rapids, Ia., adoption of commission form, 54; results, 55-60; personnel, 55.

Charleston, W. Va., mixed form, 93.

Chattanooga, Tenn., 94; tables 1-12.

"Checks" in commission cities, 214, 215; summary, 271; summary table, 273-277.

Chelsea, Mass., 80, 81; an unusual form of commission government, 283, 284.

Cities which at first rejected but later adopted commission form, 287.

Cities which have voted against commission form, 289, 290.

City planning, in Dallas, Tex., 77.

Classification of commission cities on basis of few or many "checks," 271, 272; 277, 278.

Colorado Springs, Col., 103; tables 1-12.

"Commission government," meaning of term, 127; essential features, 127-129; table of commission-governed cities, 131-138; definition, 284, 285.

Compensation of commissioners, 169; table, 170-179.

Concentration of legislative and administrative authority in same body, 181-196.

Contracts, officers prohibited from interest in municipal, 269.

INDEX

Corpus Christi, Tex., charter, 76, 77; tables 1-12.
Cumberland, Md., tables 1-12.

Dallas, Tex., charter, 76; results, 77, 78; departments, 198; tables 1-12.
Definition of commission government, 284, 285; 127-129.
Denison, Tex., charter, 76; tables 1-12.
Designating authority for heads of departments, 200; table, 201-203.
Des Moines, Ia., report by James G. Berryhill, 33; general act passed, 34; former government, 34; main features of general act, 35-44; nominating provisions, 40; publicity, 41; referendum, 42, 43; initiative, 42, 43; recall, 43; civil service commission, 43; results, 45-50; personnel, 51; constitutionality, 52, 53; departments (Iowa law), 198; tables 1-12; text of Iowa law, 312-338.
Division into departments, 197-200; Galveston, 198; Houston, 198; Iowa law, 198; Tacoma, 198; Kentucky law, 199; San Diego, 199; Oakland, 199; Kansas (2), 199; High Point, N.C., 199.
Duncan, Okla., tables 1-12.
Duties of departments, 204.

Election at large, 162-166; table (10), 250-256.
Election of the entire commission at same time, 149, 150, 157, 158.
Elective officers other than the commissioners, 146-149; table, 151-156.
Elkhart, Tex., adoption, 76; table 1.
El Paso, Tex., tables 1-12.
Enid, Okla., tables 1-12.
Entire membership of commission elected each time, 149, 150, 157, 158.
Entire time or part time, for commissioners, 166-168; table, 169-170.
Evolution of the commission idea, 304.

Financial powers of commission, 190, 191.
Financial results, summary, 113-115. *See also under* particular cities.

Fire department, improvement in, in commission cities, 116. *See also under* particular cities.
Fort Worth, Tex., charter, 76; results, 78; departments, 198; tables 1-12.
Franchise provisions in commission charters, 117, 269. *See also under* particular cities.
Fundamental elements of commission form, 278-281.

Galveston, Great Storm, 3; former government, 4; new charter, 6-10; city club, 10; results, 10-15; a meeting of the commission, 16; personnel of commission, 17; amendment of charter in 1903, 19; reëlection of commissioners, 20; referendum on bond issues, 20; schools, 21; division into departments, 198; tables 1-12.
Gloucester, Mass., 81, 82; results, 83; tables 1-12.
Grand Junction, Col., charter, 100, 103; text, 340; tables 1-12.
Greensboro, N.C., 98.
Greenville, Tex., tables 1-12.
Gulfport, Miss., rejects plan, 95.
Guthrie, Okla., rejection of plan, 78; adoption, 79; tables 1-12.

Harbor Beach, Mich., tables 1-12.
Harlingen, Tex., adoption, 76; table 1.
Haverhill, Mass., 81, 82; results, 83-86; tables 1-12.
Health department in commission cities, improvement in, 117.
High Point, N.C., 97, 98; division into departments, 199; tables 1-12.
Houston, Tex., adoption of commission form, 23; main features, 23-27; large power of mayor, 24-25; referendum on franchises, 26; results, 27-29, 31; personnel of commission, 30; departments, 198; tables 1-12.
How much time should commissioners give, 166-168; table, 169, 170.
Huntington, W. Va., 88, 89; division of officers between parties, 90; results, 91-93; tables 1-12.

INDEX

Hutchinson, Kan., results in, 68; table 1.

Idaho, general act, 108, 109; tables 1–12.
Illinois, legislative committee visits Texas, 73, 74; commission act, 74, 75; tables 1–12.
Initiative, 220; table of percentages required in petition for use of initiative, in commission cities, 229–232.
Iowa general act, tables 1–12. *See also under* Des Moines.

Kansas, two commission laws, 63, 65; cities adopting, 65; cities rejecting, 65; results in Leavenworth, 66, 67; in Wichita, 68; Hutchinson, Independence, Topeka, Kansas City, 68; departments in cities of second class, 199; tables 1–12.
Kansas City, Kan., results in, 68, 69.
Kenedy, Tex., adoption, 76; table 1.
Kentucky general act, 96; tables 1–12.

Large cities, is the commission form applicable to, 297, 298.
Leavenworth, Kan., results in, 66, 67; table 1.
Length of term of commissioners, 159–161.
Lewiston, Ida., commission charter, 71, 72; tables 1–12.
Lexington, Ky., rejects plan, 96.
Limitations of commission government, 291–298.
List of cities rejecting commission form, 289, 290.
List of commission-governed cities, 131–138.
Lockport, N.Y., proposed charter, providing for business manager, 124.
Louisiana general act, 97; Shreveport adopts, 97; tables 1–12.
Lyford, Tex., adoption, 76; table 1.
Lynn, Mass., 85; tables 1–12.

McAlester, Okla., tables 1–12.
McAllen, Tex., adoption, 76.

Main features of commission government, 126–129.
Mankato, Minn., tables 1–12.
Marble Falls, Tex., adoption, 76; table 1.
Marshall, Tex., charter, 76; tables 1–12.
Mayor, position under commission form, 204–207; both vote and veto in Houston, etc., 205, 206; veto only, 206.
Meetings of commission, 219.
Meetings of commission open to public, 215.
Memphis, Tenn., commission charter, 94; tables 1–12.
Michigan, cities adopting plan, 75; tables 1–12.
Minnesota, commission act, 73; tables 1–12.
Mississippi, general act, 95; Hattiesburg and Clarksdale, 95; cities rejecting, 95, 96; tables 1–12.
Modesto, Cal., tables 1–12.
Montana, general act, 109; tables 1–12.
Monterey, Cal., tables 1–12.
Municipal civil service commission, under the commission plan, 262–265; table of provisions, 265–268.
Muskogee, Okla., rejection, 79; adoption, 79; tables 1–12.

Nebraska, general act, not received in time for inclusion, 111.
New Jersey, general act, 109; tables 1–12.
New Mexico, general act, 107; Roswell, 107; tables 1–12.
Newport, Ky., adopts commission plan, 96.
Nominating and election provisions, table (10), 250–256.
Nomination at large, table (10), 250–256.
Nonpartisan primary and election provisions, 247–249; table of provisions, 250–256.
North Carolina cities under commission form, 97, 98.

INDEX

North Dakota, commission act passed, 70; cities rejecting plan, 71; municipal departments, 198; tables 1–12.

Oakland, Cal., 104, 105; departments, 199; tables 1–12.
Objections to commission government, 299–303; too brief a trial, 300; too much power in few hands, 301, 302; constitutionality, 303.
Oklahoma cities, 78, 79; Guthrie, 78, 79; Oklahoma City, 79; tables 1–12.
Oklahoma City, rejection of commission plan, 79; adoption, 79.
Other officers elective than the commissioners, 146, 149; table, 151–156.

Palestine, Tex., charter, 76, 77; tables 1–12.
Parkersburg, W. Va., 93; tables 1–12.
Partial commission forms, 282–287.
Partial or complete renewal of the commission, 149, 150; 157, 158; table, 151–156.
Partisanship eliminated, in commission cities, 118. *See also under* particular cities; and Chap. XXI; table, 250–256, and 260–261.
Party designation prohibited on ballot, table (10), 250–256.
Percentage of signatures required to invoke referendum, table (7), 223–228; initiative, table (8), 229–232; recall (9), 238–243; nominate candidate (10), 250–256.
Personnel of the commissions, Galveston, 17; Houston, 30; Des Moines, 51; Cedar Rapids, 55; Haverhill, Mass., 83.
Petitions required for nomination, table (10), 250–256.
Police regulations and law enforcement, summary of results in commission cities, 115, 116. *See also under* particular cities.
Pontiac, Mich., tables 1–12.
Port Huron, Mich., charter framed, 75; tables 1–12.
Port Lavaca, Tex., adoption, 76.

Powers of the commission, 181–183; general powers, 184, 185; summary, 191–196.
Preferential ballot, Grand Junction, Col., 100–103; 258, 260.
Publicity as a "check," 214–219; meetings open to public, 215; periodical reports of proceedings, 218.

Qualifications of commissioners, 179.
Quasi-commission charters, 282–287.

Recall, 234–238; table of recall provisions in commission charters and acts, 238–243; percentage which should be required, 244; use of recall, 245, 246.
Referendum, 220–222; table of percentages required for referendum petitions in commission cities, 223–228.
Renewal of commission complete or partial, 149, 150; 158; 157; table, 151–156.
Representation, an altered conception of, 305.
Restrictions on commissioners, 180.
Riverside, Cal., partial commission form, 286.
Roswell, N. Mex., not a commission form, 107; city manager, 124.

Sacramento, Cal., departments in proposed charter, 199.
St. Joseph, Mo., partial commission form, 286–287.
Salaries of commissioners, 169; table, 170–179.
San Antonio, Tex., commission form not yet adopted, 287.
San Diego, Cal., 104, 105; division into departments, 199; tables 1–12.
San Luis Obispo, tables 1–12.
Santa Cruz, Cal., tables 1–12.
Sapulpa, Okla., rejection of commission plan, 79; adoption, 79; tables 1–12.
Separation of powers not necessary in cities, 305.
"Short ballot," 139–141; table, 143–145, 280.

INDEX

Shreveport, La., operating under commission form, 97.

Simplicity of organization of city government under commission form, 207.

Small board, table showing numbers of commissioners, 139-141; value of the short ballot, 144-146; prompt action possible, 145, 146; 280.

South Carolina general act, 97; tables 1-12.

South Dakota, commission act passed, 70; results in Sioux Falls, 71; cities rejecting plan, 71; departments under commission plan, 198; tables, 1-12.

Spokane, Wash., 106; tables 1-12.

Staunton, Va., city business manager, 119-124.

Streets cleaner in commission cities, 117. *See also under* particular cities.

Summary of results in commission cities, 112-118; finances, 113-115; law enforcement, 115, 116; fire department, 116; health department, 117; streets, 117; franchises, 117; elimination of politics, 118.

Tables, (1) list of commission cities, 131-138; (2) number of commissioners, 139-141; (3) terms of commissioners and other provisions, 151-156; (4) time required of commissioners, 169, 170; (5) salaries of commissioners, 171-179; (6) who assigns departments of commissioners, 201-203; (7) referendum, percentages required, 223, 228; (8) initiative, 229-232; (9) recall, 238-243; (10) nominating and election provisions, 250-256; (11) civil service commission; (12) summary of principal provisions, 273-277.

Tacoma, Wash., 106; departments, 198; tables 1-12.

Taunton, Mass., not a commission government, 288, 289.

Temple, Tex., aldermanic form of government, 286.

Term of mayor-commissioner, table (3), 151-156.

Term of other commissioners, 159-161; table (3), 151-156.

Terrell, Tex., adoption, 76.

Texas, general act, 76; cities operating under, 76; tables 1-12.

Time requirement in commission cities, 166-168; table, 169, 170.

Topeka, Kan., results in, 68.

Tulsa, Okla., tables 1-12.

Twice as many candidates nominated as elected, table (10), 250-256.

Unusual and partial forms of commission government, 282-287.

Utah, general act, 110; tables 1-12.

Vallejo, Cal., tables 1-12.

Waco, Tex., charter, 76; tables 1-12.

Ward representation *vs.* election at large, 161-166.

Washington, D.C., 282; an unusual form of commission government, 283.

Washington, general act, 110; tables 1-12.

Wichita, Kan., results in, 68.

Wilmington, N.C., 98; tables 1-12.

Wisconsin, commission act passed, 72; amended, 73, 111; tables 1-12.

Wyandotte, Mich., tables 1-12.

Wyoming, general act, 111; tables 1-12.

A GREAT WORK INCREASED IN VALUE

The American Commonwealth
By JAMES BRYCE

New edition, thoroughly revised, with four new chapters
Two 8vo volumes $4.00 net

"More emphatically than ever is it the most noteworthy treatise on our political and social system." — *The Dial*.

"The most sane and illuminating book that has been written on this country." — *Chicago Tribune*.

"What makes it extremely interesting is that it gives the matured views of Mr. Bryce after a closer study of American institutions for nearly the life of a generation." — *San Francisco Chronicle*.

"The work is practically new and more indispensable than ever." — *Boston Herald*.

"In its revised form, Mr. Bryce's noble and discerning book deserves to hold its preëminent place for at least twenty years more." — *Record-Herald*, Chicago, Ill.

"Mr. Bryce could scarcely have conferred on the American people a greater benefit than he has done in preparing the revised edition of his monumental and classic work, 'The American Commonwealth.'" — *Boston Globe*.

"If the writer of this review was to be compelled to reduce his library of Americana to five books, James Bryce's 'American Commonwealth' would be one of them." — *Evening Telegram*, Portland, Ore.

THE MACMILLAN COMPANY
Publishers   64-66 Fifth Avenue   New York

The Citizens' Library of Economics, Politics, and Sociology

Edited by RICHARD T. ELY, Ph.D., LL.D.

Director of the School of Economics and Political Science in the University of Wisconsin; author of "Outlines of Political Economy," "Monopolies and Trusts," etc.

Each volume, cloth, leather back, $1.25 net

American Municipal Progress

Chapters in Municipal Sociology

By CHARLES ZUEBLIN, Ph.B., D.B., Professor of Sociology in the University of Chicago.

This work takes up the problem of the so-called public utilities, — schools, libraries, children's playgrounds, parks, public baths, public gymnasiums, etc. Also such heavier questions as those of rapid transit, sanitation, care of streets, etc. The discussion is from the standpoint of public welfare, and is based on repeated personal investigations in the leading cities of Europe, especially England and the United States; and the legal aspects of these subjects are dealt with.

Municipal Engineering and Sanitation

By M. N. BAKER, Associate Editor of Engineering News; Editor of "A Manual of American Water Works."

It is designed to be a review of the whole field of municipal engineering and sanitation rather than an exhaustive study of one or a few branches of the subject. The most vital points, however, under each class of activities and interests have been dwelt upon, the underlying principles stated, and in many instances details from actual practice given. The book must appeal to all classes interested in the improvement of civic conditions.

Democracy and Social Ethics

By JANE ADDAMS, Head of Hull House, Chicago.

Wage-Earning Women

By ANNIE MARION MacLEAN, Brooklyn.

While these volumes are not limited to city life, they contain much which is illuminating of the social conditions in large cities.

THE CITIZENS' LIBRARY — *Continued*

World Politics

By PAUL S. REINSCH, Professor of Political Science in the University of Wisconsin.

The full title reads: **World Politics at the End of the Nineteenth Century as Influenced by the Oriental Situation.**

"By every one who in any measure realizes the wonderful change that has been wrought in international affairs during the last couple of decades it will be eagerly welcomed. If there are any who are not conscious of this change they will find here new and fascinating material for thought." — *Pioneer Press*, St. Paul.

Colonial Government

By PAUL S. REINSCH, Ph.D.

With fascinating style and deep insight into the relation of a state to its colonies, the author has gone straight to the root of the problem with which the United States is dealing in connection with the establishment of a permanent form of government in those islands which it has lately acquired. Starting with the framework of colonial government, he treats briefly the motives and methods of colonial expansion from the historical view point and with intense interest traces the forms of colonial government, with legislative methods necessary for each separate race involved.

Colonial Administration

By PAUL S. REINSCH, Ph.D.

"If it were possible to require every Senator and Representative to pass a competitive examination in the contents of this little volume as a condition of appointment to committee work having to do with the dependencies, the prospect for the sane treatment of the tremendous question now confronting the American people would be measurably improved." — *New York Times*.

THE CITIZENS' LIBRARY — *Continued*

Studies in the Evolution of Industrial Society

By RICHARD T. ELY, Ph.D., LL.D., University of Wisconsin, Editor of this Series.

Professor Ely discusses in a straightforward way the progress of the working classes, the changes in their condition, their tendencies toward better and brighter things, and the effect of these tendencies on society generally. The benefit of competition and the improvement of the race; municipal ownership and concentration of wealth are treated in a sane, helpful, and interesting manner.

Monopolies and Trusts

By RICHARD T. ELY.

In this work the *man who wants to know* may find in condensed form the causes of trusts, the laws establishing their prices, their limits, and their efforts to control production. The evils of Monopoly are plainly stated and remedies are proposed. This book should be a help to every man in active business life.

The American City: A Problem in Democracy

By DELOS F. WILCOX, Ph.D.

The problem of city government is a live one to-day. Dr. Wilcox believes that the great political and social reforms of the future will come through the city. By tracing the causes of city growth, the peculiarities of life in the city and its ideals of democracy, he has tried to make plain to all the breadth of a city's influence, the foundations of its organization, the extent of its responsibility and the sources of its revenue in this country.

THE CITIZENS' LIBRARY — *Continued*

The Spirit of American Government

By Professor J. ALLEN SMITH, of the University of Washington.

This book treats in a clear, concise manner the growth of the effort from early Revolutionary times to limit the power of the ruling classes, its relation to the constitution and its effect upon the political development of the United States.

Dr. Smith is a candid reasoner, a careful collector of facts. . . . The book is a noteworthy study of our Constitution, and deserves the attention of all interested in good government, good politics, good citizens. — *Education*, Boston.

History of Political Parties in the United States

By JESSE MACY, LL.D., Professor of Political Science in Iowa College.

"A statement of facts so clear and exhaustive as to call for unqualified admiration and praise." — *The Nation*.

"Deserves to be placed in libraries by the side of Bryce's 'American Commonwealth.'" — *The Sun*, New York.

"Among the books relating to American party history, this is one of the most stimulating." — *Political Science Quarterly*.

Foundations of Sociology

By EDWARD ALSWORTH ROSS, Ph.D., Professor of Sociology in the University of Wisconsin.

The man of to-day who, pressed with business cares, yet feels the need of giving some little aid to the weaker part, has small chance to obtain special data and experience. The heaping together of all the facts at once will not equip him to deal successfully with the drink problem, race friction, or the factory labor of children. For a quick, comprehensive view he will find this book an immense help, a straight, sympathetic stroke toward the heart of things.

THE CITIZENS' LIBRARY — *Continued*

Social Control: A Survey of the Foundations of Order

By the same author.

"Briefly put, the question to which he seeks an answer is: How far is the orderliness of the individual due to his own morality and how far to social control? And he goes further into the subject in an attempt to determine the origin of this morality of the individual. . . . The entire subject is handled with lucidity and in a style that wins the reader to an interested study of the problems presented." — *Public Ledger*, Philadelphia.

Newer Ideals of Peace

By JANE ADDAMS, Head of "Hull House," Chicago; author of "Democracy and Social Ethics," etc.

"No brief summary can do justice to Miss Addams's grasp of the facts, her insight into their meaning. It should interest all who seek a first-hand view of modern city conditions." — *New York Examiner*.

International Commercial Policies: With Special Reference to the United States

By GEORGE M. FISK, Ph.D., Professor of Commerce, University of Illinois. Formerly Second Secretary of American Embassy at Berlin.

Government in Switzerland

By JOHN MARTIN VINCENT, Ph.D., Associate Professor of History, Johns Hopkins University.

"This is a good book on a good subject," said the *Political Science Quarterly*. "It gives a clear and instructive statement of the nature and operations of the Swiss Government; and it is full of interest for any student of politics." — *The Outlook*.

THE CITIZENS' LIBRARY — *Continued*

Irrigation Institutions: A Discussion of the Economic and Legal Questions Created by the Growth of Irrigated Agriculture in the Arid West.

By ELWOOD MEAD, C.E., M.S., Chief of Irrigation Investigations.

An Introduction to the Study of Agricultural Economics

By HENRY C. TAYLOR, M.S., Agr., Ph.D., Assistant Professor of Political Economy in the University of Wisconsin.

Money: A Study of the Theory of the Medium of Exchange

By DAVID KINLEY, Ph.D., Professor of Economics in the University of Illinois.

In view of the recent movement for a complete revision of our present currency system, this book will prove for the business man who will indirectly feel the effect of such changes, a means of assistance in grasping, with least effort, a subject vital to his interests.

Essays in the Monetary History of the United States

By CHARLES J. BULLOCK, Ph.D., Assistant Professor of Political Economy, Harvard University.

Railway Legislation in the United States

By BALTHASAR H. MEYER, Ph.D., Professor of Political Economy, University of Wisconsin, and Member of the Railroad Commission of Wisconsin.

Some Ethical Gains through Legislation

By FLORENCE KELLEY, Secretary of the National Consumers' League.

This interesting volume is by one who knows and sympathizes with the abject poverty to be found in certain sections of the country.

It has grown out of the author's experience in philanthropic work in Chicago and New York, and her service for the State of Illinois and for the Federal Government in investigating the circumstances of the poorer classes, and conditions in various trades.

THE CITIZENS' LIBRARY — *Continued*

Economic Crises

By EDWARD D. JONES, Ph.D., Junior Professor of Economics and Industry, University of Michigan.

That "acute malady to which business appears to be increasingly subject," called the *crisis*, is the subject of this book: an analysis of its causes and recommendations for its treatment. It is clear and comprehensive, treating of the causes for fluctuation in prices, its relation to bountiful harvests, and the recurrence of periodical crisis.

Introduction to Business Organization

By S. E. SPARLING.

The aim of this book is to furnish a practical help to clerks and others entering business.

The Principles of Anthropology and Sociology in Their Relations to Criminal Procedure

By MAURICE PARMELEE.

The Elements of Sociology

By FRANK W. BLACKMAR, Ph.D., Professor of Sociology and Economics in the University of Kansas.

The general reader will find in this book a brief outline of sociology founded on the principles established by standard authorities. With wide knowledge and ability for selecting the most important points, Dr. Blackmar covers the whole field in brief and pithy paragraphs.

Education and Industrial Evolution

By FRANK T. CARLTON, Ph.D., Professor of Economics and History in Albion College.

The Economics of Distribution

By JOHN A. HOBSON, author of "The War in South Africa: Its Causes and Effects."

The man who has small time to study economics will find this clever book of great value. By its critical, constructive work it helps to force readers out of the deep rut of the old ideas of bargaining and sale, the use of land, labor, and capital, and relation of prices to the market.

THE MACMILLAN COMPANY
Publishers   64-66 Fifth Avenue   New York